T0370351

The Jeremiah Project Part 1—
✂ *The Scrapbook*

By

A. J. Foltz

WESTBOW
PRESS®
A DIVISION OF THOMAS NELSON
& ZONDERVAN

WestBow Press books may be ordered through booksellers or by contacting:

WestBow Press
A Division of Thomas Nelson & Zondervan
1663 Liberty Drive
Bloomington, IN 47403
www.westbowpress.com
1-(866) 928-1240

ISBN: 978-1-4497-8386-0 (sc)
ISBN: 978-1-4497-8385-3 (e)

Library of Congress Control Number: 2013902291

Print information available on the last page.

WestBow Press rev. date: 01/03/2020

Contents

Preface

I can safely say without any hesitation that I have always been an avid Believer. I have believed in Jesus since I was a small child. From the virgin birth to His resurrection power, I believed. And my faith in those two things and all of the things that fell in between those two events only grew stronger as I became older. But a few years ago I began to question all of that when I stepped outside of the box that defined me and looked in.

After all of the years of believing, it was still there. All of the sin that, I believed, had been *washed away* was still visible. And if I was able to see it, so could the whole world. If gaining men to Christ is the mission for Believers, I and all that surrounded me displayed ineffectual evidence to positively support the Lord and that He lived. My Christian walk was powerless when it came to changing the attitude of non-Believers living in doubt and uncertainty. I came to the conclusion that I needed something undeniable to support that which I had so strongly believed in. I had to find some evidence that overpowered my weak and mortal witness. If I could not be convincing about what I believed, I would never be effective. I decided to move out of that box that housed me and all of the sin related to my life. I was not sure where I would end up but I piled all of that unhidden sin on top of my Christian beliefs. As I strapped that big bundle of *the truth* on my back and headed out I couldn't help but wonder how much of a liability I had actually been to the Lord all of these years.

I knew that I would be running into many other avid believers who were out there on a religious mission. No matter what type of faith is professed, the roots of any avid believer run deep. I knew that I could expect to find the resolute walking with solid steps, never turning to the right or to the left; and that's where my trouble, as an avid Believer in Jesus, only begins. It seems that nothing can jostle the other mission-goers as they stay focused on their goal that has nothing to do with Jesus. Many have proven themselves willing, and able, to sacrifice their lives for what they believe. They walk in ways that cannot go unnoticed. As I scanned the situation from under my backpack of *the truth,* I could see what the Lord was up against. It seemed to me that He was losing ground, especially, with *avid Believers* like me on His side.

At this pivotal point in my life I was definitely ready for the journey. But being contrary to others who set out on the customary Christian mission, I do not load up on all that I have learned. I (as much as I possibly can) unload all that I have learned, because my mission of faith will be a little different. I will not be out there spreading, what we Christians call, the good news. I will be out there looking for, and collecting evidence to support it. I wanted to find something that would empower and give life to my avid belief. I did not know how much evidence I was going to find, but I felt that unloading my preconceived ideas would give me extra space and take away a number of blind spots. I did not want to carry anything that would cause me to overlook or miss His presence. I was desperate to prove that He existed in some other place than my heart, my mind, and on the pages of the New Testament.

Though ready and willing, I quickly learned that the avenues and options for my search were very limited but I came up with a layman's plan as I remembered something that I had heard: The Old Testament testifies about Jesus. Although I would eventually like to use other reputable resources throughout my continual education of the Lord, the Old Testament was familiar to me. It was one source that I trusted so that is where I decided to begin my search for Jesus. Besides, the Old Testament Scriptures seemed to be a perfect common denominator. It is the one source that many other religions draw from. It was a good starting point for me and what I hoped to accomplish.

But before I even took the first step of my plan, I made up my mind. Finding one or two verses tucked tightly into one of the Old Testament books was not good enough. I needed to find more than just a few words plucked from the middle of a chapter that could be argued by unbelievers to mean something else. So I got out my son's Third Edition of the New Oxford Annotated Bible that he brought home from college. (It is a Revised Standard Edition with the Apocrypha. I suggest such a version for this study.) And I started searching in a tedious way for Jesus. I began by handwriting the books of the prophets allowing all of their words to flow through the pen that I held.

I started out with the shorter books working my way up. Word for word I began to write. But with each passing book I began to become more than just a little bit worried. The solid evidence, concerning Jesus, that I was sure I would find was not there. At this point my heart was faint. The only strength left in my chest was spent questioning my Christian beliefs and these were questions that I could not push off or forget about. It was as if a hot searing iron had made its mark on my heart. It left a deep pot hole that would never just go away. I knew that there was only one way to fix it. It had to be filled up with the answer.

I once again experienced that seemingly cruel fact of life: Things don't always go as planned. I was just trying to connect to my Lord at a different level. I wanted to be an effective tool in His hand but my efforts sent me reeling! I was in trouble now. I could not find Jesus. My only option was to follow through with my original plan. It is all I had. As I cautiously clung to the plan that included the Old Testament, me, and my pen, I was not sure what I would find or how I would feel after I found it.

Then one day I started penning the words from the book of Jeremiah on my own paper but decided to approach this particular book in a different way. I was reminded of a Bible study that I used to attend. Without fail I always found something new and exciting as I searched Scripture to answer questions. I decided to continue my search by following that old familiar

Bible study format. The only difference: I would have to come up with the questions as well as the answers. I immediately started asking myself questions about the verses in Jeremiah and then proceeded to search different parts of the Bible for the answers. Through that process, not only was the empty pot-hole in my heart getting filled up but the empty pages in front of me were getting filled up too. A story that I had never heard in all of my Christian days unfolded and I began to learn things about God I had never known. And the good news is, I found glimpses of Him and I took snapshots.

Though this book has no real photographs of Jesus each one of the ten chapters has a scrapbook page. On these specific pages you will find pictures of Him in word form. I have from the very beginning considered this search for Jesus a project. Though not a perfect piece of work this is a project which I am dedicated to and feel compelled to share it with the world. And now I present to you: *THE JEREMIAH PROJECT PART 1—THE SCRAPBOOK*. Part one, of this intended series, takes you on a journey through the first ten chapters of the book of Jeremiah.

HOW TO USE THIS STUDY

Each chapter, though different in content is common in form. Think of each chapter like a specialty sandwich from a restaurant menu. Everybody gets the same bread and the same kind of fancy toothpick that holds the sandwich together, but it's what goes *in* your sandwich that makes it taste different. Here's how each one of the ten chapters are prepared:

- The author begins each chapter with a **Prelude** or introduction. (This is the first piece of bread on your plate.)
- Then there is the **Chapter study** (the meat, cheese and relishes to your order). This is where you will spend most of your time by reading lead verses from the book of Jeremiah as well as the author's remarks before answering questions. You will need your bible, a dictionary, pencil or pen, and blank paper for your personal answers. After that,
- the **Tag-a-long** (the piece of bread that tops off that sandwich). The tag-a-long will generally be something to just think about. And then,
- the **Scrapbook page** (the fancy toothpick), a picture of Jesus in the form of words.
- At the end of each chapter you will find a section where we **Compare answers** for the **Chapter study**. Your choice of meat, cheese, and relish, may be different than mine. But even with the variations, you will get ten fully loaded sandwiches, each one will be better than the last.

(Just a note: Some of the reference verses, suggested as means of answering questions, have been transferred from the New Revised Standard Version of God's Word to this book for your convenience. The suggestions are meant to assist you. Do not allow them to limit you.)

The Jeremiah Project is meant to be read and worked on in a consecutive manner starting at chapter 1 and then proceeding to the next chapter and the next. You will work your way up to, and through, chapter 10. Some events are built upon what has happened in previous chapters so if you jump ahead or skip chapters you may misunderstand or miss what is going on. And if you start the study and stop at some point, without completing it, you may be missing the true message. The author tries to unfold events without looking ahead to what we now know. So try to live in the historical moment and block out the future. Be at Jeremiah's blind-side, of trust, as major events unfold during his life. The events that happened in and around his home town affected the whole world then and what happened then, within that small geographical area, still affects us today. And God, through Jeremiah, reveals to us, in an orderly fashion, that important chain of events.

The thing that I want you to know up front (and I will put it in parable form): you are hopping on a tour bus and your tour guide has no documented license to drive the bus or conduct the tour. Information that you receive during this tour may cause you to ask more questions, raise an eyebrow or two, and wonder. But that is encouraged. Hop off the bus and look around for yourself. Take snapshots of your own. Our goal is to become avid Believers who are effective for the Christian mission.

Introduction

The Jeremiah Project Part 1 ✂ The Scrapbook is a study guide but as Scripture is searched and questions are answered the study takes on the form of a novelette that tells a story of two women (Israel and Judah) and one man (The Lord). They are bound and policed by one contract (The Covenant) in marriage. The contract will play a major role throughout this study. It is living. It is breathing. It is just as alive as the parties that it binds. The active contract provides far over and above what is required for a faithful bride. But as gracious as the contract is with its good gifts, which come to the bride through obedience to its policing words, so it is cruel with curses for the one who is not faithful and true to what is written within its legal text.

God made it very clear to His bride about her future. The contract which united her with the Lord gave her two choices. She could choose life and prosperity or death and adversity. The legal contract which she was bound to would deliver one or the other. And with that disclosure the Lord supplied the bride with knowledge to successfully manage the contract to her advantage. Perpetual fame, fortune, and prosperity would be the payout from the contract if she managed wisely.

But as time passed, pride and vain glory caught her eye and captured her heart. She turned from the knowledge that the Lord supplied. She became unfaithful and showed contempt toward the contract that she was ever bound to. So her Lord chased her with the truth. He vehemently warned her to start acting in the manner that would warrant the contract to disperse life and prosperity for she did not want this thing to become her enemy (if she knew what was good for her). But she would not change.

The living contract took the only legal course available. It began to spew out its stored-up death and adversarial wrath on the one who broke it. As the living contract continued to follow the legal demands that had been summoned, it became a beast. If the bride who was bound to it did not run back to her Lord, the seemingly emotionless contract would destroy her and her children. Her Lord wanted to help her, but no matter what legal actions the Lord took to get her back to safety, she kept running the other way. He was her only safe place. He was the only one who could protect her from the contract that she continued to fuel.

Chapter 1

PRELUDE: *Confrontation*

CHAPTER STUDY: *Jeremiah, Jeremiah, What Do You See?*

TAG-A-LONG: *Powerhouse*

✂SCRAPBOOK PAGE: *Utter*

Chapter 1 Prelude

Confrontation

I don't like confrontation and I will do just about anything to avoid it, especially when the opponent is bigger than me. And when I say "bigger than me" I'm not talking about height, weight, or muscle mass. I'm talking about those who have a lot to say when they weigh in and throw their words around. I don't want to go toe-to-toe or face-to-face with anyone who *seems* to have a larger scale of knowledge pertaining to the debatable subject, whatever that might be. But in any given situation when you haven't been around long enough to know the ropes of the trade or all the rules of the game it just seems safer and wiser to play along and do what you're told. But there might come a time when you find out that what you have been hearing and going along with is completely wrong. At that point when you learn the truth, do you, being the little guy, face up with those who are wrong? I guess that would depend upon what you fear most. You have to ask yourself if it's those who have more seniority, longevity, and seeming power over you or the truth and what's right?

The people in Jeremiah's kingdom, Judah, believe and live lies because truth is not being served from the leaders who sit in the seats of power. Slanders, mockery, and deceit proceed from every type of throne (official office) in the land. And here in chapter one God is preparing little Jeremiah to face off with these big guys who are running His country. If Jeremiah shows any fear of the hot-shots in the face off it will mean that he really fears them more than he fears God.

God tells Jeremiah: But you, gird up your loins; stand up and tell them everything that I command you. Do not break down before them, or I will break you before them (Jeremiah 1:17 NRSV).

Chapter 1 Study

Jeremiah, Jeremiah, What Do You See

CHAPTER 1 READING, COMMENTS, AND QUESTIONS

📖READ JEREMIAH 1:1-3

A. ADDITIONAL COMMENTS FOR VERSES 1-3

"For many are called, but few are chosen" (Matthew 22:14 NRSV).

ANSWER QUESTIONS FOR VERSES 1-3

A-1: We don't have much direct information on Jeremiah's hometown life or boyhood. By doing some reading and answering some questions we will attempt to recreate his environment and the history of his environment. Section A will provide the foundation needed for this study.

We are told that Jeremiah is the son of Hilkiah and that his father was *of the priests* who were in Anathoth in the land of Benjamin and if you were *of the priests* you were counted as being from the tribe of Levi.

All of those who descended from Levi (Levi: the name of just one of the twelve sons of Israel aka Jacob) were called upon by the Lord. They received appointment and were required to perform religious duties at the tabernacle. They were given charge of all that pertained to the care of the tabernacle and its covering. All descendants of Levi were, without choice or nomination, in the Lord's service. They were not to be counted among the children of Israel in the census. They belonged to the Lord. See Numbers 1:48-50 to confirm. Numbers 3:14-17 says the Levites were enrolled. What is the definition of enrolled?

A-2: When the Levites were enrolled in Israel (Numbers 3:14-17), God told Moses to divide them into three groups according to their ancestral grandfathers: Gershon, Kohath, and Merari. Out of these three groups the Lord purposely and officially established one more family line. There would now be four groups, conducting tabernacle business, instead of three; and the fourth group, formed by God, would perform the priestly duties. The priestly duties were the most holy duties within the tabernacle; and, according to Exodus 28:1, God chose the family line of Aaron. He was the brother of Moses. See the following make-shift chart to see where the new line came from and where it began on its own.

	Gershon	Amram (had 2 sons)	Moses
Levi (had 3 sons)	Kohath (had 4 sons)	Izar	Aaron (priestly line starts)
	Merari	Hebron	
		Uzziel	

So the Levites from that time on were in four divisions instead of three:

- Priests (Aaron's descendants)
- Kohathites
- Gershonites (1Chronicles 6 shows a difference in spelling)
- Merarites

The tabernacle in the day of Moses was portable. Numbers 1:50-54 makes this clear and Numbers 4:5-33 describes the duties of each division of Levi when it was time to move. Numbers 3:5-10 will give you a brief description of other duties assigned to the tribe of Levi.

Many generations later the tabernacle came to rest. At that resting time David was king over the theocratic kingdom. In 1Chronicles 23 David assembled all the leaders of Israel, the priests, and the Levites. He said: "The Lord, the God of Israel, has given rest to his people; and he resides in Jerusalem forever. And so the Levites no longer need to carry the tabernacle or any of the things for its service" (1Chronicles 23:25-26 NRSV). At that time the Levites officially received appointments from the king concerning duties.

All of the Levites at the age thirty and older were officially counted. There were thirty-eight thousand. Those in this age bracket would serve and protect all that concerned the house of God in some capacity. Chapter 27 in 1Chronicles indicates some form of month-by-month scheduling for some of the duties. See verse 1 of that chapter to confirm this. Then turn to 1Chronicles 23:3-5 to find the following information concerning the Levites who were at the age of thirty and older:

- Twenty-four thousand had charge of the work in the house of the Lord.
- Six thousand became officers and judges.
- Four thousand were gatekeepers.
- Four thousand offered praises to the Lord with instruments that David had made for praise.

Even though not all of the Levites were in the official count (of the thirty and older group), all of the Levites at-and-over the age of twenty seemed to be organized into divisions (1Chronicles 23:27). If Jeremiah was not yet at this age (of twenty), as chapter one unfolds, he may have been close to it. 1Chronicles 23:28-32 may present a list of the duties that the younger Levites could participate in. What types of temple duties might the young Jeremiah be fulfilling as a Levite in training?

A-3: Levi was a substitute. Who originally, when Moses first led the people out of Egypt, was to be consecrated? Who, before Levi, was officially, in the word and eyes of the Lord, '*Mine*'? See the following selected verses for the answer.

(Exodus 13:1-2 NRSV): The Lord said to Moses: Consecrate to me all the firstborn; whatever is the first to open the womb among the Israelites, of human beings and animals, is mine.

(Numbers 3:44-45 NRSV): Then the Lord spoke to Moses, saying: Accept the Levites as substitutes for all the firstborn among the Israelites, and the livestock of the Levites as substitutes for their livestock; and the Levites shall be mine. I am the Lord.

A-4: When God chose the Levites; they served as a great *relief* for all of Israel. Use your dictionary and look up the meaning of relief. Write out the definition that might best describe the situation between God and Israel (Israel being the one corporation of people that He rescued out of Egyptian bondage).

A-5: By the looks of things, God is building a foundation for a new nation that He will rule. This is not your typical form of government. Look up the word— theocracy. What does it mean?

A-6: There were twelve ancestral divisions of Jacob (aka Israel) that exited Egypt. The Bible calls those ancestral divisions: tribes. Each one of the twelve tribes eventually received an assigned portion in the Promised Land. Each portion had specific boundaries and cities within those boundaries. The twelve individual assignments might be thought of as a small state and each state was named after one of the patriarchs.

What were the tribal names given to the twelve state-like divisions? Numbers 1:20-43 will be helpful.

A-7: As you can see from your last answer, Levi did not receive a state-like allotment. Instead they received towns. Their designated lands were scattered throughout all of Israel. Below you will find a breakdown of the towns (which included pasture lands) that Levi received and inhabited within the twelve tribal areas. The following information was taken from Joshua 21:13-41 (NRSV).

The Levite priests received 13 towns from the tribes of Judah, Simeon and Benjamin: Hebron (which was also a city of refuge), Libnah, Jattir, Eshtemoa, Holon, Debir, Ain, Juttah, Beth-shemesh, Gibeon, Geba, Anathoth, Almon .

The Kohathites received 10 towns from the tribes of Ephraim, Dan and half-tribe of Manasseh: Shechem (which is also a city of refuge), Gezer, Kibzaim, Beth-horon, Elteke, Gibbethon, Aijalon, Gath-rimmon, Taanach, Gath-rimmon.

The Gershonites received 13 towns from the tribes of Issachar, Asher and Naphtali and half-tribe of Manasseh: Golan in Bashan (which is also a city of refuge), Beeshterah, Kishion, Daberath, Jarmuth, En-gannim, Mishal, Abdon, Helkath, Rehob, Kedesh in Galilee (also a city of refuge for the slayer); Hammoth-dor, Kartan.

The Merarites received 12 towns from the tribes of Reuben, Gad and Zebulun: Jokneam, Kartah, Dimnah, Nahalal, Bezer, Jahzah, Kedemoth, Mephaath, Ramoth in Gilead (which is also a city of refuge), Mahanaim, Heshbon, Jazer.

By reading Joshua 21:14-19 you can figure out Jeremiah's roots. What division of Levi received the town of Anathoth? His father is associated with this city in verse one.

A-8: Our nation offers free education (up to a certain level) and equal-opportunity employment removes personal restrictions made by employers. Everyone is offered the opportunity to excel in all degrees. But this theocratic society appears to be partial. It seems to be mainly those who God claimed as, in His word, "*Mine*" (Numbers 3:45) that were groomed to work in God's system of government. See the following examples. They may reveal a biased state.

- We have those that we label as tax collectors or the I.R.S. They had Levi. (See 2Chronicles 24:5-6.)
- We have accountants who assist with the finances and value of our property and homes. They had Levi. (See Leviticus 27:14-25.)
- We have armed guards in armored trucks involved in the process of carrying our nation's currency to federal facilities. They had Levi. (See 2Chronicles 24:11; 34:9.)
- We have bankers who are put in charge of managing and securing monetary deposits and valuables. They had Levi. (See 1Chronicles 26:20-28.)
- We have the EPA. They had Levi. (See Leviticus 14:34-53.)
- We have the Supreme Court. They had Levi. (See 2Chronicles 19:8-11; Deuteronomy 17:8-12.)
- We have security guards who stand to protect our homeland, our leaders, and national treasures. They had Levi. (See 1Chronicles 9:17-32; 1Chronicles 26:12-19.)
- We have police officers in every city. They had Levi dispersed throughout all of their tribal areas. (See 1Chronicles 23:4; 26:29-32; and you may want to look at the make-shift chart in A-1 to confirm.)
- We have prisons that are staffed to hold the guilty and protect the innocent. They had cities of refuge. The cities of refuge were cities that were given to the Levites. (See A-11.)
- We have military leaders who command, teach, lead, and direct our troops. They had Levi. (See Numbers 31:6; 2Chronicles 20:13-17; then scanning through the book of Judges may give you a different idea of the military acts of judges.)
- Levi also served in military fashion. (See 1Chronicles 12:24-28; 2Chronicles 20:19-21.)
- We have medical assistants, nurses, and physicians. They had Levi. (See Leviticus 13.)

- We have reporters, recorders, clerks, stenographers, and secretaries. They had Levi. (See 2Chronicles 34:13; 1Chronicles 24:6.)
- We have many levels of politicians who are liaisons between the people and the leaders. They had Levi representing them before the Lord. (See 1Chronicles 6:49.)
- We have trained teachers and educators. They had Levi. (See 2Chronicles 17:7-9.)
- We form our own choirs and bands within our places of worship. They had Levi. (See 1Chronicles 9:33-34; 16:4-7; 23:5.)
- The Constitution of the United States has the signatures of those who accepted its stated conditions on behalf of all the people living under the new way of government. If there was one such document in Israel, many of Levi's offspring would have their signatures on the document. (See Nehemiah 9:38.)

How was the preferred *public servant number one* compensated for his official duties? See the following selected verses. See Numbers 18:21 and 2Chronicle 31:4-5.

A-9: See the following verse. Who (out of the four parties of Levi) holds the most powerful position within this theocracy? You may see a relationship that mimics master and servant.

(Numbers 8:19 NRSV): Moreover, I have given the Levites as a gift to Aaron and his sons from among the Israelites, to do the service for the Israelites at the tent of meeting, and to make atonement for the Israelites, in order that there may be no plague among the Israelites for coming too close to the sanctuary.

A-10: After coming out of Egypt and after the wandering in the desert first ended the people may have been ruled by the priests, Levi, and/or chosen judges (judges who seem to be more like great warriors). Israel had no king when they took possession of the Promised Land. Judges 21:25 (NRSV) says: In those days there was no king in Israel; all the people did what was right in their own eyes.

But the people (elders of Israel) were not happy with that set up (1Samuel 8:4-22). So change came about and additions were made to the structure of the government in Israel. Eventually, according to the verse below, God chose one family line to fill the spot of royalty. What was the family line and from what tribe did the royalty hail?

(1Chronicles 28:2-4 NRSV): Then King David rose to his feet and said: "Hear me,…Yet the Lord God of Israel chose me from all my ancestral house to be king over Israel forever; for he chose Judah as leader, and in the house of Judah my father's house, and among my father's sons he took delight in making me king over all Israel.

A-11: Who were the three kings sitting on the throne during the time that the word of the Lord came to Jeremiah? (See Jeremiah 1:2-3 for the consecutive order.)

A-12: What was the name of the high priest during Josiah's reign? Compare the selected verses below with Jeremiah 1:1-3.

(2Chronicles 34:8-9 NRSV): In the eighteenth year of his reign, when he had purged the land and the house, he sent Shaphan son of Azaliah, Maaseiah the governor of the city, and Joah son of Joahaz, the recorder, to repair the house of the Lord his God. They came to the high priest Hilkiah and delivered the money that had been brought into the house of God, which the Levites, the keepers of the threshold, had collected...

📖READ JEREMIAH 1:4-5

B. ADDITIONAL COMMENTS FOR VERSES 4-5

Jeremiah learns how special he is.

ANSWER QUESTIONS FOR VERSES 4-5

B-1: God reveals some noteworthy things about Jeremiah that he never knew about himself. What are they? (See verse 5.)

📖READ JEREMIAH 1:6-8

C. ADDITIONAL COMMENTS FOR VERSES 6-8

One can only imagine how fast Jeremiah's heart and mind must be racing when he hears these things about himself from God. There might be a feeling of being highly favored but this news was definitely accompanied with fear and doubt. He is only a boy.

ANSWER QUESTIONS FOR VERSES 6-8

C-1: What is God's answer in verse 7 to young Jeremiah's doubt?

C-2: Condescending looks and scowling faces are going to be some of the things that Jeremiah is going to have to deal with. What words of comfort does God give Jeremiah concerning his future task? (See verse 8.)

📖READ JEREMIAH 1:9

D. ADDITIONAL COMMENTS FOR VERSE 9

God furnishes Jeremiah with everything that he needs to accomplish His appointed work successfully.

ANSWER QUESTIONS FOR VERSE 9

D-1: What does God do and what does God say to Jeremiah that would surely be a vast comfort in overcoming his fear of being just a boy?

📖READ JEREMIAH 1:10

E. ADDITIONAL COMMENTS FOR VERSE 10

Jeremiah received a divine appointment from God. It is an appointment that can only be accomplished, if by man, through the power of God.

ANSWER QUESTIONS FOR VERSE 10

E-1: Have you ever heard the phrase: "Don't kill the messenger"? Though Jeremiah has never been known to say those exact words, his words in Jeremiah 26:15 come close. Approaching the leaders of Judah in order to confront them about their corrupt practices in governing the land would have been a dangerous task for anyone. What added element, in verse 10, will make Jeremiah's appointed task even more perilous?

E-2: Use your dictionary and look up the word— nation. What do you find?

E-3: The Lord, the true King, gave Jeremiah no customary official written documents. (See Nehemiah 2:6-8 for the protective passport procedure.) What protection will Jeremiah have as he carries out his appointed duty? Go back to verse 9.

📖READ JEREMIAH 1:11-12

F. ADDITIONAL COMMENTS FOR VERSES 11-12

God starts working with Jeremiah on his abilities to perceive and understand what He (God) is saying. God gives a message to the boy in a fun and interesting way. The word of the Lord came to Jeremiah saying: "Jeremiah, what do you see?" And Jeremiah said: "I see a branch of an almond tree."

ANSWER QUESTIONS FOR VERSES 11-12

F-1: Not everyone was permitted inside the tabernacle where God was known to meet with man. We see other methods of communication were used by God. When He makes Himself known to prophets, it is through visions and He speaks to them through dreams. God describes these visions and dreams with one word. What is the word? (See the selected verses below.)

(Numbers 12:6-8 NRSV): And he said, "Hear my words: When there are prophets among you, I the Lord make myself known to them in visions; I speak to them in dreams. Not so with my servant Moses; he is entrusted with all my house. With him I speak face to face— clearly, not in riddles; and he beholds the form of the Lord.

F-2 (OPTIONAL QUESTION): Look up the definition of your one-word answer in F-1?

F-3: What does God say, here in chapter 1, to let Jeremiah know that his seeing abilities are good?

F-4: In Jeremiah's language, the word that means *almond blossom* and the word that means *watch* are almost similar in spelling. *Almond blossom* is <u>shaqued</u> and *watch* is <u>shaquad</u>. Seeing the almond branch would be a fun play on words as God revealed a message to the young boy. God may be telling Jeremiah that He is watching over His Word (the Word that He put in Jeremiah's mouth) and that He is the one who will be putting the Word that Jeremiah will be speaking to work.

Jeremiah would not forget the visual. The almond branch served as comfort on the day that he saw it and conformation of his appointment for the rest of his life. Turn to Numbers 17. Write down a little history about the almond branch and God's people. What else might *seeing* the almond tree branch mean to Jeremiah?

📖READ JEREMIAH 1:13

G. ADDITIONAL COMMENTS FOR VERSE 13

God continues with one more exercise for testing Jeremiah's abilities to see clearly. Again God asks Jeremiah, what he sees. Jeremiah says: a boiling pot tilted away from the north.

ANSWER QUESTIONS FOR VERSE 13

G-1: The following verses give a picture, through words, of one type of pot that Jeremiah may have been looking at. What type of pot do you visualize as you read the following verses?

(1Samuel 2:12-14 NRSV): Now the sons of Eli were scoundrels; they had no regard for the Lord or for the duties of the priests to the people. When anyone offered sacrifice, the priest's servant would come, while the meat was boiling, with a three-pronged fork in his hand, and he would thrust it into the pan, or kettle, or cauldron, or pot; all that the fork brought up the priest would take for him-self. This is what they did at Shiloh to all the Israelites who came there.

G-2: As we speculate on what Jeremiah was actually looking at when the Lord asked him what he saw, there is another type of pot to be considered. Proverbs 17:3 calls it a crucible. A crucible is a type of pot that was used for melting down and refining metals such as silver and gold. There is one specific group that the Lord is going to refine. What group will be refined so that the offering of Judah and Jerusalem will be pleasing to the Lord? See the following selected verses.

(Malachi 3:2-3 NRSV): But who can endure the day of his coming, and who can stand when he appears? For he is like a refiner's fire and like fullers' soap; he will sit as a refiner and purifier of silver, and he will purify the descendants of Levi and refine them like gold and silver, until they present offerings to the Lord in righteousness.

G-3: God presents another allegory in Ezekiel 24:1-14 concerning a pot. What does the pot in those verses represent?

📖 **READ JEREMIAH 1:14-15**

H. ADDITIONAL COMMENTS FOR VERSES 14-15

The Lord reveals this message to Jeremiah. "….Out of the north disaster shall break out on all the inhabitants of the land" (Jeremiah 1:14 NRSV).

ANSWER QUESTIONS FOR VERSES 14-15

H-1: The following verses (which were written after the things that Jeremiah saw came to pass) may reveal a dual purpose for the pot.

(Daniel 9:10-11 NRSV): and have not obeyed the voice of the Lord our God by following his laws, which he set before us by his servants the prophets. "All Israel has transgressed your law and turned aside, refusing to obey your voice. So the curse and the oath written in the law of Moses, the servant of God, have been *poured out upon us*, because we have sinned against you.

Turn to Deuteronomy and read chapter 28. There you find a covenant (contact between God and Israel), its blessings and its curses. Make two columns. First write down some of the promised blessings *if* the people obeyed God and then write down some of the promised curses that would be poured out *if* they did not obey.

H-2: When laws are broken in our country, there are set penalties that the lawbreaker must endure in exchange for the crime that was committed. The modern day exchange usually happens by having the lawbreaker spend an amount of money or spend an amount of his or her time in jail or prison. Sometimes the price is high and the lawbreaker has to spend his or her life in order to pay up. When payment is made, the scales of justice are balanced (for at least that one crime).

Picture the scales of justice in Israel: all criminal activity is deposited on the right platform of the scale and the payment made for those penalties is deposited on the left. Though the base and the pillar (that separate the two plate-like platforms) are made to remain stable, that will not be the case as the balancing bar that is on top of the pillar, teeters, giving way to the heavier side. The scale proves that criminal activity is running rampant in Israel. As the platform reserved for offenses gets lower and lower, the platform where the payments are made continues to rise higher and higher. Justice cannot bear the heavy burden or come in balance with the offenses.

God made a way for Israel to be perfect in His eyes. He gave her the knowledge, showing her how to keep those scales in balance. But she turned from God and His plan that made her perfect. Now the scales are about to tip in the land of Israel.

You may be surprised at who you will find living in Israel. Who will be affected by the fall-out? (See some examples in 2Chronicles 2:17, 11:23; 1Kings 9:20-21, 11:1-3; Judges 1:21, 1:27-36; Joshua 6:25, 9:1-27, 13:13, 15:63, 16:10, 17:12; Numbers 31:7-9; Exodus 12:38, 12:44-50.)

H-3: Were there any exceptions for the non-citizens living in Israel when it came to the law? (See selected verses below.)

(Numbers 15:29 NRSV): For both the native among the Israelites and the alien residing among them— you shall have the same law for anyone who acts in error.

(Leviticus 24:22 NRSV): You shall have one law for the alien and for the citizen: for I am the Lord your God.

H-4: All offenses against the law had to be recognized, accounted for, and put to rest. How were unsolved or mysterious deaths supposed to be processed in Israel? (See Deuteronomy 21:1-9.)

H-5: What did the processing and ritual, from your answer to the last question, accomplish? (See Deuteronomy 21:8-9.)

H-6: Let's get back to the disastrous pot. God tells Jeremiah that this disaster will be *out of the north*. See the selected verses below for more insight. If you use your reference notes that go along with these Scriptures (in your NRSV) you will find that *Zaphon* is a word that is used instead of *North*.

(Job 26:7 NRSV): He stretches out Zaphon over the void, and hangs the earth upon nothing.

(Isaiah 14:13 NRSV): You said in your heart, "I will ascend to heaven; I will raise my throne above the stars of God; I will sit on the mount of assembly on the heights of Zaphon.

What do you envision the *north* to be after reading these previous verses?

H-7: "The law is on the way to get you Frank." That is a line that you might hear from a cop show. And when the law arrives it is not really the law (the written words). It is a man or woman dressed in uniform. It is someone who represents and carries out what the laws dictate. And the same representation of the law happens in the courtroom. When the judge enters and everyone stands, it is out of respect and reverence to the law, not the judge because you would surely not stand if you would happen to see that judge enter a restaurant where you were sitting for lunch. The law sits in a high place and holds power even over its administrators (people like the judge and police officer). Is there a parabolic place in verses 14-15 which serve as a seat for the laws by which God will judge His people?

H-8 (OPTIONAL QUESTION): If you have a dictionary, look up the word— set. Pick just two meanings that could describe the reason or motive for the thrones that God called and were then set at the entrance gates of Jerusalem and her cities.

H-9: God tells Jeremiah that these thrones shall be set at the entrance gates of Jerusalem. It seems that we could compare the city gates to our modern day courtrooms or televised newsrooms. According to the following verses, what type of events occurred at the entrance gates of the city?

(Deuteronomy 22:15 NRSV): The father of the young woman and her mother shall then submit the evidence of the young woman's virginity to the elders of the city at the gate.

(Deuteronomy 22:24 NRSV): you shall bring both of them to the gate of that town and stone them to death, the young woman because she did not cry for help in the town and the man because he violated his neighbor's wife. So you shall purge the evil from your midst.

(Deuteronomy 25:7-9 NRSV): But if the man has no desire to marry his brother's widow, then his brother's widow shall go up to the elders at the gate and say, "My husband's brother refuses to perpetuate his brother's name in Israel; he will not perform the duty of a husband's brother to me." Then the elders of his town shall summon him and speak to him. If he persists, saying, "I have no desire to marry her,"

(1Kings 22:10 NRSV): Now the king of Israel and King Jehoshaphat of Judah were sitting on their thrones, arrayed in their robes, at the threshing floor at the entrance of the gate of Samaria; and all the prophets were prophesying before them.

📖 READ JEREMIAH 1:16

I. ADDITIONAL COMMENTS FOR VERSE 16

People are ruled by the laws in their country. And even though officials may come and go, serving only a short term (to uphold the law and deliver justice to and for the people) the laws remain the same. It (the law) continues to sit in power. But the laws that God gave His people were not sitting in the power seats now. The people have forsaken their theocratic calling and that is going to be addressed. God has stepped in and will be the presiding Judge that delivers justice.

ANSWER QUESTIONS FOR VERSE 16

I-1: What is God's complaint and reason for bringing judgment?

I-2: When a nation is established there needs to be a main headquarters, Washington DC is the capitol headquarters in the United States. Through the Bible we know of God's plans to establish a special nation. This is what the Lord said to Abraham at different times in his life:

(Genesis 12:2 NRSV): I will make of you a great nation, …

(Genesis 17:4 NRSV): … You shall be the ancestor of a multitude of nations.

Turn to Jeremiah 33:2. Why did God form the earth?

I-3: Turn to Job 38:33. This verse may also hold a clue. What does God ask that may indicate His plan for earth?

I-4: Turn to Matthew 6:10. Jesus' words may give us a clue about the overall plan. How are we instructed to pray concerning His kingdom?

📖READ JEREMIAH 1:17

J. ADDITIONAL COMMENTS FOR VERSE 17

God demands full commitment from Jeremiah. This appointment comes from the highest power and Jeremiah is about to take on some duties that require allegiance and loyalty.

ANSWER QUESTIONS FOR VERSE 17

J-1: There were some major job hazards for prophets. Jeremiah may have learned about them early on, due to the fact that his father was *of the priests* in Anathoth. Deuteronomy 18:20 (NRSV) says: "But any prophet who speaks in the name of other gods, or who presumes to speak in my name a word that I have not commanded the prophet to speak— that prophet shall die."

According to Jeremiah 2:30 what becomes a personal threat as Jeremiah approaches these misled, misinformed, and defiled leaders?

J-2: Here in verse 17 is the message that Jeremiah hears from the Lord: "But you, gird up your loins; stand up and tell them everything that I command you." If Jeremiah is afraid to tell these men what God has to say; it means that he fears them more than he fears God and if that is the case, God will break him (bring him to submission) in the presence of these men. How do New Testament scholars repeat the same thought on *fearing God*? (See Matthew 10:28.)

📖READ JEREMIAH 1:18-19

K. ADDITIONAL COMMENTS FOR VERSES 18-19

God paints Jeremiah a picture with words. God compares Jeremiah to a fortified city, an iron pillar and a bronze wall.

ANSWER QUESTIONS FOR VERSES 18-19

K-1: God tells Jeremiah that he (Jeremiah) is a fortified city. What is being protected in the fortified city? See Jeremiah 1:9.

K-2: What might provide the fortification for Jeremiah? What did God surround the city walls with in verse 15?

K-3: Look up the word— pillar. How will Jeremiah be like a pillar?

K-4: Here in the United States an individual, be they governor, mayor, police officer, etc., who is elected or appointed to a civil office (a position that involves some type of overseeing the activities, needs, or ways of the public) must take an oath. In that oath they swear to support and defend the Constitution of the United States against any enemies. They take an oath to uphold the outlined laws of the land. So when any of the laws in our country are not being enforced, the leaders will be the first to answer for the disorderly conduct among the people.

It was no different in Israel and she (Israel) is about to be reminded of her lack. But there are a lot of lies going around. A lot of evidence has to be sifted through in order to find the truth. God is thorough and will start at the very beginning. Jeremiah will represent the justice and righteousness of God. Who will fight against the legal team representing justice and righteousness?

K-5: The fact that the Highest Judge is making arrangements to preside over this matter indicates how serious the charges are. He has summoned the thrones and the pot is boiling. He has appointed Jeremiah as the voice to represent His Word and every eye in heaven must be watching! The people of the land have been trying to overthrow the government that they owe their allegiance to and it looks as if charges of treason could be applied. Verse 16 here in chapter 1 reveals the act of treason in the land. What does that verse say?

K-6: Although there are some 613 laws in the Old Testament, a short version of the Ten Commands which were written in stone (see Deuteronomy 5:6-21 for the full version) are available for you on these pages. Which ones have been broken by God's people according to chapter 1?

- 1 You shall have no other gods before me.
- 2 You shall not make for yourself an idol.
- 3 You shall not make wrongful use of the name of the Lord your God
- 4 Remember the Sabbath Day and keep it holy.
- 5 Honor your father and mother.
- 6 You shall not murder.
- 7 You shall not commit adultery.
- 8 You shall not steal.
- 9 You shall not bear false witness against your neighbor.
- 10 You shall not covet anything that belongs to your neighbor.

K-7: Has Jeremiah affected you personally through chapter one? Does anything in your life need to be plucked up, pulled down, destroyed, overthrown, built, or planted? Start your to-do-list for the future. Jeremiah will give you some direction on how to proceed. And then be patient as the changes in your life lead to changes in your community, your society, and even your nation.

Chapter 1 Tag-A-Long

Powerhouse

Jeremiah the fortified is now on his way to Jerusalem. He is like a strong fortified city. He is a powerhouse, inside and out, because God is in him. God's power surrounds and protects him. When Jeremiah arrives at the gates of Jerusalem, it is God who arrives. And when God arrives it is no ordinary thing. We have read what many a spiritual eye has witnessed upon His arrival. When the human eye beholds visions of God, He is accompanied by a great entourage. The following verses suggest this idea: Ezekiel 1:4-28, Daniel 7:9-10, Psalms 68:17 and Deuteronomy 33:1-3. He's packin' power! God has whatever it takes to address the business at hand with nothing lacking. In this particular case God will go straight to the top, setting up for business at the gates of Jerusalem and the 'big bosses' will answer for their actions and the condition of Israel.

In chapter 2 we get to see Jeremiah, a God-made powerhouse, at work. He is a human just like you and me who has been fortified by God. He will be speaking as the prosecuting lawyer from the plaintiff's side of the courtroom. Jeremiah will be seeking to obtain a true confession of guilt from Israel. She was the one who was sworn-in to uphold His law but she has instead inflicted injury to God, His name, His word, and His reputation.

✂ Scrapbook Page For Chapter 1

Utter

When somebody says something that my father-in-law does not go along with or something that he thinks untrue, I've seen him wag his head back and forth and say "No sir-ree, I don't buy that." And then so clearly I can see his actions and hear the words of his voice when he agrees with someone, "Now that I'll buy!" I absolutely knew what he meant when he used those two expressions but it wasn't until I started this Jeremiah project that I realized just how relevant those responses were in the manner that he used them.

When God says: And I will *utter* my judgments against them… (Jeremiah 1:16 NRSV), I thought the word *utter* was just an old, old word that people used centuries ago; and that as our language grew in a different direction over time, the word *speak* replaced it. But when I looked up the word I found that an obsolete definition for *utter* is: *to offer up for sale*. I guess when you really think about it, every word that we *utter* is for sale. People accept it as truth and buy it, or they disagree and don't buy it at all.

God's word is about to go on the auction block at the entrance gates of Jerusalem. That is where God will *utter* His word through Jeremiah. All who hear God's word will have a choice to make. They may choose to believe Jeremiah, shake their heads yes, and say, "I'll buy that"; or they may choose to disagree, wag their heads no, and say "I don't buy that."

Though you are not at the city gate in Jerusalem to buy, or not buy, what is uttered through Jeremiah; there is something that I would like to utter.

I found that there is another definition for the word *utter*. That definition is:

to put into circulation as if legal or genuine.

When I read that I thought, 'This definition is the perfect picture of Jesus!'

How?

John 1:1 NRSV says: In the beginning was the *Word*….

(I interpret *Word* as *God's Utterances*).

John 1:14 NRSV says: And the *Word* became flesh and lived among us,

17

(I interpret *His Word* living among us as *Jesus* living among us.)

Jesus (a significant alteration of the *Word*)

came to us (was put into circulation here on earth)

as the legitimate (legal), genuine, and real God;

and God until that time, had no form but was only known by

His *Word* (*utterances*) and as *Word* (*utterances*).

Jesus is: the Word 'uttered'.

He is: God 'uttered'.

Do you buy that?

Compare Answers For Chapter 1

A-1: officially register as a member of an institution

A-2: They were to assist the descendants of Aaron (the priests) at the house of the Lord. They took care of the courts and the chambers, the cleansing of all that was holy, and any work for the service of the house God. They also assisted with the rows of bread, the choice flour for the grain offering, the wafers of unleavened bread, the baked offering, the offering mixed with oil, and all measures of quantity and size. They were also required to stand every morning and evening, thanking and praising the Lord and also whenever the burnt offerings were offered to the Lord on Sabbaths, new moons, and appointed festivals, according to the number required of them.

A-3: the firstborn that opened the womb (human or animal)

A-4: a payment made by a feudal tenant to his lord upon succeeding to an inherited estate

A-5: affairs of a 'people' are governed by officials who are regarded as divinely guided

A-6: Reuben, Simeon, Gad, Judah, Issachar, Zebulun, Ephraim, Manasseh, Benjamin, Dan, Asher, Naphtali

A-7: from the line of priests

A-8: Tithes and portions from the people.

A-9: priest

A-10: the House of David out of Judah

A-11: Josiah, Jehoiakim, Zedekiah

A-12: Hilkiah, also the name of Jeremiah's father

B-1: "Before I formed you in the womb, I knew you, and before you were born I consecrated you; I appointed you a prophet to the nations." (Jeremiah 1:5 NRSV)

C-1: "Do not say, 'I am only a boy', for you shall go to all to whom I send you, and you shall speak whatever I command you" (Jeremiah 1:7 NRSV).

C-2: "Do not be afraid of them, for I am with you to deliver you, says the Lord" (Jeremiah 1:8 NRSV).

D-1: The Lord put out His hand and touched Jeremiah's mouth and God said: "Now I have put my words in your mouth" (Jeremiah 1:9 NRSV).

E-1: He was also appointed over nations and kingdoms who served other gods.

E-2: a *nation* refers to those who were not Jewish (according to the dictionary)

E-3: God's promise to accompany him

F-1: riddles.

F-2 (OPTIONAL QUESTION): A riddle is a mystery and difficult to understand. God spoke in omens and by signs to His servants and they delivered His message.

F-3: You have seen well.

F-4: Twelve staffs were laid before the Lord. Each leader from their ancestral house (tribe) was represented before God by the staff given. The next day there was one staff that sprouted. It put forth buds, produced blossoms, and bore ripe almonds. The spouting branch was God's way of declaring whom He had chosen. (God chose the branch with Levi's leader, Aaron.) Seeing the almond branch may have been some proof of licensing for Jeremiah, by God, since it was once a sign of being chosen.

G-1: These pots (cauldrons, vessels or pots) were used by the priests when boiling the sacrificial offerings to the Lord.

G-2: Levi

G-3: the city of Jerusalem

H-1: If they obeyed the Lord He would set them high above all nations of the earth. They would receive blessings on their cities, fruit of their wombs, fruits from their ground, and the fruit of their livestock. They would be blessed coming in and going out (in all directions and all times). Their enemies would be defeated and come in one way but run in all directions to escape. God will command blessing for them in many forms. All of the people of the earth would fear those called by the name of the Lord. They would be the lenders not borrowers. They would be the head not the tail. They would be on top, not the bottom if they obeyed the commandments of the Lord.

If they did not obey the Lord, He would send disease, panic and frustration. They would be cursed in their cities, in their fields, in their baskets and bowls. Their wombs would be cursed as well as the fruit of their ground. They would be cursed when it came to their increase of cattle and issue of their flock. Curses would follow them in all directions. They will experience pestilence and it would cling to them until it consumed them off the land that God gave them. Fever, drought, and mildew as well will pursue. Enemies will be victors and they are the ones who will be fleeing seven ways. They will become repulsive to kingdoms on the earth. Birds will eat their corpses and no one will frighten them away. They will be inflicted with incurable diseases from Egypt. They will be continually abused, robbed, and driven mad by the things they see. Their children will be taken away. Foreigners will be their masters. Aliens among them will ascend higher and higher while they descend lower and lower and become a proverb.

H-2: aliens, foreigners, previous natives, captives from previous battles, slaves

H-3: No, everyone must have the same law.

H-4: Judges and elders go out to the crime scene and measure which town the body is closest to. The elders of the town nearest the body will provide the heifer for redemption. The priests, the sons of Levi, come forward to pronounce a blessing in the name of the Lord, by their decision all cases, like this, are settled. All elders wash their hands over the dead heifer saying: "Our hands did not shed this blood, (speaking of the dead victim found) nor were we witnesses to it. Absolve, O Lord your people Israel, whom you redeemed; do not let the guilt of innocent blood remain in the midst of your people Israel." This is how they purged the guilt of innocent blood.

H-5: It took away the guilt of innocent blood from the midst of the people.

H-6: The 'north' may represent a place that man does not have access to.

H-7: The laws could be sitting on the thrones.

H-8 (OPTIONAL QUESTION): 1. To furnish as a pattern or model (for His people) 2. As a dog, to point out the position of game by holding a fixed position (their duties as they are placed there are to point out the abominations)

H-9: The leaders sat at the city gates and this is where cases were settled and sentences carried out. This is where you could go to hear news from God, which came from the prophets and I suppose this is where you would hear news from other cities as well as your own. The gate was the place to sit if you wanted to be the first to hear any incoming news outside of your city or town, which was carried in by foot.

I-1: For all of their wickedness in forsaking Him and they made offerings to other gods and worshipped the works of their own hands

I-2: To establish it

I-3: Do you know the ordinances of the heavens? Can you establish their rule on the earth? (Job 38:33 NRSV.)

I-4: Your kingdom come. Your will be done, on earth as it is in heaven (Matthew 6:10 NRSV).

J-1: His very own people have a reputation of killing prophets from among their own people.

J-2: Do not fear those who kill the body but cannot kill the soul; rather fear him who can destroy both soul and body in hell (Matthew 10:28 NRSV).

K-1: God's word

K-2: The thrones (the law that administers justice)

K-3: He will be chief supporter of God's word and stand alone.

K-4: The kings of Judah, its princes, its priests, and the people of the land

K-5: And I will utter my judgments against them, for all their wickedness in forsaking me; they have made offerings to other gods, and worshipped the works of their own hands (Jeremiah 1:16 NRSV).

K-6: 1.You shall have no other gods before me. 2. You shall not make for yourself any idols.

K-7: I will work on learning about God so I can obey Him.

Chapter 2

Chapter 2 Prelude

Family Heirloom

There was a man named Abram. Isaiah 41:8 tells us that he was God's friend. God showered His friend with some great promises. Below is a list of, what we know to be, the first of the many great promises that God made to Abram:

- I will make of *you* a great nation, and
- I will bless *you,* and make *your* name great, so that *you* will be a blessing.
- I will bless those who bless *you,* and the one who curses *you* I will curse; and
- In *you* all the families of the earth shall be blessed (Genesis 12:2-3 NRSV).

As Abram invested his faith in God's promises, the promises grew at a very steady rate. By the time Genesis 17:4-12 rolled around he found out from God that the investment of faith had really paid off. The promises went up in value, big time! They could now be compared to priceless family heirlooms because they were not just for him but could be forever handed down from generation to generation. Due to the forever part these family heirlooms are better, by far, than any other inheritance ever known on earth.

It was cause for celebration. Abram received a new name from God; and he (now Abraham, according to Genesis 17:5) was going to be the ancestor of a *multitude* of nations instead of being (just) *a* great nation! And with His words God continued painting a picture of Abraham's prosperous future and that of the heirs:

- I will make you exceeding fruitful; and I will make nations of you, and
- kings shall come from you.
- I will establish my covenant between me and you, and your offspring after you throughout their generations, for an everlasting covenant, to be God to you and to your offspring after you. And
- I will give to you, and to your offspring after you, the land where you are now an alien, all the land of Canaan, for a perpetual holding; and I will be their God (Genesis 17:6-8 NRSV).

As the heirlooms maintained their value there was one particular line of Abraham's offspring that seemed to have it made-in-the-shade. Those who God had His eye on were to be inherently wealthy. They were destined to be this world's leading lenders, suppliers, and providers. They would never have to borrow, be in debt, or have a need for anything. God would make these children great and nations would seek them for help in all matters. But there was something that the children seemed to misunderstand. This everlasting position of greatness and power would come from God alone. He, and no one else, would secure this position for them. Knowing, seeing, and believing this one thing would have been a complete turn-around, not only for them but for the unsettling conditions of the world in which they lived.

One thing was sure. Israel, those in line for this great inheritance, was a rebellious bunch. God had His hands full. Getting them to the place where He can fulfill what He promised to Abraham can be easy or hard for them. It looks like they have chosen to take the difficult route. Going in the direction that God was coaxing them was something that their stubborn hearts did not want to do. They did not embrace the same sentiment, about God, as their ancestor King David. David compared God to a shepherd and said this of Him: …your rod and your staff— they comfort me (Psalms 23:4 NRSV). These children of Israel despised God's rod of correction that would lead them to green pastures and still running waters. So the wild children saw only one way to survive their many aimless wanderings and that was to strike hands and yoke up with neighboring nations.

In this chapter of Jeremiah, God compares these offspring of Abraham to an unfaithful bride who went astray. He asks the unfaithful bride who has forsaken Him: What then do you gain by going to Egypt, to drink the waters of the Nile? Or what do you gain by going to Assyria, to drink the waters of the Euphrates? (See Jeremiah 2:18 NRSV.)

Chapter 2 Study

Showing Legal Grounds for Divorce

CHAPTER 2 READING, COMMENTS, AND QUESTIONS

The gavel sounds.

And these are the words that broke the silence inside the courtroom that day:

"Hear ye, Hear ye! Now all will hear the history of the defendant in this case of:

God-v-the bride.

The name of the defendant is Israel.

Abraham became the defendant's grandfather

on the day that Isaac became his father.

They called the defendant Jacob but

God gave him promise and announced his new name, Israel. (See Genesis 35:10.)

Twelve sons descended from Israel and the descendants of the twelve sons are known as

the twelve tribes of Israel.

There was a great famine in the land where Jacob (aka Israel) and his small clan dwelt.

All of them ended up in the land of Egypt where there was food-a-plenty.

It was from human deceit and long-suffering, both out of Jacob's loin,

by which God created a plan of provision that kept them all alive." (See Genesis 37-50.)

The courtroom still sits in silence and the bailiff continues:

"This God-planned provision is how we, as a chosen and holy nation,

stand here today in this courtroom.

While living in Egypt, the children of Israel became very numerous in the land.

The Egyptians feared their great numbers and forced them into slavery.

God heard them suffering and called on a man named Moses.

Moses delivered God's plan and led them out of bondage.

He brought them to the door of the land that God promised

the forefather Jacob. (See Genesis 28:13.)

The great numbers of those in the exodus were divided by their twelve ancestral fathers

and each one of the tribes (eventually) settled to his own inheritance in the new land of promise.

But the twelve tribes became rivaling powers and the whole of Israel was split into two kingdoms.

(Turn to 1Kings 11:29-40 to see God's hand at work in this split.)

The northern kingdom carried on the name of

Israel,

and the southern kingdom was called

Judah.

As this case comes about, we all must realize that Israel, the northern kingdom,

has been ravaged by war and taken captive.

But, we, the southern kingdom of Judah,

still have cities that are controlled by rulers from among our own people.

Israel's capitol *was* known as

Samaria.

Judah's capitol *is still*

Jerusalem."

As warring Assyria continued to eat-up the northern kingdom bit by bit (with Jerusalem still on its menu) it seemed that God was nowhere to be found. And while kinsmen were still facing turbulence and living with the evidence of war torn lives, evil words and evil thoughts of arrogance were growing out of control among those who were feeling safe and sound in Jerusalem.

📖READ JEREMIAH 2:1-3

A. ADDITIONAL COMMENTS FOR VERSES 1-3

God sends Jeremiah to Jerusalem. It is Judah's capitol city and it will serve as God's courtroom in this court case of: God-v-the bride. God will recap the history between Him and Israel (in earlier days, when it was still a whole) in a picturesque manner comparing Israel to a young bride. He has fond memories and tells of the time when she was younger, purer, and devoted to Him.

ANSWER QUESTIONS FOR VERSES 1-3

A-1: If someone told you: "go to the capitol and proclaim this news in the hearing of Washington D.C." who comes to your mind as being the targeted audience?

A-2: As you picture Jeremiah proclaiming the message from God where would he probably stand to deliver God's word? (See 1Kings 22:10.)

A-3: Though unseen who may be present at this time? (See Jeremiah 1:15.)

A-4 (OPTIONAL QUESTION): God says that He remembers her (Israel's) devotion and love as she followed Him through the desert. Exodus 13:21-22 tells us that the Lord was a pillar of cloud by day and a pillar of fire by night and that was how He led her. Why do you suppose He did not instruct His bride to follow a certain star or the position of the sun?

A-5: Israel eats at God's table and she lives under His roof, but she takes the perpetual privilege for granted. From generation to generation, Israel does not act in accordance to the house rules. All of Israel proves to be defiant and out of control. According to the law, what have those who perpetually enjoy the good life become? (See the last part of verse 3.)

📖READ JEREMIAH 2:4-8

B. ADDITIONAL COMMENTS FOR VERSES 4-8

A loving husband lays His life open. He starts from the very beginning when He brought her out of Egypt. He presents the devotion and powerful care He has shown, toward His bride, in this relationship.

ANSWER QUESTIONS FOR VERSES 4-8

B-1: When the leader of our country (the president) makes a speech that pertains to our nation, he first addresses those to whom he is talking. His speech might start out like this: "Mr. Speaker, Mr. Vice President, Members of Congress, distinguished guests and fellow Americans…" Though the speech that follows is for all Americans to hear, not all do. But the leader will continue as if all citizens were right in front of him because the elected representative, of the people, is there to be the eyes and ears of the absent multitudes.

When God addresses the people of His nation He starts out like this: "O house of Jacob, and all the families of the house of Israel..." God is expecting the present day bride to not only answer for those not present, but she will also answer for the past generations. God cannot understand the past actions of the wayward bride. Maybe someone in the courtroom has knowledge of what happened and can answer. What does He ask in verse 5?

B-2: When a president campaigns for re-election he or she might run on all of the positive things that had been accomplished during the time spent in office. God gives His bride a quick reminder of what He has done for her. What had God done for His bride in her earlier days that she seems to have forgotten about?

B-3: Once the bride entered into her new home she defiled it. Who is being charged here in this chapter for being slack in their duties? (See verse 8.)

B-4: It is a leader's duty to exercise authority and govern. Do you think that a leader should be called to account when those they are responsible for act unjustly, cause harm, or break the law?

📖 **READ JEREMIAH 2:9**

C. ADDITIONAL COMMENTS FOR VERSE 9

(Let's get back to the courtroom.) Penalties are cruel, inconsiderate, and far reaching. Even innocent victims are affected when the law is broken.

ANSWER QUESTIONS FOR VERSE 9

C-1: Out of the ten laws that were written in stone, by God, the people of God are, so far, being charged with breaking the first two. (See Jeremiah 1:16.) There is a *rider*, in one of these first two laws, for the participant's children. The *rider* could be very beneficial or very detrimental depending on the actions of the responsible party. What is the *rider* and how would the violation of this law prove the past generations to be arrogant and unconcerned about the future generations? (See Exodus 20:1-6 below.)

(Exodus 20:1-6 NRSV): Then God spoke all these words: I am the Lord your God, who brought you out of the land of Egypt, out of the house of slavery; you shall have no other gods before me. You shall not make for yourself an idol, whether in the form of anything that is in heaven above, or that is on the earth beneath, or that is in the water under the earth. You shall not bow down to them or worship them; for I the Lord your God am a jealous God, punishing children for the iniquity of parents, to the third and fourth generation of those who reject me, but showing steadfast love to the thousandth generation of those who love me and keep my commandments.

C-2: Stiff penalties that would bring hurt to children in future generations should have increased the desires of parents and grandparents to do what was right. But that was not the case. There were many grandchildren who became victims. They unfortunately, but legally, suffered not only for their own trespasses but they also suffered for trespasses that they inherited.

God has always expected more from His people. Not only must they be responsible for current social conditions but they must carry the burdens left behind by their less responsible ancestors. And then on top of that they are expected to display positive actions of concern for the future social conditions. Though God will not prevent justice from being served, He provides Israel with a pill to dull the pain that she must endure. He tells us about the pain-reliever that fights against the ill-inheritance and worries of her future. (The following verse shows the future acts of God concerning this case. He constantly fights to relieve, rehabilitate, and find some sort of freedom for the defendant whom the law is most violent against.) God provides Israel with a legally court appointed Advocate. God's faithful friend will be the pill that relieves. The friend that He calls is named: Comfort. What does Isaiah 40:1-2 say?

C-3: 1Kings 15:1-5 presents evidence of the law at work. See the verses below and answer: how did King David stabilize future conditions for his grandchildren?

(1Kings 15:1-5 NRSV): Now in the eighteenth year of King Jeroboam son of Nebat, Abijam began to reign over Judah. He reigned for three years in Jerusalem. His mother's name was Maacah daughter of Abishalom. He committed all the sins that his father did before him; his heart was not true to the Lord his God, like the heart of his father David. Nevertheless for David's sake the Lord his God gave him a lamp in Jerusalem, setting up his son after him, and establishing Jerusalem; because David did what was right in the sight of the Lord, and did not turn aside from anything that he commanded him all the days of his life, except in the matter of Uriah the Hittite.

C-4: Here is another example of the law at work. This is one instance where the victims, who could not escape the long arm of the curse, would call on Comfort, the pill that God provides. How did the actions of King Jeroboam earn him a spot with those who are considered to be less responsible? (See the selected verses below.)

(1Kings 14:7-11 NRSV): Go, tell Jeroboam, 'Thus says the Lord, the God of Israel: Because I exalted you from among the people , made you leader over my people Israel, and tore the kingdom away from the house of David to give it to you; yet you have not been like my servant David, who kept my commandments and followed me with all his heart, doing only that which was right in my sight, but you have done evil above all those who were before you and have gone and made for yourself other gods, and cast images, provoking me to anger, and have thrust me behind your back; therefore, I will bring evil upon the house of Jeroboam. I will cut off from Jeroboam every male, both bond and free in Israel, and will consume the house of Jeroboam, just as one burns up dung until it is all gone. Anyone belonging to Jeroboam who dies in the city, the dogs shall eat; and anyone who dies in the open country, the birds of the air shall eat; for the Lord has spoken.' (The following verses may also be of interest: 1Kings 12:28; 13:33.)

📖 **READ JEREMIAH 2:10-13**

D. ADDITIONAL COMMENTS FOR VERSES 10-13

(Back to the trial in progress) God brings in surprise witnesses. And what a surprise it is when the illicit behaviors of other nations serve as character witnesses against the defendant Israel.

ANSWER QUESTIONS FOR VERSES 10-13

D-1: God says: "*My people* have changed their glory." What did *God's people* change their glory for?

D-2: I have always had a difficult time pinpointing what the word glory means. But I think I have found a word that could stand in its place and that word is stellar. Stellar means: composed of stars, of or relating to the stars, chief, leading, outstanding, first-rate, or principal.

God gave *His people* that high in the sky status when He told Abraham: "….I will make your offspring as numerous as the stars of heaven…." (Genesis 22:17 NRSV). God gave Israel a make over. She had a new image. But she reverted back to her old self. The result of this change would cause a great turmoil, a great shift in the mood of the heavens. What does verse 12 say?

D-3 (OPTIONAL QUESTION): Wisemen from the East followed one bright and shining star to find the Savior (Matthew 2:1-2). Imagine the little sparkles of glory, the heavens may have held, at the time that Israel was created as a nation. But God reorders the heavens. Look up the words: appalled, shocked, and desolate. These words reveal the state of the heavens and God's people. What are the definitions of the descriptive words?

D-4 (OPTIONAL QUESTION): Isaiah 14:12-16 gives some bits and pieces of some confusion in (or about) the heavens. What does Isaiah 14:13-14 say?

D-5: Does God seem to be angry at the witnessing nations (verses 10-11) for serving other gods?

D-6: God's people have forsaken Him. Though He provided them with a perfect fountain they ventured out and dug cisterns for themselves. These actions are inappropriate when it comes to God's people. They acted with negligence as they gambled with future generations as well as their own lives. What does God call their reckless acts?

D-7: Think of a time when your actions proved you to be negligent. Can you see how your actions were a gamble? When you take risks that could cause injury or loss of life to someone or even something, do you think that God gives your reckless acts the same name that He gave to Israel's reckless acts?

📖 **READ JEREMIAH 2:14-19**

E. ADDITIONAL COMMENTS FOR VERSES 14-19

The bride is still on the stand and the questioning continues. God makes His bride take a good look at herself and her actions. God had set her free from the bonds of Egypt and placed her high above other nations but she was back to her old self. She has somehow managed to once again become the plundered. God brings up her past involvement with Egypt and Assyria (Jeremiah 2:18). You are provided below with some known facts of her demise. This is a lot of information to keep up with so you may want to draw five symbols to represent each kingdom as you read. This method of using symbols helped me to keep who-is-helping-who-out, straight.

Pekah, the king of Israel along with the king of Syria,

tried to enlist Ahaz, the king of Judah, to fight with them against Assyria.

When Ahaz of Judah would not join them, the two kings attacked him.

So Ahaz of Judah turned to Assyria for help in this struggle against the two kings.

Assyria did comply but because of this protection Judah became a suffering vassal of Assyria.

Reverential regard and honor were paid by the subservient Judah.

Many years later, the strong Assyria overthrew Syria and Israel,

while Judah, the vassal servant, yet had kings from among her own people.

Hezekiah, son of Ahaz, becoming king at a later point in time, tired of the vassalage,

attacked Assyria with support from Egypt.

But the support from Egypt was not readily available.

So the Assyrian king successfully conquered the cities surrounding Jerusalem.

History says that Hezekiah prevented this fate for the capitol city Jerusalem only by paying tribute.

ANSWER QUESTIONS FOR VERSES 14-19

E-1: The defendant has not gained anything by going to Egypt or Assyria. These allies and their gods were useless when it came to helping God's bride. No priest, ruler, or prophet in Jerusalem can blame the fall of Israel on these other nations or their gods. Israel's failure lies in her own personal wickedness. God says: Your wickedness will punish you, and your apostasies will convict you… (Jeremiah 2:19 NRSV). What words in the last part of verse 19 pinpoint what wickedness is?

📖 **READ JEREMIAH 2:20-22**

F. ADDITIONAL COMMENTS FOR VERSES 20-22

The bride's condition is presented as perplexing.

ANSWER QUESTIONS FOR VERSES 20-22

F-1: God speaks to His bride in a parable: "I planted you as a choice vine, from the purest stock. How then did you turn degenerate and become a wild vine?" (Jeremiah 2:21 NRSV). Even though it is not yet clear how the pure vines changed, turn to Matthew 21:33-41. The condition of the vine is not the main subject in this parable, but what were the surrounding circumstances that contributed to the ill produce at harvest time?

F-2: The bride tried to hide some evidence of her guilt before coming to court today. But what does God say about her fuddled attempts to cover up evidence?

📖 **READ JEREMIAH 2:23-25**

G. ADDITIONAL COMMENTS FOR VERSES 23-25

God's bride looks at herself and tries to say that she is not defiled. But the whole courtroom can see the truth. Evil does not have to come looking for her. She has worn herself out trying to keep a good hold on it.

Let's rewind and take a look at Israel as she walks up to take her place on the witness stand. God has made her beautiful. She is like a queen with perfect etiquette. But look at the way she's walking today. Therein you will find evidence of her wanderings. Each step that she takes, toward the witness stand, seems to bring pain. Some of those inside the courtroom snicker at the hobbling beauty queen who has tried to shove a size ten foot into shoes that are only size five. God has provided great growth but she is never home long enough to get new shoes that fit her growing body. And to top it all off, the heel of her once beautiful left shoe is broken off. But she still holds her head high. She is not ashamed of her condition.

Before she turns to seat herself on the witness stand (after the long and painful walk), it is plain to see; there is no way to hide that big sparkling libation cup that hangs like a purse from her right shoulder. It is empty and full of dust. It has not held anything to quench her thirst for quite some time.

ANSWER QUESTIONS FOR VERSES 23-25

G-1: Once Israel is on the stand all evidence of her guilt is hidden behind the podium. But God has not forgotten what He saw as she approached the stand. As He stands between her and the whole courtroom, He compares her to a restive young camel.

"At first, she starts out faithful and follows. She goes straight....then all of the sudden she takes an odd notion and goes to the left for a while. Left, left, left….. Only after numerous tugs does she allow herself to be led back. And as if nothing had ever happened, she follows faithfully. But all evidence will reveal that she can stay true to her straight path for only a short period of time. Because without warning or cause…there she goes again…wandering off to the right, to the right, to the right…Her weaving to the right and weaving to the left, like a young camel, will not be stopped."

God goes on to compare His bride to a donkey who is 'at home' (comfortable, fits in well) out in the desert, looking for any and everyone who passes by. He has called her. He has told her time and time again: "Keep your feet from going unshod and your throat from thirst."

Though we don't know if her words are to be considered as an admission or a confession, she says: "It is hopeless, for I have loved strangers, and after them I will go" (Jeremiah 2:25 NRSV). Use your dictionary to find the difference between confession and admission.

📖 READ JEREMIAH 2:26-28

H. ADDITIONAL COMMENTS FOR VERSES 26-28

Though this case will lead to numerous investigations against others who have committed criminal acts, that injure God's reputation, the house of Israel is on trial here. They, their kings, priests, and prophets will be shamed just like a thief (as per God).

ANSWER QUESTIONS FOR VERSES 26-28

H-1: God has a further complaint about the house of Israel, their officials, kings, priests, and prophets in Jeremiah 2:27-28. How have they contributed to, and continue to contribute to, the ills that are being experienced in this (one of a kind) society?

H-2: In verse 27, God's people infringe on another one of the ten commands that were written in stone (Ten Commandments). Who, besides God, receives dishonor through these particular rebellious acts found in Israel?

H-3: Just when Judah (the southern kingdom) arrogantly thinks that Israel (the northern kingdom) is the only one in trouble here. God throws a quick left hook. Judah has not escaped the heavy handed words of God. As God is in the middle of addressing Israel, what does He suddenly say to Judah?

H-4: Judah is arrogant and her words prove it. What arrogant thing is Judah known to have said about, exiled Israel, her kinsfolk? (See Ezekiel 11:15.)

H-5: The southern kingdom has managed to survive. Judah and Benjamin (1Kings 11:29-35; 12:21; 2Chronicles 11:1-3; 14:8; 15:2) are the only tribes still in possession of their inheritance. So which group of Levi's offspring is still in possession of their assigned towns and pasture lands? Review the assigned settlements of the four groups of Levi in A-11 back in chapter 1 for the answer.

H-6: The United States Congress consists of two houses; the lower house can be addressed as the House of Representatives and the upper house can be addressed as the Senate. God addresses two houses in this chapter. What are the two houses? Go back to Jeremiah 2:4 for the answer.

H-7: You may wonder how and why the trial for Israel (the northern kingdom which has already been exiled) is taking place in Jerusalem right now. What very notable and important event took place, previous to this trial, according to 2Chronicles 11:13?

📖 READ JEREMIAH 2:29

I. ADDITIONAL COMMENTS FOR VERSE 29

As God speaks the whole truth, the people (I would imagine mostly to be leaders) inside the courtroom don't like it. They see God as a trouble-maker instead of the truth-and-justice-seeker that He is. They are now complaining about God and blame Him for the condition of the nation.

ANSWER QUESTIONS FOR VERSE 29

I-1: The whole courtroom erupts in an uproar about God's comments. He has hit a nerve. Some have their fists in the air. Some are grumbling to one another and rising up in their seats. "God is not doing His part." "Where has He been?" "Look at the condition of our nation!" "He certainly is not rolling up His sleeves around here!" What does God say to them in verse 29?

I-2: Even though the priests and the Levites left Israel (the northern part of the kingdom) due to the circumstances that you stated in your answer to H-7, why do you think they are still on trial?

📖 READ JEREMIAH 2:30-32

J. ADDITIONAL COMMENTS FOR VERSES 30-32

Those who are representing Israel in the courtroom had been openly blessed by God's way; and He gave them wisdom and power in order to lead, guide, and teach the people in the land. They show their appreciation by running off with the all loot (wisdom) and abandoning their post. Bride-Israel may also be looking at charges of abandonment and (child) endangerment.

ANSWER QUESTIONS FOR VERSES 30-32

J-1: Read chapter 26 in Leviticus. This will give you a good idea of the weapons, specifically contracted, to be used if something like this should happen between Israel and her Lord. When the bride, who instead of remaining devoted to her husband (her calling) and taking care of the family affairs, decides to break the law that binds them; the family that she has abandoned will suffer. God asks Israel how she can say (so flippantly) "we are free". What understanding does God want bride-Israel to come to, concerning this whole situation that led to courtroom litigation? (See Leviticus 26:40-42.)

J-2: Women enhance their beauty and proudly identify their status by what they wear. Young girls adorn themselves with ornaments which signify their availability and a bride adorns herself with her children. But Israel has a whole new look inside this courtroom today. She is not wearing the jewels that God gave her. God is concerned about what she leaves behind in her act of abandonment. What does Zechariah 9:16 say?

J-3: Those who God called *"Mine"* (Numbers 3:44-45) were, in allegory, the shepherds and these chosen shepherds are the ones who would care for His many flocks. But in order to keep sheep, something is needed. Go back to Joshua 21:7-41. Glance over all of those verses. What is specifically named to accompany all of the towns that the Levites received from Israel? (You may be able to parabolically relate this to the shepherd-sheep relationship between the leaders and the common people.)

J-4: In Exodus 20:8, the people were commanded to: Remember the Sabbath day, and keep it holy. How do we know that *His people* have broken this law too? Breaking this law only contributes to the tragedy of this family and is another infringement on one the ten commands written in stone.

J-5: Who would be held responsible and have to make answer when Sabbath Day laws were broken? (See Numbers 18:1.)

📖 READ JEREMIAH 2:33-35

K. ADDITIONAL COMMENTS FOR VERSES 33-35

"I'll be there with bells on!" This is an enthusiastic response to an invitation. I believe that God would have loved to hear those enthusiastic words, from Israel, as she was summoned to appear before her Lord and King. This response would have been the expected response from a loving and faithful bride. Exodus 39:25-26 describes what should have been on the hem of His bride's garment. There should have been pure bells of gold between pomegranates. But as the prosecution continues to question the bride He notices something else there instead and makes some comments.

ANSWER QUESTIONS FOR VERSES 33-35

K-1: In these verses God brings attention to some bloodshed that He notices on the fashionable skirt of the bride. Even though someone else is serving a term in the *official uniform* (so to speak), there is clearly evidence of her guilt on the skirt (which has been passed down from generation to generation). That evidence alone, presented reason to review some old cases. The court reopened and reviewed some cold case files.

God has tried everything over the years to keep this girl from destruction and annihilation. He tried talking through His prophets but words didn't work. Even severe punishment would not change her ways. If this were a western made for television, God would be the loyal and faithful serving sheriff and the people would be the outlaws. Every time God sends a deputy (true prophet) out with a warrant, they (being armed only in spirit with the truth) are murdered. The sheriff has used every available resource that He has to get this outlaw to come in and be rehabilitated so that the town can once again be a good place to live and bring up a family.

In Jeremiah 2:34 God says that even though the innocent poor were not caught breaking in, their blood is on her skirt. What do you suppose God means by that? Though God addressed this, a few verses back, in the last part of verse 30 the answer may also be found in Matthew 23:29-39.

K-2 (OPTIONAL QUESTION): The actions of the leaders were shameful. Are you ashamed of anything that your ancestors or the leaders of your country have done in the past? Are there any actions that left a nasty and stubborn stain or burden of shame for your generation? Do you feel any remorse or responsibility to those who were injured and left scarred by a shameful act?

K-3 (OPTIONAL QUESTION): Have you, yourself, made any decisions that have had a bad effect on your family, your children, or your grandchildren? Have you done anything that will 'sting' them later? Where do you fall short as a leader?

K-4: Israel will not stop throwing the kindling onto the fire (that which serves to feeds God's anger). Why will God open up and give full vent to His wrath? (See the selected verses that follow.)

(Lamentations 4:11-14 NRSV): The Lord gave full vent to his wrath; he poured out his hot anger, and kindled a fire in Zion that consumed its foundations. The kings of the earth did not believe, nor did any of the inhabitants of the world, that foe or enemy could enter the gates of Jerusalem. It was for the sins of her prophets and the iniquities of her priests, who shed the blood of the righteous in the midst of her. Blindly they wandered through the streets, so defiled with blood that no one was able to touch their garments.

K-5: Even though the evidence (blood on her skirt) has been found, the bride still says she is innocent. She believes she is only following ordinance number 20 found in section 18 of Deuteronomy (Deuteronomy 18:20). But as she sits on the stand she lies to the court and to herself. She again thinks she has done absolutely nothing wrong, even after God, who is all wisdom, tells her that she has. In verse 35, God says He is going to bring her to judgment for this untrue statement which only serves to harm His reputation. What do we call it when someone gets up on the stand in a courtroom and tells a lie? What is that crime?

READ JEREMIAH 2:36-37

L. ADDITIONAL COMMENTS FOR VERSES 36-37

Have you ever stood in front of a trick mirror? Well Israel apparently has one of those. Even though God has told her what she looks like, the bride will not face the truth about her appearance or what her future holds. Her cup is empty. Her shoes are worn out. Her skirt is soaked with blood. But in light of all this she steps down from the witness stand with the mind to continue on the same path and it will only lead to her destruction.

ANSWER QUESTIONS FOR VERSES 36-37

L-1: The bride is wearing herself out looking for something that is not and will never be as good as what the Lord has given her. What does God have to say about the nations that the bride runs to and trusts in?

L-2: Turn to Ezekiel chapter 23 for a detailed version of what God has to say about His bride. What is the warning to the unrepentant bride in Ezekiel 23:45?

L-3 (OPTIONAL QUESTION): Who do you think the righteous judges (from the last question) could be?

L-4: Although there are some 613 commands in the Old Testament, here are the 10 commands that God wrote in stone and gave to the people of His nation. Check the ones that have been broken and give the verses, from chapter 1 and 2, that indicate the infringement.

- 1 You shall have no other gods before me.
- 2 You shall not make for yourself any idols.
- 3 You shall not make wrongful use of the name of the Lord your God.
- 4 Remember the Sabbath Day and keep it holy.
- 5 Honor your father and mother.
- 6 You shall not murder.
- 7 You shall not commit adultery.
- 8 You shall not steal.
- 9 You shall not bear false witness against your neighbor.
- 10 You shall not covet anything that is your neighbors.

L-5: Has Jeremiah affected you? Is there something in your life that needs to be plucked up, pulled down, destroyed, or overthrown? Is there something that you should build or plant?

Chapter 2 Tag-A-Long

Remorse

You here on earth, as well as those in heaven, have witnessed the unfolding of this courtroom case: God-v-the bride. When I heard God, expressly in no uncertain terms, tell this ol' girl what she had done wrong I thought He was looking for some remorse. But there were no signs of that coming from the witness stand. She felt no shame and she did not seem to care that her actions brought on the ravaged condition of her fellow man, as well as herself.

Maybe God wanted the leaders of His people to take the first step and do something like our leaders did. In the year of 2009, in Washington DC, the Senate passed a resolution apologizing for a great injustice that our nation had committed. It apologized for the practice of slavery. The resolution was an attempt for the federal government to take responsibility for the wrongs that had been committed for over a period of 250 years. The national leaders took the first step in making repairs by admitting guilt and apologizing. They expressed regret over the injustices.

But this prideful bride felt no sorrow or regret. She was not ready to apologize. She was not going to take any blame or carry any guilt for the degenerate acts which led to the ravaged condition of her twelve states. All of the Promised Land was a mess due to the injustice that was found there. Yet she felt no pain for the suffering that her unchecked guilt had caused throughout the land.

At this point the leaders in Jerusalem still had some power to make change. What if the gadabouts would have admitted their error? What if they would have given their heritage the same consideration that Frederick Douglas gave his heritage? (Frederick Douglas was an influential African-American who expressed his convictions through powerful public speeches.) What would have happened if the kings and priests, the lawyers and the prophets, would have stood up and said words similar to those of Douglas?

The following words of Douglas are rendered to you with some change to fit Jerusalem.

Fellow citizens, above your tumultuous, busy chatter, I hear the mournful wail of millions, whose chains are heavy and grievous. Their pain questions the joy of my freedom today. If I do forget our past gross injustices— if I do not remember our brothers suffering to this very day, may my right hand forget her cunning and may my tongue cling to the roof of my mouth. (Compare Psalms 137:5-6 to the words in Douglas's speech.)

Even though their fingerprints were all over the broken pieces (of the nation), the leaders refused to bend and pick up any of the mess. As they walk through all of the damage, that God says they were responsible for, they prove themselves to be arrogant and unconcerned.

✂ Scrapbook Page For Chapter 2

Cistern

Due to my desperate need for help in comprehending God's Word, there is something that stays close by my side, actually at an arm's reach. It is Webster's Dictionary. I have three editions and I look up a lot of words quite frequently. So my search for the Lord is at a pace that I am not happy with. But this help at my right hand, Webster, is something that I have learned to depend upon and highly respect.

When I got to chapter 2, the word *cisterns* in verse thirteen immediately caught my attention. It reminded me of the meditation prayer for my daughter and son-in-law. My meditation prayer for them, for many years, has been a verse from Proverbs 5:15: Drink water from your own cistern, flowing water from your own well (NRSV). Dedicating this verse to them was a way for me to speak a blessing over their marriage. I believed that God would hear me and establish those words in their lives. Now I have come to the realization that I have been asking and believing on the Lord to provide something for others that He lacked from His own bride. I felt sorrow for His lack.

I decided to do a little investigating on the word *cistern*. As I did my sorrow concerning this relationship between God and His bride continued to grow as one meaning of the word led me to another and then another. The word *cistern* can also be used to describe a common every day large vessel for holding water. And large vessels were definitely needed at the temple. Cisterns played a big part when it came to processing the payments that were made by the lawbreakers.

Today, when we break (trespass) the law, we appease the law by paying appropriate fines. We satisfy the law by spending our money. But the legal system in Israel was different. The shed-blood of animals served as precious currency. That was the required settlement according to the Law of Moses which ruled God's people. When I read Leviticus 1:1-9, I picture a priest at work in front of a water-filled *cistern*. That was one of his designated jobs, to processes the incoming payments that covered the errors of society.

That definition of the word led me to another. I found that another word for cistern is: *trough*, you know… that thing that a farm animal drinks and eats from. Immediately my thoughts were led to that trough that was filled with hay the night that the heavenly hosts sang and shepherds heard their song. But we don't call that *trough* a trough in that story. We don't call it a *cistern* either. We call it a manger. And I thought this definition of the word provided a great snapshot for the scrapbook. But the manger scene described in this snapshot may not leave you with the familiar warm and fuzzy Christmas feeling that you are used to:

The barn was not the best place to birth a baby but Mary and Joseph had to work with what they had that night. Mary was in labor and Joseph was busy moving some hay around trying to make her comfortable. He was doing anything and everything possible to be ready. So he dragged it a little closer to Mary. Though it was not what the *trough* was for, tonight it (*the trough*) would serve purposes that it was never intended to.

So (in this personal rendition) Joseph built a fire, warmed some water and poured it in the *trough*. When the baby arrived Joseph took the newborn from Mary's arms and placed the child inside the bath-water that he had prepared. As Joseph (like a priest) took the baby (like a payment) from Mary (like a lawbreaker) and placed Him in the bath-water that soon turned red (like a *cistern* where payments were processed), did anything about that act seem uncanny to them? Was God speaking to them (with tears in His eyes as He thought about His Son's purpose?) Was God trying to communicate a message that night? Did He ask Joseph and Mary, does He ask you and me the same question that He asked Jeremiah back in chapter one, "what do you see?"

In this snapshot Jesus fulfills the demands made by the Law.

Through Jesus we can see that God lives by the same law that is given to bride-Israel.

When God's leaders were lacking,

God's leaders were expected to answer and make payment for the lack.

It is true. The Word (before it was flesh) was just like the leaders.

It (the Word) was not doing the job it was created to do,

at least not in Israel.

The people were still committing crimes even though the Word was dispersed and

lived with them, in them, and among them.

The stiff Law required a payment from the responsible One (in leadership).

The Word could not successfully fulfill the duties to which He was appointed.

So the Word became flesh and took the blame and

paid for (what legally appeared to be) His own lacking.

Compare Answers For Chapter 2

A-1: The leaders of the nation

A-2: the city gates

A-3: thrones from the north

A-4(OPTIONAL QUESTION): He gave those (the stars, sun, etc.) to everyone according to Deuteronomy 4:19. But by this strange method of leading, Israel would be special as she followed God. He was with her, leading and guiding her. The sun, moon, and stars are mere creations, just like humans. They each had a certain purpose and performed so. But God's power could be seen in the signs (the cloud and the fire). The actions of the cloud by day and fire by night were contrary to their normal nature (their usual pattern) but obedient to God.

A-5: guilty

B-1: What wrong did your ancestors find in me?

B-2: God brought them up from the land of Egypt. He led them through the wilderness, a land of deserts and pits, a land of drought and deep darkness, in a land that no one passes through, where no one lives. God brought them to a land of plentiful to eat its fruit and its good things.

B-3: priests, rulers, prophets

B-4: A leader is put into the position of leadership to lead and guide. If those who are under his (or her) care are being unruly it may be due to negligence on the part of the leader. The leader must make gain and take correct steps to successfully fulfill the assigned duties.

C-1: The *rider-* if they bowed down to idols, God would punish their children to the third generation. But He would show steadfast love to the thousandth generation of those who love Him and keep His commandments. They showed little concern for the future generations as they turned from God to idols.

C-2: Comfort, O comfort my people, says your God. Speak tenderly to Jerusalem, and cry to her that she has served her term, that her penalty is paid, that she has received from the Lord's hand double for all her sins (Isaiah 40:1-2 NRSV).

C-3: David did what was right in the sight of the Lord.

C-4: He brought destruction to his grandchildren when he did things during his life that fueled the anger of the Lord God.

D-1: something that does not profit

D-2: Be appalled, O heavens, at this, be shocked, be utterly desolate, says the Lord (Jeremiah 2:12 NRSV).

D-3 (OPTIONAL QUESTION): the definition of appalled- obsolete definition is: weaken; fail/ the definition of shocked- sudden or violent disturbance / the definition of desolate- to deprive of inhabitants, lay waste

D-4 (OPTIONAL QUESTION): You said in your heart, "I will ascend to heaven; I will raise my throne above the stars of God; I will sit on the mount of assembly on the heights of Zaphon; I will ascend to the tops of the clouds, I will make myself like the Most High" (Isaiah 14:13-14).

D-5: no

D-6: evil

D-7: I have never considered myself evil or a gambler but I can now see that I have been both. I risk the eternal life of my children and grandchildren when I neglect to live for the Lord and teach them about God.

E-1: Forsaking the Lord your God and not fearing God is wickedness in Israel.

F-1: The landowner sent his slaves to collect produce from the tenants who were left in charge of the produce. But the tenants kept killing those sent by the landowner.

F-2: Though you wash yourself with lye and use much soap, the stain of your guilt is still before me, says the Lord God (Jeremiah 2:22 NRSV).

G-1: Confession- a disclosure of one's sins in the sacrament of penance. Admission- the granting of an argument or position not fully proved

H-1: They say to a tree, 'you are my father' and to a stone, 'you gave me birth'. They turned their backs to God instead of their faces. But in the time of their trouble they say (to God), 'come and save us' because their gods will not answer.

H-2: father and mother

H-3: You have as many gods as you have towns (last part of Jeremiah 2:28 NRSV).

H-4: Then the word of the Lord came to me: Mortal, your kinsfolk, your own kin, your fellow exiles, the whole house of Israel, all of them, are those of whom the inhabitants of Jerusalem have said, "They have gone far from the Lord; to us this land has been given for a possession" (Ezekiel 11:14-15 NRSV).

H-5: priests

H-6: house of Jacob and families of the house of Israel

H-7: The priests and the Levites who were in all Israel presented themselves to him from all their territories. The Levites had left their common lands and their holdings and had come to Judah and Jerusalem, because Jeroboam (king in the northern kingdom) and his sons had prevented them from serving as priests of the Lord, (2Chronicles 11:13-14 NRSV personal interpretation added). Some, if not all of Levi, defected to Judah.

I-1: Why do you complain against me? You have all rebelled against me, says the Lord (Jeremiah 2:29 NRSV).

I-2: They were the leaders and teachers in Israel. God considered their move an act of rebellion because they abandoned the land, leaving the people at the mercy of the abominations. They were also apparently being negligent in their appointed duties. If they were being responsible, the land would not have gotten to this point.

J-1: (Leviticus 26:40-42): But if they confess their iniquity and the iniquity of their ancestors, in that they committed treachery against me and, moreover, that they continued hostile to me— so that I, in turn, continued hostile to them and brought them into the land of their enemies; if then their uncircumcised heart is humbled and they make amends for their iniquity, then will I remember my covenant with Jacob; I will remember also my covenant with Isaac and also my covenant with Abraham, and I will remember the land.

J-2: …for they are the flock of *his people*; for like the jewels of a crown they shall shine on his land.

J-3: …and their pasture lands

J-4: God says: …Yet *my people* have forgotten me, days without number (Jeremiah 2:32 NRSV).

J-5: all of Levi

K-1: These leaders were getting away with murder. They killed many innocent prophets who served at the hand of God for His people. They shed innocent blood and treated them all like common thieves who were breaking into the Lord's house.

K-2 (OPTIONAL QUESTION): When I was in grade school I remember learning about the bomb that the U.S. dropped on Hiroshima. It disturbed me greatly as I thought about all of those kids, just like me, that died and got hurt. I guess what I felt, about that tragedy, might fall under the category of shame.

K-3 (OPTIONAL QUESTION): I am afraid that I have not passed enough of the Word onto my children and therefore my grandchildren too will suffer. They will undoubtedly incur guilt because of knowledge that they do not have. When I see my own children struggling in certain situations, I know that I could have changed that but I failed. They suffer because of my lack as a teacher and leader.

K-4: It was for the sins of her prophets and the iniquities of her priests.

K-5: perjury

L-1: ...the Lord has rejected those in whom you trust, and you will not prosper through them (Jeremiah 2:37).

L-2: But righteous judges shall declare them guilty of adultery and of bloodshed; because they are adulteresses and blood is on their hands (Ezekiel 23:45 NRSV).

L-3 (OPTIONAL QUESTION): maybe the thrones from the north in chapter 1

L-4: This is a running list from the previous chapter.

Number 1: You shall have no other gods before me (broken law according to Jeremiah 1:16)

Number 2: You shall not make for yourself an idol (broken law according to Jeremiah 1:16)

Number 5: Honor your father and mother (broken law according to Jeremiah 2:27)

Number 6: You shall not murder (broken law according to Jeremiah 2:30b and 34)

Number 4: Remember the Sabbath day and keep it holy (broken law according to Jeremiah 2:32)

L-5: I need to break down the wall that keeps me from seeing the suffering that sin causes (which I am also a contributor to). I need to plant seeds of responsibility and change what I can.

Chapter 3

Chapter 3 Prelude

She Looks Clean Now

Josiah was just one of the kings in Judah during the life and times of Jeremiah (Jeremiah 1:2). Josiah was eight years old when his kingly reign began. But I can't imagine him feeling safe in the place he called home. Finding a secure place where he could fully relax in peace and be comfortable with his surroundings was probably not an easy task, especially after what happened to his father. It is written that the servants of his father (his father was King Amon), conspired with one another and killed Amon. Even though justice was served and the servants ended up paying the ultimate price for their crime, the tragedy must have left unseen scars on Josiah. I would imagine that he carried the memory of that conspiracy around with him for his whole life. Living with and through such a tragedy may have caused him to turn to God for protection and wisdom.

The Bible says that in the eighth year of his reign (at about age 16) Josiah began to seek the God of his ancestor King David. And in the twelfth year (at about age 20) he began to purge Judah and Jerusalem of the high places, the sacred poles, and the carved and cast images (2Chronicles 34:3). And it was in the very next year (which would have been year number thirteen of his reign) that the word of the Lord, according to Jeremiah 1:2, started coming to Jeremiah. This crusading king used his power to bring the words of the covenant to the attention of those who legally lived under it. He recognized his position and what God demanded from him in his times. Who knows what heights Jerusalem could have reached? With all of the powers that God had promised to those under His theocratic covenant, Jerusalem could have been a world ruler if she would have been chaste to her Lord.

As I read about Josiah and what he did during his reign (2Kings 22-23:30 and 2Chronicles 34-35), I was honestly a little shocked at what was going on. God's people had turned away from the Lord and violated the land as well as the law that ruled over them. The following verses reveal some of the restoration that Josiah is credited for.

At the temple: The king commanded the high priest Hilkiah, the priests of the second order, and the guardians of the threshold, to bring out of the temple of the Lord all the vessels made for Baal, for Asherah, and for all the host of heaven; he burned them outside Jerusalem in the fields of the Kidron, and carried their ashes to Bethel...He brought out the image of Asherah from the house of the Lord, outside Jerusalem, to the Wadi Kidron, burned it at the Wadi

Kidron, beat it to dust and threw the dust of it upon the graves of the common people. He broke down the houses of the male temple prostitutes that were in the house of the Lord, where the women did weaving for Asherah (2Kings 23:4, 6-7 NRSV).

He removed the horses that the kings of Judah had dedicated to the sun, at the entrance to the house of the Lord, by the chamber of the eunuch Nathan-melech, which was in the precincts; then he burned the chariots of the sun with fire. The altars on the roof of the upper chamber of Ahaz, which the kings of Judah had made, and the altars that Manasseh had made in the two courts of the house of the Lord, he pulled down from there and broke in pieces, and threw the rubble into the Wadi-Kidron (2Kings 23:11-12 NRSV).

All of the tearing down that Josiah had to do, to restore the house of the Lord, to the Lord, sounds a bit like a demolition project that would have called for some major restoration (2Chronicles 34:8-10). After the major clean-up, Josiah set the temple in order and offerings were once again (in the eighteenth year of Josiah) made by the priests to the Lord (2Chronicles 35:16-19).

In and around the city of Jerusalem: He deposed the idolatrous priests whom the kings of Judah had ordained to make offerings in the high places at the cities of Judah and around Jerusalem; those also who made offerings to Baal, to the sun, the moon, the constellations, and all the host of the heavens (2Kings 23:5 NRSV).

… he broke down the high places of the gates that were at the entrance of the gate of Joshua the governor of the city , which were on the left at the gate of the city (2Kings 23:8 NRSV).

He defiled Topheth, which is in the valley of Ben-hinnom, so that no one would make a son or daughter pass through fire as an offering to Molech (2Kings 23:10 NRSV).

The king defiled the high places that were east of Jerusalem, to the south of the Mount of Destruction, which King Solomon of Israel had built for Astarte the abomination of the Sidonians, for Chemosh the abomination of Moab, and for Milcom the abomination of the Ammonites. He broke the pillars in pieces, cut down the sacred poles, and covered the sites with human bones (2Kings 23:13-14 NRSV).

Outside of Jerusalem: He brought all the priests out of the towns of Judah, and defiled the high places where the priests had made offerings, from Geba to Beer-sheba; …(2Kings 23:8) Moreover Josiah put away the mediums, wizards, teraphim, idols, and all the abominations that were seen in the land of Judah and in Jerusalem, so that he established the words of the law that were written in the book that the priest Hilkiah had found in the house of the Lord (2Kings 23:24 NRSV).

Outside of his territory: Moreover, the altar at Bethel, the high place erected by Jeroboam son of Nebat, who caused Israel to sin— he pulled down that altar along with the high place. He burned the high place, crushing it to dust; he also burned the sacred pole (2Kings 23:15 NRSV).

Moreover, Josiah removed all the shrines of the high places that were in the towns of Samaria, which kings of Israel had made, provoking the Lord to anger; he did to them just as he had done at Bethel. He slaughtered on the altars all the priests of the high places who were there, and burned human bones on them... (2Kings 23:19-20 NRSV).

In the towns of Manasseh, Ephraim, and Simeon, and as far as Naphtali, in their ruins all around, he broke down the altars, beat the sacred poles and the images into powder, and demolished all the incense altars throughout all the land of Israel. Then he returned to Jerusalem (2Chronicles 34:6-7 NRSV).

By the looks of things, Josiah's mission of reformation was a complete success; but there was an unseen problem. Although Josiah was able to clean up the temple, the city, and even the whole country, it is apparent that he could not clean up the hearts of the people. Josiah had the power to clean up and create an illusion of that which is acceptable in the physical world. But all of that cosmetic work seemed to be in vain. Verse 6 in this next chapter of study tells us that the Lord spoke to Jeremiah in the days of this king Josiah. I believe that this particular exchange between God and Jeremiah took place after or at least sometime during the reform because God says, in verse 10, that Judah did not return to Him with her whole heart.

Chapter 3 Study

Israel and Judah's Dirty Laundry

CHAPTER 3 READING, COMMENTS, AND QUESTIONS

There are signs of war all over Israel. She, the northern kingdom, has been ravaged by hostiles and left with nothing. Those who managed to remain alive throughout the widespread devastation now cry out to God. They are affectionately calling Him an old friend from the past. But it will take a lot more than sweet talk to get God to the point where He can forget about what His bride has done. It will take a lot of earnest work. Her heart would have to show signs of a rekindled desire for the ways of the Lord. Her words are not enough.

In Matthew 13:3-9 Jesus tells a parable. He compares human hearts to the different types of soil. Some hearts, like some soils, are fertile and readily fit for sowing seed; but some are resistant to any new planting. The hearts in Israel are showing resistance to God's seed. God finds the heart very inhospitable, even refusing to open up and accept Him.

We know that God (the owner of the heart-land) had not been lax in His duties with Israel. He showed His persistent concern and desire for her by continuing to send His servants with instruction to assist in the upkeep and maintenance of her heart. But still her heart had managed to become settled and satisfied in dry compromise. Her heart could not maintain the healthy support system that God's word required for existence and survival.

But Israel's heart was not always like this. It changed. If we continue on with the parable that Jesus was telling in the New Testament, we might find an explanation for the changes that occurred in the Old Testament. In Matthew 13:24-30, Jesus explains another problem that arises when God's seeds are planted in His fields: "...The kingdom of heaven may be compared to someone who sowed good seed in his field; but while everybody was asleep, an enemy came and sowed weeds among the wheat, and then went away" (Matthew 13:24-25 NRSV). This parable may be one that best suits the situation that Israel was in. God gave Israel His word (His seed). He planted it in her heart but something else sprouted. Some wild weed was growing and taking over His field.

This is what God says in Jeremiah 3:19 and I believe that He is talking directly to the heart, (His seed that had been sown there). The author's personal interpretation will make this observation clear.

"I thought how I would set *you* (*you* being His seeded word)

among my *children* (*children* being all of the people known as Israel),

and give *you* (*you*, again being His seeded word)

a *pleasant land,* (*pleasant land* being the pure heart(s) of Israel),

the most beautiful heritage of all the nations."

God sent His seed to be planted unsparingly. With each sack of seed that He sent (parabolically), His hopes, of getting His homestead ready for a great future, must have grown; but the keepers of the land became negligent. Somehow, someone else got in; and that someone else secretly planted seeds that produced thick weeds. The beautiful heritage where God had thought to live, via His word forever, became polluted. And now there was God's beloved word tangled in the midst of the weeds. That which was purchased by God, from out of Egypt (the hearts of Israel), to be the most beautiful piece of real estate for His word to abide in, was now a waste land suitable for nothing and His word, that had been planted there, was suffering.

📖 READ JEREMIAH 3:1-5

A. ADDITIONAL COMMENTS FOR VERSES 1-5

As the court case of God-v-the bride from chapter 2 convenes, the gavel sounds and whole courtroom comes to a hushed order. Bride Israel is about to get her final ruling as half-hearted Judah sits in Israel's shadow waiting and watching. From the evidence that has been presented things are not looking good for insolent Israel. (Though all of Israel is not present, her negligent representatives and overseers stand in for her. They will be expected to answer for her unacceptable condition.)

ANSWER QUESTIONS FOR VERSES 1-5

A-1: Israel, was a people who, considered her lovers to be dependable but they abandoned her in her time of need. She looks around the courtroom to see if any of them came to show support, but none can be found. So she holds her dirty heart in her hand and asks God to take it. But God wastes no time in pointing out what she has done to herself by having many lovers. What questions does God ask her? Answer only with the questions that you find in verse 1.

A-2: Other evidence against the bride could have been presented early on, but the Lord wanted to give the bride as much time as possible to make a free and willing confession. So this final piece of evidence was not revealed to the court or to the bride until the very end. The final remarks from the prosecution will prove beyond a reasonable doubt that she is the guilty one and God is the injured party in this case.

After all of the witnesses had been questioned, after all evidence was presented, and after the bride said all that she wanted to say, the prosecuting attorney speaks and God opens up His domain to the whole courtroom. His rooms (the hearts of Israel) should have been filled with evidence of love for Him, but that was not the case. The evidence showed signs of a cover-up. His domain was dusted for fingerprints and blood samples were taken. And then finally, when the lights were turned off, the infrared eye of God revealed her undeniable infidelity. The Lord tells her to look up to the bare heights and see! What does He ask her about the evidence? (See verse two.)

A-3: Pollution contaminates, causes instability, disorder, and harm when it is introduced into a natural environment. God calls Israel "a land that is greatly polluted". What was she polluted with? (See the last part of verse 2.)

A-4: What has been withheld from the land because of the man-made pollution? (See verse3.)

A-5: Were you ever so angry at someone that you just quit speaking to them? Turn to Deuteronomy 32:2. What does this verse talk about and could this be the most important thing that God is really withholding from His people when He uses the word: showers?

A-6: Now that her land (her heart) is like a toxic dumpsite, Israel has offered God her polluted land (her heart) and He refuses the offer. In verse 5 of this chapter, as Israel continues to play the innocent victim in this case, she asks: "will He be angry forever, will He be indignant to the end?" Now that she has done everything that she could possibly do to make God angry, Israel is calling Him indignant for holding something back from her. Instead of feeling shame (shame or regret is what we expect to see from our children when we hold something back or take something away like the car keys, video games, or a favorite toy because they have done something wrong) how is she still acting when God takes away the rain and showers? (See verse 3.)

📖 READ JEREMIAH 3:6-10

B. ADDITIONAL COMMENTS FOR VERSES 6-10

Jeremiah reminisces over the time that God opened up and revealed His thoughts concerning the one(s) He loved.

ANSWER QUESTIONS FOR VERSES 6-10

B-1: During the time of Josiah's reign, what were God's thoughts concerning Israel as He watched Israel cheat on every high hill and under every green tree?

B-2: According to the following verse, what was built on every high hill and under every green tree?

(1Kings 14:23 NRSV): For they also built for themselves high places, pillars, and sacred poles on every high hill and under every green tree.

B-3 (OPTIONAL QUESTION): God describes Israel as faithless in verses 6, 8, 11, and 12. She has not been true to her country (her land, her heart). She has been disloyal and not true to her allegiance (her vows). Here in the United States when someone is disloyal to the government, participating in war crimes against our homeland, attempting to overthrow the government, allowing known hostile and foreign powers to secretly abide in the land; what crime are they charged with when they are caught?

B-4: Israel's actions did not reflect the good thoughts God kept about her so what did God do?

B-5: What has God been competing against as He tried to maintain this relationship with Israel? (See verse 9.)

B-6: God needed help as He competed for the affection of His sheep in Israel, but no help was found. Who had abandoned God, abandoned His land, abandoned His sheep, and apparently taught the abandoned sheep inadequate and haphazard skills for maintaining the perpetual possession? (See 2Chronicles 11:13-14 or H-7 in chapter two.)

B-7: Stop for a moment to take a look at the little sister who sits in the back of the courtroom. Instead of fearing God and learning from big sister's mistakes she (she being Jerusalem the capitol of Judah) followed and will continue to follow in the footsteps of her bigger sister. For more details concerning these two turn to Ezekiel and read chapter 16.

- God says that Samaria (the capitol or heart of Israel) was the older sister and that
- Sodom (infamous Sodom and Gomorrah) was the younger sister of Jerusalem
- Jerusalem (the capitol or heart of Judah), whom God has yet to deal with here in this book of Jeremiah, followed the ways of her sisters and acted according to their abominations.

How will the cities of Sodom and Samaria size up as they stand next to Jerusalem? (See Ezekiel 16:51.)

READ JEREMIAH 3:11-13

C. ADDITIONAL COMMENTS FOR VERSES 11-13

(Now back to the official sentencing of exiled Israel.) Israel receives her sentence and does not have much of a choice at this low point in her life. She finally opens the door of her heart. She calls out to God and wants to hear what God has to say. Through this act, she has shown herself to be less guilty than Sister Judah. So God sends out words of consolation to Israel, she who is now His ex wife. Though the curses are hot on her trail, God tells her that: no, He will not be angry forever.

ANSWER QUESTIONS FOR VERSES 11-13

C-1: There is a line of succession, that every country follows, in the absence of its leader. (If you have access, review the current 'list of the U.S. presidential line of succession'.) Having to follow some line of succession in the absence of the priests and Levites, she, the people, becomes successor and takes the position that was abandoned by the leaders. God tells the new one in command how to alleviate His anger and her pain. How can she relieve the grief and pain that she and God share? She is the only one that can do it.

C-2: The Lord will scatter you among all peoples, from one end of the earth to the other… (Deuteronomy 28:64 NRSV). That was one of the pursuing curses noted in the covenant. Knowing that God's people will be scattered from one end of the earth to the other, may cause you to wonder why God's message, to Israel, is being directed to the north. Turn ahead to Jeremiah 23:8. These verses speak of God bringing Israel out of two places. It seems that one could be a spiritual place and the other could be a physical place. What are the two places?

C-3 (OPTIONAL QUESTION): The covenant curse, from Deuteronomy 28:64 in the last question, concerning a scattering seems to have a familiar ring to it. We have heard about a scattering before in this study. What was it? Go back to chapter one, question A-9.

C-4: In relation to C-2 (previously in this section): What else is produced or comes from the land of the north? (See Jeremiah 1:15; 3:18 and 6:22.)

📖 READ JEREMIAH 3:14

D. ADDITIONAL COMMENTS FOR VERSE 14

Now that Israel no longer sits on her high horse, God finally gets the opportunity to speak to His offspring. His offspring are the *words* that have been planted (like a seed) in the heart of Israel. He has not been able to see or hear from them in years. He must be excited to see how much, or even if, His planted seeds have grown. And His offspring must be excited as well. Hearing the voice of their Father (God) could be the hope that the dying offspring, who live in a polluted land (polluted heart), need to hear. Words from their true Father are like cleansing rain. Now that the power has reached the people by line of succession (see C-1), God finally gets the chance to speak heart to heart and word to word with His offspring who have been kept from Him for far too long.

ANSWER QUESTIONS FOR VERSE 14

D-1: When seeds of tradition and personal convictions are planted in the heart and presented as something to be equal with God's word the heart struggles. Add seeds of cultic and occult beliefs into the mix and the struggle escalates. Israel has God and man-made beliefs all growing in their heart together and the heart struggles. Turn to the parable in Matthew 13:24-30. After reading, answer this question. Should we expect to see an immediate fix, for the struggling heart of Israel, during this study?

D-2: What did Jesus tell His disciples in Matthew 15:13?

D-3 (OPTIONAL QUESTION): What can a person do, in the meantime, to ease the struggle?

D-4: Now that the dispersed have opened up their hearts, God takes this open window of opportunity to plant a new message in the heart. It is a message of direction and hope. If Israel (the people) will listen (to the heart), what will the heart now say?

D-5: "Listen to your heart." When is that good advice and when is that not good advice?

D-6: Have you ever just planted a flower-seed in your garden not knowing what type of flower the seed would produce? Well it seems that God has planted some beautiful words that will not come to full fruition for a while. God's words were: "I will take you, one from a city and two from a family, and I will bring you to Zion." Though it's hard to know what that planting will grow to mean, dispersed Israel can expect to see the answer pop-up if she takes care of the seed that God planted. But for now, answer this. What city and what tribal families seem to be the focal point in this study?

📖 **READ JEREMIAH 3:15-18**

E. ADDITIONAL COMMENTS FOR VERSES 15-18

It seems that God's Word has some kind of hierarchy. This is no surprise. God shows organization and rank through all that He does.

ANSWER QUESTIONS FOR VERSES 15-18

E-1: God wants His offspring to be safe; but His seed was planted in a place that turned out to be, an all-out war zone. They are in deep jungles, struggling to just exist in the land (heart) that is overgrown with briars and wild trees (false teachings). But now that Israel has opened up her heart, God takes this opportunity to give consolation to His offspring by telling them that He will send other ranks (of their kind) with certain capabilities. He is going to send shepherds. What will these shepherds be like and what will they do? (See verse 15.)

E-2: Have you ever felt a prick in your heart? That is what the heart of Israel is feeling as God continues to speak to His offspring. As Israel listens with the eyes of her heart wide open, the words of God that were slowly dying are being revived. His dormant words lying within the heart find hope from their Father. His voice now brings a peace that cannot be described; giving strength, understanding, and knowledge. God tells them (them being the words that have had no power in the hearts where they now exist) of the power that they will have someday. As He speaks directly to the words (His offspring) in the heart He says: And when you have multiplied and increased in the land, (in the hearts), in those days, says the Lord, *they* shall no longer say, "The ark of the covenant of the Lord." It shall not come to mind, or be remembered, or missed; nor shall another one be made (Jeremiah 3:16 NRSV with personal interpretation added).

As God speaks to His word that is in the heart, the heart is listening. He gives them a message with hope. Who, in your opinion, is the '*they*' that God refers to when He says: "....*they* shall no longer say, "The ark of the covenant of the Lord"?

E-3: Turn to Exodus 25:17-22. Why was the ark of the covenant of the Lord so important to God's people?

E-4: God uses two verbs in verse 16. They are used in the past tense. One verb is multiplied and the other is increased. I looked up the words in my dictionary. The word *increase* showed an obsolete definition: propagation (propagate). This word, propagate, might better describe what (I think) God meant. Some definitions are: to pass along to offspring; to cause to spread out and affect a greater number or a greater area; publicize; the spreading of something (as a belief) abroad or into new regions.

So what will happen to the ark of the covenant because of this increase of God's seeded word (His offspring)?

E-5: God shares His plans and from the sounds of things the ark of the covenant will no longer be the dwelling place for His presence, which seems to be the original plan in Exodus 25:8. Though there is no specific time mentioned for this event, where will the nations gather to find God's presence?

E-6: "Again, the kingdom of heaven is like a merchant in search of fine pearls;" (Matthew 13:45 NRSV).

Finding that which is considered precious is not an easy task. Many people work hard and search years for that one gold nugget or perfect pearl. When they find what they have been searching for it is joy unspeakable! Finding God and being able to put His words of wisdom into our hearts is like that. And like a precious pearl, that is under full guard at all times, so should be God's word.

We often say that God is everywhere and therefore we think He is easy to find. But I think that God might like us to consider Him to be a treasure that is of the rare kind. In fact, He did not make Himself so available back in the Old Testament. You could not go to every high hill or under every green tree and expect to find Him there. Although God's people were instructed to put God's word (the portable part of Him) into their hearts, He was stationary. Visiting God sometimes took great effort on the part of those who wanted to be in His presence. Read the following verses and then answer: Where did God's people have to go to find *Him*?

(Deuteronomy 12:2-6 NRSV): You must demolish completely all the places where the nations whom you are about to dispossess served their gods, on the mountain heights, on the hills, and under every leafy tree. Break down their altars, smash their pillars, burn their sacred poles with fire, and hew down the idols of their gods, and thus blot out their name from their places. You shall not worship the Lord your God in such ways. But you shall seek the place that the Lord your God will choose out of all your tribes as his habitation to put his name there. You shall go there, bringing there your burnt offerings and your sacrifices, your tithes and your donations, your votive gifts, your freewill offerings, and the firstlings of your herds and flocks.

E-7: What do these following verses reveal? 1Kings 8:30; Matthew 5:16; Mark 11:25.

E-8: God needs to have open lines of communication with His planted word (God needs a circumcised heart). His offspring (His seed) must receive nourishment from their Father in order to survive. Even though the heart does not understand it now, God's seeded offspring will eventually comprehend and interpret the message that God plants. What message will the heart eventually interpret for Israel if she nurtures the seed and allows it to grow? (See verse 18.)

📖READ JEREMIAH 3:19-20

F. ADDITIONAL COMMENTS FOR VERSES 19-20

God continues to speak to the heart. His seeds and offspring that have been planted there listen as they are tangled, trampled, deformed and some holding on to their last breath. But the weeds around them thrive in a glory of false hope.

ANSWER QUESTIONS FOR VERSES 19-20

F-1: What were God's hopes and plans concerning His planted word (seed)? See verse 19.

F-2: The heart is the chamber where God's spiritual seed is planted. But His little seedlings are distressed. They are like prisoners of war. Some of His seeds cannot even be found. They are like soldiers missing in action. They are miserable as they dwell in the hearts of men. The two men in the following verses have opened up their hearts. As they reveal what's inside, these are not the kinds of words that God expected to spring up and flourish from the seed that had been planted on His property.

(Jeremiah 20:14-18 NRSV): Cursed be the day on which I was born! The day when my mother bore me, let it not be blessed! Cursed be the man who brought the news to my father, saying, "A child is born to you, a son," making him very glad. Let that man be like the cities that the Lord overthrew without pity; let him hear a cry in the morning and an alarm at noon, because he did not kill me in the womb; so my mother would have been my grave, and her womb forever great. Why did I come forth from the womb to see toil and sorrow, and spend my days in shame?

(Job 3:11, 13, 16-19 NRSV): "Why did I not die at birth, come forth from the womb and expire? ... Now I would be lying down and quiet; I would be asleep; then I would be at rest... Or why was I not buried like a stillborn child, like an infant that never sees the light? There the wicked cease from troubling, and there the weary are at rest. There the prisoners are at ease together; they do not hear the voice of the taskmaster. The small and great are there, and the slaves are free from their masters.

Do not neglect God's word that dwells in your heart. Remember that we are the guards of His precious word. Reassure the word of God, which is living in you, that you are aware of the dangers, that you are concerned about the welfare of every word that belongs to God.

Tell His word that you are officially on duty working to protect it. God's seeded word is in dangerous territory as it struggles to survive in the heart of mortal man and with the other mortal hearts within its environment. It is repressed, hindered, and held in chains. There is good news for those captives (God's word that was planted like a seed in the heart). The good news is tucked inside Luke 4:18. You will find the good news at the end of verse 18. Write it down and tell it to your heart today.

F-3: What lifesaving message do you hear from these following verses?

(James 1:21 NRSV): Therefore rid yourselves of all sordidness and rank growth of wickedness, and welcome with meekness the implanted word that has the power to save your souls.

(1Peter 1:23-24 NRSV): You have been born anew, not of perishable but of imperishable seed, through the living and enduring word of God. For "All flesh is like grass and all its glory like the flower of grass. The grass withers, and the flower falls, but the word of the Lord endures forever."

F-4: What cry and what action does God want from the heart? (See the last part of Jeremiah 3:19.)

F-5: God got two things from that which He purchased out of Egypt. What did He get? (See verse 20.)

📖 READ JEREMIAH 3:21-25

G. ADDITIONAL COMMENTS FOR VERSES 21-25

God (He is Word) has penetrated the crusty and uncircumcised heart of Israel. And for the first time, in a long time, as the eyes of her heart are opened, God's offspring (that have been seeded in the heart) see their true Father (the One from which they sprang). The wall that Israel had built to keep God away was beginning to crumble. Israel now had a broken heart.

ANSWER QUESTIONS FOR VERSES 21-25

G-1: In verse 2 the bare heights held evidence that could be seen, evidence of the bride's infidelity. But now that God has truly been heard there is another mood on the bare heights. What is happening on the bare heights due to the break through made by God?

G-2: What, unfortunately, had to precede the great break through, making a way for God to gain entrance to the heart?

G-3 (OPTIONAL QUESTION): What, or where, are the *bare heights* and why are they bare?

G-4: In Deuteronomy 6:6-7 (NRSV) you will find words of instruction that were given to the people of Israel: Keep these words that I am commanding you today in your heart. Recite them to your children and talk about them when you are at home and when you are away, when you lie down and when you rise.

But Israel did not provide a nurturing home for the words of God to grow and she did not pass the treasures on to her children. God sent them everything that was needed to start His future homestead and He continued to send portions (by true prophets).

His 'sent portions' were like deposits that had been sent from a soldier (who was away in battle) to his wife back home. But the wife became negligent. She did not take good care of their home or the portions that God sent ahead of Himself. His intentions, hopes, and dreams, for their future together, should have been made clear, through the abundance of 'sent portions'. (You might consider the 'sent portions' as God's word. God might consider the 'sent portions' as His sons, daughters, flocks and herds.) The eyes of the chosen bride were not focused on the precious cargo that God entrusted to her. She allowed strangers into their house and seeds of perversion were planted on God's property. Perverse ways sprouted, grew, and molested God's portions and property. Because of this, the treasures that God sent have been compromised and cannot function properly. The enemy has now infiltrated God's homeland and established ground. The battle has hit the shores of home.

In verse 24 they say that the devourer was a shameful thing. The shameful thing may be the seed of deceit which was planted in the heart (the heart which was meant for God's seed only). After many years of investigation, who is named as the father of this illegitimate seed? (See John 8:44 and Matthew 13:37-39.)

G-5: Although there are about 613 laws in the Old Testament; here is a list of the laws that God gave to Israel in stone. Check mark the ones that have been broken, giving the chapter and verse that indicates the infringement. (Use only references from the first three chapters of Jeremiah.)

- ➢ 1 You shall have no other gods before me.
- ➢ 2 You shall not make for yourself any idols.
- ➢ 3 You shall not make wrongful use of the name of the Lord your God.
- ➢ 4 Remember the Sabbath Day and keep it holy.
- ➢ 5 Honor your father and mother.
- ➢ 6 You shall not murder.
- ➢ 7 You shall not commit adultery.
- ➢ 8 You shall not steal.
- ➢ 9 You shall not bear false witness against your neighbor.
- ➢ 10 You shall not covet anything that belongs to your neighbor.

G-6: The verdict handed down, for Israel, in the courtroom on this day: "guilty." Even though the courtroom is filled with tears, the law (covenant or contract that does not rest) is there in full force and does not back down. But in the next chapter we will find that God, the presiding Judge, has outlined that guilty verdict with mercy. But first the law must be satisfied. It is always hungry for its violators.

Has Jeremiah's message and Israel's verdict brought about change in your life? If so how will that change affect others?

Chapter 3 Tag-A-Long

Admit Your Guilt

Copping a plea, it is an acceptable legal avenue for many criminals. If you have committed a crime and make a bargain to just plead guilty to (even sometimes a lesser degree of) that crime, you may be offered a lighter sentence. So, many times the criminal will present a confession to receive a lighter sentence. A punishment *will* be handed down but the up front plea lessens the severity.

Maybe that's how it was for Judah. When she saw the severe sentence that was handed down to sister Israel, *copping a plea* seemed like the safest way out. In verse ten, God said that Judah did not return to Him with her whole heart but only in pretense. Judah may have returned to God but it was not because she was burdened by all pain that sin had brought to her fellow man and she did not return to God because she was sorry for all the wrong she had personally committed which contributed to the hurting nation. It just sounds as if she returned to God because she didn't want to get it as bad as her big sister Israel. She wanted God to think she had changed. Maybe her new outward appearance caused her to be deceived herself. Yes, she was definitely changed on the outside. She had a whole new look but she did not make any changes where it counted. There were no good changes in her heart.

Judah was going through great rehabilitation. King Josiah was cleaning up her environment (see Chapter 3 Prelude) and God's word, through Jeremiah, was making its rounds, trying to clean up the heart. But she is just like her older sister Israel. The heart of little daughter Judah, as we will see later, is still in love with someone else.

The first step to any rehabilitation is acknowledging that you have done things that cause damage to someone or something. Here is an example of just one man who took that first step on the road to recovery. But it came only after he was carried away into captivity. The written confession is found in Daniel 9:4-18 (NRSV):

I prayed to the Lord my God and made confession, saying, "Ah, Lord, great and awesome God, keeping covenant and steadfast love with those who love you and keep your commandments, we have sinned and done wrong, acted wickedly and rebelled, turning aside from your commandments and ordinances. We have not listened to your servants the prophets, who spoke in your name to our kings, our princes, and our ancestors, and to all the people of the land. "Righteousness in on your side, O Lord, but open shame, as at this day, falls on us, the people of Judah, the inhabitants of Jerusalem, and all Israel, those who are near and those who are far away, in all the lands to which you have driven them, because of the treachery that they have committed against you. Open shame, O Lord, falls on us, our kings, our officials, and our ancestors, because we have sinned against you. To the lord our God belong mercy and forgiveness, for we have rebelled against him, and have not obeyed the voice of the Lord our God by following his laws, which he set before us by his servants the prophets. "All Israel has transgressed your law and turned aside, refusing to obey your voice. So the curse and the oath written in the law of Moses, the servant of God, have been poured out on us, because we have sinned against you. He has confirmed his words, which he spoke against us and against our rulers, by bringing upon us a calamity so great that what has been done against Jerusalem has never before been done under the whole heaven. Just as it is written in the law of Moses, all this calamity has come upon us. We did not entreat the favor of the Lord our God, turning from our iniquities and reflecting on his fidelity. So the Lord kept watch over this calamity until he brought it upon us. Indeed, the Lord our God is right in all that he has done; for we have disobeyed his voice.

"And now, O Lord our God, who brought your people out of the land of Egypt with a mighty hand and made your name renowned even to this day— we have sinned, we have done wickedly. O Lord, in view of all your righteous acts, let your anger and wrath, we pray, turn away from your city Jerusalem, your holy mountain; because of our sins and the iniquities of our ancestors, Jerusalem and your people have become a disgrace among all our neighbors. Now therefore, O Our God, listen to the prayer of your servant and to his supplication, and for your own sake, Lord, let your face shine upon your desolated sanctuary. Incline your ear, O my God, and hear. Open your eyes and look at our desolation and the city that bears your name. We do not present our supplication before you on the ground of our righteousness, but on the ground of your great mercies.

Other verses of interest: Ezra 9:6-15 and Nehemiah 9:6-37. The confessions are for the whole corporation. (Just saying, that may be something to remember as we pray.)

✂ Scrapbook Page For Chapter 3

Mama Makes Me Crazy!

"My Dad and I are inseparable but me and my keeper, my mom— well that's a different story. Even though Dad would like me to be as close to mom as I am to Him, it just seems like after all of this time, that close bond will never happen. He would love it if His chosen bride would hold me tight and never let me go. He sends me to her but she just rejects me by sitting me aside. He keeps hoping she will change. He would love to see her looking out the window every day, or sitting by the door in anticipation as she anxiously awaits for my every visit.

I try to be strong every time I'm sent. I want to be perfect so others will appraise her highly. But no matter how hard I try or how strong my desire is to make her look good, she just makes even the smallest part of me look bad. She never pays me any good attention. Her house is always cold and dark and she leaves me there to be continuously attended by some crazy weirdo. Even though it is always dark I can tell that the house is full of confusion and I can smell the dirt. And as if all of that is not bad enough I have to share this place, that I call home, with all of her other visiting guests. Even though I am the only good thing that she has in this place she allows everyone else to talk lies about me. She won't even stand up and defend me.

Of course that hurts and I suffer so I cry. When I cry out to Dad it makes Him cry too. But after He thinks for a while about the way she treats me (His word) He gets angry. Why should His wife, who lives in this foreign land, be permitted to do such a thing to the planted seed of God (the offspring that He sends)?

But Dad loves that woman and I can only do the same, because I, His Son, can do only what He says. I am (just a small part of) Him. So, when He sends me I go and I do it willingly without any reservations. He keeps sending me whenever He can. He sends me and she rejects me, He sends me and she rejects me. It is the same old heartbreak every time. But this last time something happened. She looked at me in a different way. All of His efforts seem to have paid off.

She finally admits that she has broken the law (a part of what I am, right in two) and she realizes that all of these penalties that she is paying right now are due to her own evil acts against me! Dad said she really needed to see that because He never wanted her life to end up this way and she was totally blaming Him for all of the bad stuff that was happening to her, when in truth, Dad was really just being true to their covenant. He was bound to it and she was bound too. Maybe she will accept me now without abusing me and trying to turn me into something that I am not. I can't wait until Dad sends more of Himself (more of me) to her again."

The words of God may be welcomed by some of the people who have been captured by the Assyrian army because they are in desperate need right now but sending His word to the people in Judah, well— that is just another heartache-waiting-to-happen for the kid.

This is a snapshot of Jesus (who is yet word).

He anticipates spending better times with a mother who, in the past, has not been so caring.

Compare Answers For Chapter 3

A-1: If a man divorces his wife and she goes from him and becomes another man's wife, will he return to her? Would not such a land be greatly polluted? You have played the whore with many lovers, and would you return to me? (Jeremiah 3:1 NRSV.)

A-2: Where have you not been lain with?

A-3: whoring and wickedness

A-4: showers/spring rain

A-5: 'teaching' could also be the meaning of showers being withheld

A-6: She has the forehead of a whore who refuses to be ashamed. She will not lower her head in disgrace or shame.

B-1: God thought that after Israel has done all of this, on every high hill and under every green tree: "she will return to me".

B-2: They built high places, pillars, and sacred poles on every high hill and under every green tree for themselves.

B-3 (OPTIONAL): high treason

B-4: God sent her away with a decree of divorce.

B-5: rocks and trees

B-6: the shepherds (priests and Levites)

B-7: Samaria and Sodom appear more righteous.

C-1: Acknowledge her guilt of rebellion against the Lord her God and admit that she has scattered her favors among strangers under every green tree and that she has not obeyed His voice.

C-2: out of the land of the north and out of all the lands where He had driven them

C-3 (OPTIONAL QUESTION): Jacob (aka Israel) spoke of scattering Levi and Simeon, not throughout the earth, but throughout Israel.

C-4: tribes of the kingdoms of the north, the house of Judah who has joined the house of Israel, and a people

D-1: No the struggle continues but God will at some time separate the righteous word from the useless word. It sounds like the fix will come in a time of great restoration.

D-2: .... "Every plant that my Heavenly Father has not planted will be uprooted" (Matthew 15:13 NRSV).

D-3 (OPTIONAL QUESTION): receive and plant God's seed unsparingly

D-4: Return, O faithless children, says the Lord, for I am your master; I will take you, one from a city and two from a family, and I will bring you to Zion (Jeremiah 3:14 NRSV).

D-5: When God's word is the Ruler in your heart, it is good advice.

D-6: Jerusalem, Judah, Levi, Israel

E-1: They will be 'after' God's own heart and they will feed the children with knowledge and understanding.

E-2: 'they' is the people, the keepers of His word

E-3: It is the mercy seat (throne) of God. It is the place from which God delivered His commands to Israel.

E-4: The ark of the covenant will not come to mind or be remembered.

E-5: Jerusalem

E-6: They had to seek the place that God chose, out of all the tribes, as His habitation to put His name there.

E-7: God is in heaven.

E-8: In those days the house of Judah shall join the house of Israel, and together they shall come from the land of the north to the land that I gave your ancestors for a heritage (Jeremiah 3:18 NRSV).

F-1: He would set it (His word, His offspring) throughout and amongst His chosen children (hearts on earth, Israel), giving them (them being His planted words) the most pleasant land and most beautiful heritage of all nations.

F-2: Jesus says: ...He has sent me to proclaim release to the captives...to let the oppressed go free.

F-3: the word of God is the only thing that is eternal. If you have the truth of God's word, you have life, so work to provide a good home for the Word

F-4: The cry would be "My Father!" The act would be, *not* turning from Him (God).

F-5: a faithless heart and a faithless people that left Him

G-1: The people finally see their wickedness and their eyes are opened to the truth. There may be new hope for growth in the land that has become dry and parched and bare.

G-2: Application of the curses

G-3 (OPTIONAL QUESTION): The bare heights may be places of beauty where the people went to worship other gods but at this point in time God has made those beautiful places (where she met the other gods) barren, ugly, and dry by withholding rain. (It could be a reflection of their hearts).

G-4: The devil, he is also a murderer. He kills or chokes off all of God's seed (offspring) by planting his own seed (offspring).

G-5: This is a running list from the previous chapter.

Number 1: You shall have no other gods before me (broken law according to Jeremiah 1:16)

Number 2: You shall not make for yourself an idol (broken law according to Jeremiah 1:16)

Number 5: Honor your father and mother (broken law according to Jeremiah 2:27)

Number 6: You shall not murder (broken law according to Jeremiah 2:30b and 34)

Number 4: Remember the Sabbath day and keep it holy (broken law according to Jeremiah 2:32)

Number 7: You shall not commit adultery (broken law according to Jeremiah 3:6)

G-6: This chapter has opened up my eyes to my responsibility toward God's word. I should be careful not to contaminate its space with that which will destroy it and make it a prisoner. As I am changed so is my attitude which is passed on through my actions in my everyday life. I hope that others will see that He lives as I carry His word in my heart.

Chapter 4

Chapter 4 Prelude

Ketubah

The *ketubah* (something like a prenuptial contract) has long been established as part of the Jewish marriage. It is signed and read aloud at the marriage ceremony. It traditionally contains what is required from the husband. He is to support his wife providing her with food, clothing, and marital relations. As long as she is faithful, the *ketubah* polices the actions of the man and binds him to care for her. Not only does he agree to provide these things for the bride during the marriage but at this point he is also responsible to provide for the bride, who has been faithful, in case of divorce.

As outlined in Exodus 21:10-11, if the husband marries another (having more than one wife was acceptable) and is neglectful and does not provide these things for her, she may freely leave the marriage. She owes the husband nothing yet he still must pay the price for the faithful bride. But this was not the case for bride Israel. Even though the Lord had made great provision for Israel, she was not a faithful bride.

God's prenuptial (His promises written within the law) provides for His bride far over and above what is her due. For any new bride this offer would have been a dream come true. But as freely as God blesses her, gives gifts, and showers her with His riches, so He curses her for her unfaithfulness. The payment for her unfaithfulness, toward God, is disclosed in the covenant and the payment is dreadful. The prenuptial curse includes terms of forfeiture concerning any promised assets, as a result of divorce on the grounds of adultery. The prenuptial contract is powerful and not only dictates what will happen if the parties divorce but it dictates what can happen far into her future. The agreement reveals God's holy will to eliminate all rights concerning Israel's homestead allowances. The predetermined heir (wife) no longer holds rights to His estate when adultery is committed. As she turns from God to other gods everything is lost and she can legally claim nothing from her husband except the penalties that the marriage contract outlines for unfaithfulness. (See Deuteronomy 28 for the details.)

Chapter 4 Study

Matters of the Heart

CHAPTER 4 READING, COMMENTS, AND QUESTIONS

📖**READ JEREMIAH 4:1-2**

A. ADDITIONAL COMMENTS FOR VERSES 1-2

God has been waiting a long time for His people to acknowledge that they are the guilty party in this relationship. In the last chapter, Israel broke down and listened to God. Even though Israel is remorseful she still must serve her sentence (as the covenant stated) in strange lands but she carries something with her. It is a prize that will change the nations forever.

ANSWER QUESTIONS FOR VERSES 1-2

A-1: Going back to her past we see God's proposal to Israel. On bended knee He agrees to be her God if she will trust, honor, and obey Him. This is what the Word, on bended knee between them, says as it turns to face the bride:

Today you have obtained the Lord's agreement: to be your God; and for you to walk in his ways, to keep his statutes, his commandments, and his ordinances, and to obey him (Deuteronomy 26:17 NRSV).

She agrees and signs on to be His treasured bride and keep His commands. For her loyalty she will receive greatness. And this is what the Word, which stands between them, says once God hears that His official proposal has been accepted:

Today the Lord has obtained your agreement: to be his treasured people, as he promised you, and to keep his commandments; for him to set you high above all nations that he has made, in praise and in fame and in honor; and for you to be a people holy to the Lord your God, as he promised (Deuteronomy 26:18-19 NRSV).

The bride was to receive great fame and fortune if she would only provide a nurturing environment and tenderly care for that which was most important to God. God gave her His precious word. She was to keep it safe in her heart, nurture it, allow it to grow and rule her life. But we know that Israel did not do that. So she was sent away with a decree of divorce (Jeremiah 3:8). She was thrown out of her home and landed in the hands of her enemy. But if she returns to the words and ways of God and removes her abominations (the other gods) and if she swears "As the Lord lives!" in truth, in justice, and in uprightness, what will the nations gain through her return to the Lord? In this answer you will find the goodness and grace from a merciful God is still extended to the ex wife and her new (in a manner of speaking) husband!

A-2: Think about it for a moment. Compare how a man planting a seed in the womb of a woman is parabolic to God planting His seed (His word) in the heart of man. Then answer this question. Who do you think God is referring to when He says "*him*" in verse two? In leading you to get the same answer that I did, I will say: the other nations will become step-parents, fit and unfit alike, of something that is really not from them. They will receive something that Israel brings with her into her new relationship.

A-3: Read the following verses (which have personal interpretation added) from a previous chapter and then answer the question that follows.

God's question in Jeremiah 2:14-15: Is Israel (the bride) a slave? Is *he* (the planted word) a homeborn servant? Why then has *he* (the planted word) become plunder? The lions have roared against *him* (the planted word), they have roared loudly. They have made his land (the heart) a waste; his cities are in ruins, without inhabitant. (When God looks at His home, the heart, He asks: How can this be; the bride of the king and the son of the king look like slaves in their own land?)

How has Israel (the bride) been a neglectful bride concerning the *he* and/or *him* (the planted word)?

A-4: Let's return to the courtroom scene one more time. Israel has officially received her sentence. God watches and Israel is escorted out of the courtroom in handcuffs but she has left something behind. God picks up the, one-of-a-kind, wedding ring (the promise) that He gave her. He looks at it and wonders if she will become a changed woman after serving the time required by law. Who, even though unfaithful, is the carrier of *him*— that which will bless all nations?

📖READ JEREMIAH 4:3-4

B. ADDITIONAL COMMENTS FOR VERSES 3-4

God, like a surgeon had taken steps to save his beloved bride Israel. 2Kings 10:32 gives the time when some of her lifesaving treatments began. He had been cutting away (the cancer) that which brings death. But now Judah is what is left of the once vibrant body (with Jerusalem being the heart which is also weak with disease). The years have not been kind and she has not been able to break free from the disease that has defiled and destroyed the biggest part of her body. Even though she does not recognize or acknowledge her poor and sickly condition, God tries to warn her.

ANSWER QUESTIONS FOR VERSES 3-4

B-1: What two tribes, from Jacob's (Israel's) offspring, still hold onto their Promised Land in the southern kingdom called Judah? (See the following verses for available clues.)

(1Kings 12:21 NRSV): When Rehoboam came to Jerusalem, he assembled all the house of Judah and the tribe of Benjamin, one hundred eighty thousand chosen troops to fight against the house of Israel, to restore the kingdom to Rehoboam son of Solomon.

(2Chronicles 11:3): Say to King Rehoboam of Judah, son of Solomon, and to all Israel in Judah and Benjamin.

(2Chronicles 14:8): Asa had an army of three hundred thousand from Judah, armed with large shields and spears, and two hundred eighty thousand troops from Benjamin who carried shields and drew bows; all these were mighty warriors.

(2Chronicles 15:1-2): The spirit of God came upon Azariah son of Oded. He went out to meet Asa and said to him, "Hear me, Asa, and all Judah and all Benjamin: The Lord is with you, while you are with him. If you seek him, he will be found by you, but if you abandon him, he will abandon you.

B-2: Who else can we assume is there? (See 2Chronicles 11:13-14 and Joshua 21:9-19.)

B-3: Did you notice that Jeremiah 4:3 seems to make some distinction between the *inhabitants of Jerusalem* and the *people of Judah*? See Ezekiel 45:1-5. If these verses hold the customary layout for the city of Jerusalem, who is mentioned as being among the inhabitants of Jerusalem?

(Ezekiel 45:1-5 NRSV): When you allot the land as an inheritance, you shall set aside for the Lord a portion of the land as a holy district, twenty-five thousand cubits long and twenty thousand cubits wide; it shall be holy throughout its entire extent. Of this, a square plot of five hundred by five hundred cubits shall be for the sanctuary, with fifty cubits for an open space around it. In the holy district you shall measure off a section twenty-five thousand cubits long and ten thousand wide, in which shall be the sanctuary, the most holy place. It shall be a holy portion of the land; it shall be for the priests, who minister in the sanctuary and approach the Lord to minister to him; and it shall be both a place for their houses and a holy place for the sanctuary. Another section, twenty-five thousand cubits long and ten thousand cubits wide, shall be for the Levites who minister at the temple, as their holding for cities to live in.

B-4: One that occupies a particular place regularly, routinely, or for a period of time. That is the definition of the word inhabitant. Why would priests and Levites (and even the king) fit the definition of those who are inhabitants of Jerusalem? (See 1Chronicles 27:1 and Luke 1:5-9; 39-40 for clues.)

B-5: God, who upholds and abides by the law, has gone above and beyond the call of duty when it comes to being a good landowner. Even though He doesn't have to, He continues to send His servant Jeremiah to deliver help to those who attend His property. Though He knows that the bride must endure the consequences handed down by the law, the contract has no clauses concerning mercy. He can toss out all of the life preservers that He wants. What instructions does He send by way of Jeremiah to the tenants of His land? (See the last part of verse 3.)

B-6: If you were the overseer, supervisor, or governor (a tenant) of God's land and He sent you the same instructions, how would you interpret the instructions and what would you do?

B-7: God's *people* must open up their (crusted) hearts or else— What will happen if they do not circumcise themselves (which is the acceptable legal code for land in such a state of emergency) and allow Him to plant His seed successfully?

📖READ JEREMIAH 4:5-8

C. ADDITIONAL COMMENTS FOR VERSES 5-8

As Jeremiah speaks the words of prophecy, it is probable that he is at the city gates. That is where the largest and most powerful audiences can be found (1Kings 22:10). The things that are heard at the city gates will be carried into the city, by those who enter; and out into the countryside, by those who are leaving.

The land has shown signs of nothing but resistance toward its Owner (the Lord). The tenants are stubborn and clueless so therefore they are also useless when it comes down to any kind of recovery. God can wait no longer. The day is here! Jeremiah tells the people at the gates: Declare it in Judah and proclaim it in Jerusalem: Evil from the north and great destruction! The message of disaster and destruction is old news at the gates but maybe today holds new hope as the month-by-month shifts change. New temple worshippers and workers (Levites) arrive for appointed duties. Jeremiah delivered this same message, to those who attend to God's properties, some time ago, but as each day and month pass, the danger is closer. Review your answer for question H-1 in chapter 1 and be reminded what the evil from the north might involve or include.

ANSWER QUESTIONS FOR VERSES 5-8

C-1: When a country is under attack as ours was, on what we now call 9/11, leaders (president, vice president, top staff members) are whisked off to secured facilities. Moving the nation's leaders to a secured facility ensures that the country continues to be under the command of the present government.

When disaster strikes, our authorities are kept in secured locations where they can make decisions that continue the pursuit of that for which we stand: freedom and liberty. God uses one word to describe the secured facility where *His people* must go to make lifesaving decisions for the survival of the nation. What city is the only city mentioned?

C-2: Security for the homeland is an important issue in any country. Building fortified cities seems to be the way the issue is addressed in Israel. Building the cities of fortification is an ongoing project with every new king. What were some of the fortified cities in Judah and what was kept inside the fortified cities? (See 2Chronicles 8:3; 11:5-12; 14:6; and 17:12.)

C-3: God now gives a more detailed explanation of why He is bringing evil from the north and what the evil from the north is after. A lion has gone up from its thicket. The lion is the one who (like a cancer) has already wasted and spoiled the nations. And it is absolutely clear and evident that the lion in-the-thicket is at large in Israel. He wants to waste all of God's covenanted people too. We know that the place in which the lion lives is a jungle (which God calls a thicket) originating from shoots and root suckers. Moses warned God's people about this danger long ago.

This is the warning that Moses gave as they exited Egyptian slavery and traveled toward the land of promise. In a manner of speaking, they had been taken on a tour of many nations and Moses speaks to these people concerning the things that they saw and experienced during the long-haul. They knew what the lion-in-the-thicket's dwelling looked like.

(Deuteronomy 29:16-20 NRSV): You know how we lived in the land of Egypt, and how we came through the midst of the nations through which you passed. You have seen their detestable things, the filthy idols of wood and stone, of silver and gold, that were among them. It may be that there is among you a man or woman, or a family or a tribe, whose heart is already turning away from the Lord our God to serve the gods of those nations. It may be that there is among you *a root sprouting poisonous and bitter growth*. All who hear the words of the oath and bless themselves, thinking in their hearts, "We are safe even though we go our stubborn ways" (thus bringing disaster on moist and dry alike)— the Lord will be unwilling to pardon them, for the Lord's anger and passion will smoke against them.

Where or what is the overgrown and wild thicket, that the lion is living, thriving, and growing stronger in, day by day? Jeremiah 4:4 will give you a clue just as well as the verses that you just read.

C-4: Concerning Deuteronomy 29:16-20 (from C-3 in this section), all who took the oath and blessed themselves but yet had evil in their hearts (a root sprouting bitter and poisonous growth), would cause disaster to fall on all (the moist and the dry alike). Make up a parable to explain how some *small evil* in a good place can spread and grow out of control. Then explain how the actions that must be taken to get rid of that once *small evil* but now *larger-out-of-control-evil,* can also affect that which is still *good* around it?

C-5: With all of these warnings God is trying to save something in the midst of the disaster. God is warning these people to flee for safety. If He is telling them of the pending disaster and to take cover, what is it that He really wants to destroy?

📖 **READ JEREMIAH 4:9-10**

D. ADDITIONAL COMMENTS FOR VERSES 9-10

God is talking to Jeremiah and reveals to him what will happen on "that day".

ANSWER QUESTIONS FOR VERSES 9-10

D-1: What will be the reaction of (each particular branch of) the leaders when they discover that the thing, that God is after, is living and growing in their very own hearts?

D-2: Have you ever seen a documentary, show, or movie about a person who is entangled in a cult and the beliefs of a cult? There is usually only one way to rescue those people and that is to hog-tie, drag, and kid-knap them. Well God has a knife at the throats of His people (that's the way Jeremiah puts it) in order to get them to where they should be. What is God saying as He holds the knife to the throat?

D-3: These people now find themselves in the middle of a raging war between their Lord and the lion-in-the-thicket. The actions that God required from His weak and diseased people, back in Jeremiah 4:3, were steps that would have prepared them for this day of war. Even though what God wanted them to do did not seem like aggressive war efforts, it was. This move, of breaking up fallow ground and not sowing among thorns, would have not only supported Him but they also would have protected themselves. How? (See Deuteronomy 6:6 and Psalms 32:7 for clues.)

📖 **READ JEREMIAH 4: 11-14**

E. ADDITIONAL COMMENTS FOR VERSES 11-14

God does not have a stronghold in the hearts of the people that He has chosen for rulers. God warns in verse 14: "O Jerusalem, wash your heart clean of wickedness so that you may be saved…." Cleaning up a dirty heart, which God calls a land full of pollution, is not easy. God is like the head of the environmental protection agency or EPA of Zion. Through this environmental protection agency, warnings have been handed out, fines have been issued, and sentences are being served. But the land (heart) is not changed. The evil seems to be lodged within at a hopeless angle.

ANSWER QUESTIONS FOR VERSES 11-14

E-1: You could compare God's people to criminals and addicts who are court ordered to go through rehabilitation time and time again. No matter what they do, they cannot get rid of the bad habit. Even though they are washed and put *through the wringer* (that expression arises from the old-fashioned washing machines) so to speak, they come out with the same stain. What do you do with the stained clothes that refuse to become clean?

E-2: The people back then, depended on strong winds. They laid out the harvested wheat in places where the wind would hit it just right to blow away the useless chaff. They also built their fires for refining metals in places where the strong winds would blow hard enough to keep the fire under the pots going strong. They depended on the winds to assist them in refining products. So they knew exactly what God meant when He spoke about the winds coming against them.

God has sent the refining winds but nothing is being refined. God cannot get any support from his own people to defeat this enemy. Since the refining winds have not worked God's people are going to get a wind so strong that nothing will be left. It will not be a prophet who speaks God's words but God will speak Himself, using His own methods of speech.

The strong winds are blowing right now (examples of the wind are war, famine, plague, etc.). It is a sure sign that total destruction is on its way to Jerusalem. Jeremiah sees the force that no one can reckon with. How does he describe his vision of the refining force that comes to destroy the lion-in-the-thicket (which lives in the hearts of God's people)?

📖 **READ JEREMIAH 4:15-17**

F. ADDITIONAL COMMENTS FOR VERSES 15-17

The prophecies, that the people are hearing at the city gates of Jerusalem, probably have the same measure of effect on those people as the book of Revelation has on modern day listeners. Everyone can see that destruction looms for all; but no one seems to know exactly what to do about it. So the matter is put on the back burner; and if not totally forgotten about, it is dangerously neglected.

ANSWER QUESTIONS FOR VERSES 15-17

F-1: In Numbers 10:25, we find that the tribe of Dan was *rear guard,* of the military, in the days of Moses. Symbolically, what message comes from the rear guard, which has already been chased as far south as Ephraim and ready to enter Benjamin and then Judah, the home of that great city of Jerusalem? (See verse 15.)

(For your personal information: Dan was the northern most tribe in Israel. Some maps may indicate Dan to be located on the western coast of Israel, next to the Mediterranean Sea. But Dan moved to the northern most borders of Israel. You can see Judges, chapter, 18 for the details of the move.) Now back to the original question: What message is heard from Dan?

F-2: God has been talking about a destructive lion-in-the-thicket. Read the following verses and then answer: What is the moral from the battle that was fought in the forest of Ephraim? It can be applied to the battle going on in the heart of not only sister Israel but Judah too. (They seem to be unaware that the most destructive war rages, out of control, inside of them.)

(2Samuel 18:6-8 NRSV): So the army went out into the field against Israel; and the battle was fought in the forest of Ephraim. The men of Israel were defeated there by the servants of David, and the slaughter there was great on that day, twenty thousand men. The battle spread over the face of all the country; and the forest claimed more victims that day than the sword.

F-3: God's *people* (the remnant of the bride) continues to aid and abet His enemy. In our legal system today, the person who is aiding and abetting the criminal is just as guilty because they facilitate or purposely assist and promote the unlawful act. Judah is the aider and abettor. Here, in these verses, the hot wind takes on the form of besiegers. It is said that *besiegers* come from a distant land. Besiege means to surround with armed forces and to cause worry or distress. If these people were merely hostages of the lion and on the right side of the law, this surrounding (from a distant land) would be seen and heralded as "heroes coming to save the day!" Who are (possibly) the powerful besiegers that will not only cause worry and distress to God's people but will also be the fear in other nations when they hear about the war that God has declared on His enemy, the lion-in-the-thicket? Go back to the first chapter. (See Jeremiah 1:15-16 for one optional answer that is available to us at this point of the study.)

F-4: What will these besiegers do? What two actions will reveal that they (the policing forces) are against Judah at this time? (See Jeremiah 4:16-17 for the actions that seem more like a violent protest of warning.)

F-5: Jeremiah 4:16 (NRSV) says: Tell the nations, "Here they are!" In your opinion, why tell the nations?

F-6: As you remember that Jeremiah is at the city gates, make speculation and answer: how will the nations hear about the besiegers that Jeremiah prophesies about?

📖READ JEREMIAH 4:18

G. ADDITIONAL COMMENTS FOR VERSE 18

It is certain. Destruction has reached Israel's heart.

ANSWER QUESTIONS FOR VERSE 18

G-1: According to the dictionary, another word for *heart* is *intellect*. Look up the word—intellect. What doom has come to God's people?

📖READ JEREMIAH 4:19-22

H. ADDITIONAL COMMENTS FOR VERSES 19-22

The people of Judah and inhabitants of Jerusalem get a detailed report of the raging war that is now in progress and headed their way. The report comes from an Eye-witness.

ANSWER QUESTIONS FOR VERSES 19-22

H-1: Sister-Israel is getting hit spiritually (by the lion-in-the-thicket) and she is getting hit physically (by the curses of the covenant). What words describe the scenes of war?

H-2: The disaster is imminent. The disaster is unavoidable. When God says that His tents are destroyed, what is this prophecy about? Scan over Exodus 25-27 for a description of the *physical* tent. Then see Numbers 3:21-37 for a description of the *spiritual* tent.

H-3: God's shepherds, (His chosen line of rulers), did not properly disperse the wisdom that God had given them. They were negligent not only in duty but they showed negligence by not passing all of the wisdom on. So now as the wars (of the spiritual and physical kind) ensue, what else may God be grieving over? What is going to be buried with the mortal men who housed God as this war escalates? (See Deuteronomy 10:9 and 6:6.)

H-4: There is no stopping the curses of the covenant. God's people have legally ordered-up these besiegers by their own acts. God's people continue to feed the beast that destroys them. The people are running in all directions, but not the right one. God describes His people. What does He say? (See Jeremiah 4:22.)

📖READ JEREMIAH 4:23-28

I. ADDITIONAL COMMENTS FOR VERSES 23-28

No matter what Judah does or does not do, the hot wind is coming and it is her choice to face the hot wind protecting the lion-in-the-thicket or giving up the lion-in-the-thicket. But she appears to be deaf and blind to God's directions.

ANSWER QUESTIONS FOR VERSES 23-28

I-1: Can you see any metaphors in verses 23-26? Compare the physical descriptions in those verses to something else.

I-2: The Lord has spoken desolation and He will not relent. What do you think is meant by: the earth shall mourn, and the heavens above grow black?

I-3: Human beings as well as their fingerprints are unique. No two are the same. I like to think that God's offspring (the word that He plants in the heart of man) has that same unique quality. When God plants His seed in the heart of a man, He becomes like an expectant father. He cannot wait to see what sprouts and comes to life. Let's take a look at some surprising words that grew in the heart of a man named Moses. When Moses spoke these words from the heart, God must have been surprised what had sprung up. It was words of a leader who cared about His (God's) own people. God must have felt like a proud father who, for the first time, sees his son taking a stand for something he believes in.

Back in Exodus 32:7-14, God was angry at His people. He wanted to destroy them. But Moses was someone who nurtured God's seed; and his care caused the seed to grow into strong and healthy vines that produced fruits of wisdom and compassion. Moses picked two pieces of fruit from the vine and gave them to God. He showed God two reasons why He should not destroy His people.

- The first: The Egyptians would say, 'It was with evil intent that he brought them out to kill them in the mountains, and to consume them from the face of the earth.'
- The second reason: Remember Abraham, Isaac and Israel, your servants, how you swore to them by your own self, saying to them: 'I will multiply your descendants like the stars of the heaven, and all this land that I have promised I will give to your descendants, and they shall inherit it forever.'

Do you believe that God's seeded word, growing in your heart, has the power to change God's mind or affect God's decisions? What does Exodus 32:14 say?

📖 READ JEREMIAH 4: 29-30

J. ADDITIONAL COMMENTS FOR VERSES 29-30

The land that God gave to His covenanted people as a perpetual holding had been brutally abused, broken, and degraded. The land served as a reflection of their hearts (the place God wanted to dwell). Just like the land their hearts became a breeding ground for wickedness. Wickedness had grown strong and taken root. The evil lion had taken over and now its hold on them would cause their end. Even though they were warned, idols and places where other gods were worshipped could be found in every town. The people lived their day-to-day lives in the wild environment with the lion-in-the-thicket.

ANSWER QUESTIONS FOR VERSES 29-30

J-1: At the noise of the horseman and archer every town takes flight (Jeremiah 4:20 NRSV). God describes one of their hiding places as a *thicket*. A thicket is a cluster of tangled small trees or bushes. What do God's people say to the small trees that they run to? (See Jeremiah 2:27.)

J-2: The people are also trying to hide among the rocks on the hills. What are the people of God saying to the rocks that they try to hide behind? (See Jeremiah 2:27.)

J-3: Judah has apparently returned to her true love. Where are the people really running when they hear the sound of the horseman and archer?

J-4: It has been heard that the horseman and archer are on their way. You will find Levi at the temple praying to God in these devastating times, while many others are under every green tree and on every high rock praying too, but not to God. One thing is sure throughout Judah and in Jerusalem; everyone is dressed-to-impress their saviors. No matter which one shows up first, they want to look good during the dramatic rescue as they play the part of damsel in distress (they avidly believe that their salvation is near). God says: in vain you beautify yourself. Your lovers despise you, they seek your life. Who are the lovers?

J-5 (OPTIONAL QUESTION): How do we know that worshippers dressed-up before worship? (See 2Kings 10:21-22; 22:14; and 2Chronicles 34:22.)

J-6: In Genesis 35:1-4 we will find Jacob and his family getting prepared for the worship. What did Jacob tell everyone to do in order to get ready? See below and answer in your own words.

(Genesis 35:1-4 NRSV): God said to Jacob, "Arise, go up to Bethel, and settle there. Make an altar there to the God who appeared to you when you fled from your brother Esau." So Jacob said to his household and to all who were with him, "Put away the foreign gods that are among you, and purify yourselves, and change your clothes; then come, let us go up to Bethel, that I may make an altar there to the God who answered me in the day of my distress and has been with me wherever I have gone." So they gave to Jacob all the foreign gods that they had, and the rings that were in their ears; and Jacob hid them under the oak that was near Shechem.

J-7: Jacob's family probably did some actual cleaning up (bathing, hair washing, cleaning of clothes) but I think that God desires a different kind of cleaning up. He wants our insides to be cleaned. How do we work on getting to that cleaned up state? (See 1Peter 1:22.)

📖READ JEREMIAH 4:31

K. ADDITIONAL COMMENTS FOR VERSE 31

A cry is heard and here is how the cry is described: For I heard a cry as of a woman in labor, anguish as of one bringing forth her first child, the cry of daughter Zion gasping for breath, stretching out her hands, "Woe is me! I am fainting before my killers!"

ANSWER QUESTIONS FOR VERSE 31

K-1: (OPTIONAL QUESTION): Read Revelation 12:1-6. Could these particular verses in Revelation be related to Jeremiah 4:31? If so, what happened to the child and what happened to the woman in labor?

K-2: When you read the words: Zion gasping for breath (Jeremiah 4:31), what do you think God is saying through the metaphor? See the following verse, it may help you. (Isaiah 2:3 NRSV)… For out of Zion shall go forth instruction, and the word of the Lord from Jerusalem.

K-3: Even though there are about 613 laws all together, here is a list of the ten laws (taken from Deuteronomy 5:6-21) that God wrote in stone and gave to His people. Has any been broken in this chapter? If yes give reference from chapters 1-4.

- ➢ 1 You shall have no other gods before me.
- ➢ 2 You shall not make for yourself any idols.
- ➢ 3 You shall not wrongfully use the name of the Lord your God.
- ➢ 4 Remember the Sabbath Day and keep it holy.
- ➢ 5 Honor your mother and father.
- ➢ 6 You shall not murder.
- ➢ 7 You shall not commit adultery.
- ➢ 8 You shall not steal.
- ➢ 9 You shall not bear false witness against your neighbor.
- ➢ 10 You shall not covet anything that belongs to your neighbor.

K-4: What message do you hear from the fourth chapter of Jeremiah?

Chapter 4 Tag-A-Long

Laying Blame

As I watched the evening news they were reporting on a group of protesters. The protesters were identified as a Christian group and the messages on their picket signs revealed that this was an anti-gay protest. If I had to summarize their message in ten words or less, I would have to say that they were operating on the notion that: God brings suffering on America because of gay people.

Imagine if this picketing was done by *God's people* back in Jeremiah's day. Imagine if *God's people* would have lined the streets of their cities proclaiming that all of their suffering (war, famine, and pestilence) was due to the acts of the foreigner's. Imagine if they laid that blame on foreigners who did not follow the laws and ordinances that God prescribed for His people, Israel. As far as we have come in this study, we know that claim would be absolutely false. *God's people* and all of their land was suffering because of the sins they (*God's people*) committed against God as His bride.

The people in the other nations had no responsibility to follow the law of God's people. God's covenant was given to Israel. He entered into a contractual agreement with one group of people and those people were then, *His people*. The nations had no such legal relationship with Him. In fact, God seems to reveal an attitude of calmness toward them and their ways at this time. (See Deuteronomy 32:8-9 and Jeremiah 2:10-12.)

It's a little scary to think that all of the suffering today could be because of those who come under the heading of: God's people, those who are a part of the one body to which Believers belong (the body is called *the church* in the New Testament). The *church* is not just those in the place you go to worship. It's all the Christians in your town. It's all the Christians in your state, country, across the borders of your country, and across the seas. Some of your *church* may have passed from this earth and some of your *church* is not yet born. It's a big, big, big, body. Admitting and confessing that your body (as a whole) has done sinful things against God and that your body (as a whole) has done things to damage others, may not seem like your responsibility. But there is only one body and if you are in Christ, you are part of that body and the acts of your body are your responsibility. What are you going to do today to have a healthier body so that we can deliver blessings with strength and not curses due to weakness and confusion?

It seems that the worst tragedies and disasters are in nations who have traditionally served *gods*. It is great that the body of Christ is growing worldwide but some members of our body may be struggling like Judah. They may be interlacing their tracks by holding the gospel in one hand but yet they do not have the ability to let go of old ways and traditions from the past. Many Believers are like Jacob in Genesis 35:1-4. They just hide the old traditions in a secure place. The traditions still lie buried somewhere in the heart. Is turning away from God to serve other gods still a problem of God's people (of one body) today? I don't have the answer but I am just asking you to examine and know your own body.

✂ Scrapbook Page For Chapter 4

Home

Praise the Lord, O Jerusalem!

Praise your God, O Zion!

For he strengthens the bars of your gates;

He blesses your children within you

(Psalms 147:12-13 NRSV).

The verses above give a good description of what happened, spiritually, to Jeremiah back in chapter 1. God put (planted) His word inside the gates of Jeremiah's heart and then fortified it all around. God's *word* is His precious child (His offspring). He calls His child the finest wheat in verse 14 of Psalms 147. If you read further down, in verse 15 He says He sends His word out to the earth and it runs swiftly. Then verse 18 shows the power of it. And finally in verse 19 and 20, we hear about *mom*. We see how special she (the bride) is to God. She is the chosen one to carry His child (His seed). He has dealt with no other woman like He has dealt with her.

But she is not providing a very good home for the word. In Jeremiah 4:3 God warns her about the bad condition of the home. It is not a safe place and if she does not get it cleaned up herself, He, God is going to do it for her. But He warns her, if He has to do it, it is not going to be pretty.

I have always heard that— home is where the heart is. I would like to change that cliché to— the heart is where the home is (the home of God, the home of His word.) I would pray for safety upon each home and that the child (the planted word of God) would be safe and grow strong. I pray that it would always go out prepared and come home with a great story of how it changed the world that day or how it changed someone in the world that day. I would especially pray that predators would not break in or be permitted to enter the home and corrupt the child and turn it into something that it was never meant to be. I would pray that the caretakers would be good providers, keeping the word safe and ever alive. I would pray that the word would be strong enough to survive and move into the homes of the next generation and the next and the next, forever.

Throughout all of Israel, much of God's word has died prematurely and at an early age because there has been great neglect concerning their righteous duty toward God's word and their perpetual care of God's word. And because of this God's people are instructed to put on sackcloth, lament and wail: "The fierce anger of the Lord has not turned away from us" (Jeremiah 4:8 NRSV).

Be a good tenant. Be wise and responsible. Choose life for the child (the word) in your care and hear comments like this: "I noticed your Word out-and-about the other day and you should be filled with joy. He is really making a difference around here! I told Him so and he said it was all because he had a great home."

This snapshot portrays Jesus as a happy child who is loved, well nourished, and active.

Compare Answers For Chapter 4

A-1: The nations will be blessed by Him and by Him they shall boast.

A-2: I think the '*him*' in that verse is the living Word of God (which is somewhere in their hearts).

A-3: They have not raised or nourished the seed to be a ruler. He, the seed in their hearts, has become like a servant as the lions of deceit roar against Him and the people allow this as they let the deceitful lion take priority in their hearts.

A-4: Israel holds the blessings of the nations in her heart, if she would only turn back to serving God.

B-1: Judah and Benjamin

B-2: the priests and Levites from all the territories of Israel

B-3: Levites and priests

B-4: They came to Jerusalem to serve at the temple for periods of time as scheduled. And then, with every new king, a new cabinet full of members usually follows.

B-5: …Break up your fallow ground, and do not sow among thorns (Jeremiah 4:3 NRSV).

B-6: If I were the tenant (at this particular time) I would understand the corrective steps to starting the planting process all over and not plant the seed in a weeded field. As one who is responsible to oversee the production of fruits, I guess I would have to start with those who are as children, having a clean and undamaged soil.

B-7: Circumcise yourselves to the Lord, remove the foreskin of your hearts, O people of Judah and inhabitants of Jerusalem, or else my wrath will go forth like fire, and burn with no one to quench it, because of the evil of your doings (Jeremiah 4:4 NRSV).

C-1: Zion

C-2: Some fortified cities were Bethlehem, Etam, Tekoa, Bethzur, Soco, Adullam, Gath,

Mareshah, Ziph, Adoraim, Lachish, Azekah, Zorah, Aijalon, and Hebron. Inside them were commanders, stores of food, oil, wine, shields, and spears. They were storage cities.

C-3: the heart

C-4: When you have cancer, the unfriendly and foreign force moves in and starts taking over all of your good vital body parts. Then the treatment that must be used, to destroy the cancer, not only destroys the foreign matter, when it is at work, but it also destroys a lot of good body tissue also.

C-5: the lion in the thicket and/or the evil that dwells in the heart

D-1: Courage shall fail the king and officials. The priests shall be appalled and the prophets astounded.

D-2: It shall be well with you.

D-3: They would have been planting (hiding) God (God's word) in a spot by itself and not among the enemy. His word would grow and gain some strength for what was to come. God needs a stronghold in order to be ready for the enemy and the people could have provided that for Him. It (the heart) was His purchased ground to begin with and He had to now fight to reclaim it.

E-1: tear them up and use them for rags, they then help me to keep everything else clean

E-2: Look! He comes up like clouds, his chariots like the whirlwind; his horses are swifter than eagles— woe to us for we are ruined! (See Jeremiah 4:13 NRSV.)

F-1: disaster from Mount Ephraim— The besiegers are here!

F-2: The forest claimed more victims that day than the sword. The evil living in their hearts will destroy more of them than the sword from God.

F-3: judgment (represented by the thrones from chapter one) of justice and righteousness

F-4: shout against the cities of Judah and close in around her like watchers (compare to Jeremiah 1:15)

F-5: He wants the nations to know that He is coming to destroy that (lion in the thicket). The lion-in-the-thicket is the destroyer of ALL nations. God will go wherever He has to in order to destroy the lion. The nations have been officially warned. God's coming and this war is no surprise.

F-6: Maybe people from other nations have come to Jerusalem for some sort of business (See Jeremiah 27:3).

G-1: intellect: the power of knowing as distinguished from the power to feel and to will. The intellectual powers (power of knowledge), of God's people, have been destroyed. They seem to have been taken over by personal feelings and desires.

H-1: There is desolation and destruction.

H-2: The Levites, those who were claimed by the Lord were being destroyed.

H-3: God's truth and wisdom, by inherited word, were going to the grave.

H-4: God says: "For my people are foolish, they do not know me; they are stupid children, they have no understanding. They are skilled in doing evil, but do not know how to do good" (Jeremiah 4:22 NRSV).

I-1: Heavens had no light could mean that no light (wisdom) was coming to earth to show the way. The mountains and hills quaking could be the leaders who fear the situation that they are in. All the birds had fled could mean that there was no human life. The fruitful land was a desert could mean that the there was no spiritual fruit to be found anywhere. The heart (land) has been destroyed, if not by the lion, by the war.

I-2: The heavens, like a store, at closing time will grow black. The earth will receive 'no good' from the heavens. Also Micah 3:5-6 speaks of darkness (no knowledge from God) being disclosed from the heavens. (Micah 3:5-7 NRSV): Thus says the Lord concerning the prophets who lead my people astray, who cry "Peace" when they have something to eat, but declare war against those who put nothing into their mouths. Therefore it shall be night for you, without vision, and darkness to you, without revelation. The sun shall go down upon the prophets, and the day shall be black over them.

I-3: And the Lord changed his mind about the disaster that he planned to bring on his people. (See Exodus 32:14 NRSV.)

J-1: "You are my father."

J-2: "You gave me birth."

J-3: They were running to their idols and seeking answers from other gods.

J-4: For those under green tree and on high rock, lovers are the gods who will destroy them; but for those in the temple, it is the covenant curses.

J-5(OPTIONAL QUESTION): These verses speak of vestments for worship and a person who was in charge of a wardrobe living in the Second Quarter.

J-6: put away foreign gods that are among you, purify yourselves, change your clothes

J-7: Now that you have purified your souls by your *obedience to the truth* so that you have genuine mutual love, love one another deeply from the heart (1Peter 1:22 NRSV). From this verse I think that I, as a believer in Jesus, must be obedient to the truth. Obedience to the truth is how I purify my soul. Being obedient to Jesus, who brought the truth, is my plan for purification.

K-1: (OPTIONAL QUESTION): The child was taken to God and His throne and the woman fled to the wilderness, to a place God prepared so that she could be nourished.

K-2: I think instruction (from Zion) is: the directions. And the word (from Jerusalem) is: the parts. It's like something that has to be assembled. Zion gives the step by step directions of how to assemble the words so that the thing that you put together is useful. I think Zion may be a spiritual place. We have the word, but it is apparent that everyone does not have the same instructions in hand. Instruction from God struggles and has a hard time breathing among us. It even faints off.

K-3: This is a running list from the previous chapter.

   Number 1: You shall have no other gods before me (broken law according to Jeremiah 1:16)

   Number 2: You shall not make for yourself an idol (broken law according to Jeremiah 1:16)

   Number 5: Honor your father and mother (broken law according to Jeremiah 2:27)

   Number 6: You shall not murder (broken law according to Jeremiah 2:30b and 34)

   Number 4: Remember the Sabbath day and keep it holy (broken law according to Jeremiah 2:32)

   Number 7: You shall not commit adultery (broken law according to Jeremiah 3:6)

K-4: One thing is sure. I am going to suffer in my lifetime. But I have a choice to suffer for the Lord's cause or suffer for the selfish evil that lives in my heart. I want to be on the Lord's side and give up the lion-in-the-thicket. I will hide God deep inside. He will spring up in strength and glory if I give Him a good spot and continue to care for His seeded word.

Chapter 5

Chapter 5 Prelude

As the Lord Lives

IN GOD WE TRUST. This is the proclamation written on United States currency. But if you step back and take a look at our nation and its people as a whole you will see that our actions do not always reflect that proclamation. If we truly trusted in God we would follow Him in all His ways. This worldwide proclamation far outweighs the evidence found within our nation.

A foreigner who has seen that proclamation on the nation's currency decides that he wants to come and visit the people who make this declaration. He thinks this land must be like heaven on earth! When he arrives he has great expectations but unfortunately as well as unavoidably he witnesses some disturbing events. The actions of many do not reflect the great proclamation. They are not being truthful about themselves or the land in which they live. He has witnessed arrogant boasters, abusive, uncaring, and inconsiderate attitudes. He sees people who are insensitive and true haters of justice. Any means are deemed lawful by the inhabitants if it gets them to the place they want to be. They love to collect a lot of money that makes the great proclamation but they never stop to read what the wad in their back pocket really says. They are fakers who hold onto false identification. He thinks that these people hide behind and abuse the words: In God We Trust.

The visit proved to be a very disappointing one for the foreigner. As he boards the air bus to return home his opinion of this people and the God they boast of is not the one he had originally planned to leave with. He finds the passenger seat that corresponds with the numbers and letters on his ticket stub. He sits down and allows his head to fall back and relax. He closes his eyes for a moment to find some much needed solitude only to come face to face with that ongoing feeling of discontentment that he has been trying to shake off since his first day here in the strange land full of (how he sees it) delusion.

So in an attempt to make peace with himself he reaches deep inside his pocket to pull out that one last crisp dollar bill. He had wanted to keep it as a souvenir. He studies this piece of currency long and hard for, what he knows will be, the very last time. He pulls out his pen and writes something defacing the currency. Neatly he folds it up and stuffs it down inside the crevice of the passenger seat that he occupies. Then with no expression on his face he turns his head and watches out from his window seat. The jet takes off and the land of the people who trust in God gets smaller and smaller. He wonders how a land of people could proclaim, in such great magnitude, that they trust in God when they don't even trust their God enough to do what He says. They trust and live by something other than what they profess to the world.

If this foreigner would have visited Jerusalem, the capitol of Judah, he would have found the same kind of unfounded proclamation in that city too. The proclamation in Jerusalem was: 'As the Lord lives!' But finding any evidence of that being true is not going to happen in that capitol, at least not on this day, in this chapter.

Oh by the way when the foreigner's crisp new bill was found and unfolded it revealed the same thing as the hearts of the people in Jerusalem revealed. The word 'God' was crossed off with a big X. And above it, the word 'evil' was written. But the inhabitants in Jerusalem and the people of Judah still will not see it (their hearts) the way God sees it. They will not admit the truth. She (Jerusalem) holds the evil and she will not give it up. She does not see the danger as her heart is the hide-out for that which is the cause of her destruction. Nothing good will be left if the destroyer, living in her heart, has his way.

Chapter 5 Study

One Can Make a Difference

CHAPTER 5 READING, COMMENTS, AND QUESTIONS

In the last chapter God warned the people to run to the fortified cities of Judah and take cover. The trumpets sounded and the standard (warning flag) was raised. Even though this destruction coming from the north will prove to be a real physical problem for these people, we looked at that warning in a spiritual sense; because Judah's biggest enemy of destruction is herself. If she doesn't get the spiritual matter of the heart taken care of, she, as a holy people, will be destroyed.

The words in the covenant from God were meant to bring a faithful people security and peace of mind in knowing that God would never leave them or forsake them. The words of His covenant gave promise and protected a faithful bride and her children from a wandering husband. But she was the wanderer in this relationship and now God is rounding her (Judah) up and bringing her in. She will have to face the law for her rejection and answer for her criminal acts. I imagine the Lord wants to see if this remnant of Israel wants to try to work things out with Him. So the fortified cities of Judah are packed but we will focus on Jerusalem; that is where we will find the most powerful leaders of Judah.

📖 READ JEREMIAH 5:1-2

A. ADDITIONAL COMMENTS FOR VERSES 1-2

God tells Jeremiah to run through the streets of the mighty fortified city of Jerusalem and take note of anyone who acts justly and seeks truth.

ANSWER QUESTIONS FOR VERSES 1-2

A-1: What type of physical evidence will Jeremiah look for as he searches the streets for someone who acts justly and seeks the truth? (See the following verses.)

(Isaiah 36:22-37:2 NRSV): Then Eliakim son of Hilkiah, who was in charge of the palace, and Shebna the secretary, and Joah son of Asaph, the recorder, came to Hezekiah with their clothes torn, and told him the words of Rabshakeh. When King Hezekiah heard it, he tore his clothes, covered himself with sackcloth, and went into the house of the Lord.

(Jonah 3:6-7 NRSV): When the news reached the king of Nineveh, he rose from his throne, removed his robe, covered himself with sackcloth, and sat in ashes. The he had a proclamation made in Nineveh: "By the degree of the king and his nobles: No human being or animal, no herd or flock, shall taste anything…"

A-2: Have you ever heard the phrase 'Long Live the King!'? It is a phrase used by the people in a kingdom or society that signifies continuity of the king's place of sovereignty. 'As the Lord lives' was probably a phrase used in Jerusalem with the same significance. When someone said, 'As the Lord lives' it was a proclamation that the Lord their God (and His ways) ruled the land. It was Jerusalem's creed. If they, would have, had currency it would have been inscribed on every dollar bill and coin that was made but the currency would be declaring a lie. 'As the Lord lives' would have been a false swear by God's people. From what you know about the ways of the people, why would God say they swear falsely?

A-3: Do you remember the conversation back in Genesis 18:16-33 between God and Abraham? God was going to destroy Sodom because the outcry against that city was great. And after the conversation was over it was decided by the Lord that if ten righteous people could be found in Sodom, it would not be destroyed. But ten could not be found. So Sodom was destroyed. How many people will it take for God to pardon Jerusalem?

A-4: What was the reason God destroyed Sodom? (See Ezekiel 16:49-50.)

A-5: This is what God says concerning Sodom: …"How great is the outcry against Sodom and Gomorrah and how very grave their sin! I must go down and see whether they have done altogether according to the outcry that has come to me; and if not, I will know" (Genesis 18:20-21 NRSV).

When cities are misbehaving and God hears about it, He makes a visit. Jerusalem is about to receive some company and according to Jeremiah 1:15 some heavy back-up (tribes of the kingdoms of the north who bring thrones) will show up too. What is God hearing from Jerusalem? Look ahead to Jeremiah 6:7.

A-6: Back in Jeremiah 1:13, Jeremiah saw a boiling pot. It was tilted away from the north. We reviewed the physical possibilities of what that pot (which provided a vision) could be; but I would like to build another analogy concerning that pot. Think about this: Every nation has its own pot in heaven. Each pot gets filled up by the actions of the nation. When the pot of any nation begins to overflow God gets ready. He is going on a trip! God does not have to decide what to bring. The sort (kind, type, or character) of overflow will decide if blessings or punishment will accompany Him. I imagine that God expects the leaders to be the first to greet Him upon arrival. They should have been watching for Him with either fear or great expectation, depending upon the overflow that their nation has been experiencing.

Judah's pot has been filled up. But she has not deposited anything good and the overflow is slowly beginning to prove that. But the leaders in Jerusalem are not fearful even though the pot is boiling and about to explode. As they confidently walk the streets of the walled Jerusalem;

they have their hands in the air, saying: "We are saved!", "The Lord Lives!", and "We shall not see sword of famine!" What got them to this point of feeling so safe, even though the pot lurks, and boils dangerously, overhead? (See the following verses.)

(2Kings 8:19 NRSV): Yet the Lord would not destroy Judah, for the sake of his servant David, since he had promised to give a lamp to him and to his descendants forever.

(2Kings 19:34 NRSV): "For I will defend this city to save it, for my own sake and for the sake of my servant David."

(Jeremiah 3:17 NRSV): At that time Jerusalem shall be called the throne of the Lord, and all nations shall gather to it, to the presence of the Lord, in Jerusalem....

A-7: This situation, of feeling safe, reminds me of a game that I used to play when I was a kid. Here's how the game was played: One child in the group was chosen to be 'it'. The child who was 'it' had to tag (or tap) the other kids before they reached the safe place called home. If you (not wanting to be tagged) could reach that place called home (before you were tagged) and hold onto it, calling out "I'm safe!", you were indeed safe from the one who was 'it'. I think that Jerusalem was the place that God's people held onto and yelled out "I'm safe!" God's people held onto places and people for protection.

Have you ever been in a situation where knowing someone in particular got you out of trouble when you mentioned their name or when you said 'I know so-and-so'? Or has anyone treated you with respect because of who your friends or relatives are? Have you ever avoided a speeding ticket or fine by dropping a name? God's people had such pillars for support. Whose names were powerful enough, in heaven, to bring protection to Israel and Judah? (See the following verses as well as the verses in the last question.)

(2Kings 13:23 NRSV): But the Lord was gracious to them and had compassion on them; he turned toward them, because of his covenant with Abraham, Isaac, and Jacob, and would not destroy them; nor has he banished them from his presence until now.

(Deuteronomy 9:5 NRSV): It is not because of your righteousness or the uprightness of your heart that you are going in to occupy their land; but because of the wickedness of these nations the Lord your God is dispossessing them before you, in order to fulfill the promise that the Lord made on oath to your ancestors, to Abraham, to Isaac, and to Jacob.

A-8: The inhabitants of Jerusalem must have been feeling pretty secure with these promises under their belts. Not only did they have the promise that God made to David (which Israel did not receive) but they also fell under God's promise to Abraham and others still had the priestly covenant (promise) on their side. We have already viewed this verse once, but turn again to Ezekiel 11:15. After reading the verse, explain, in your own words, how those in Jerusalem viewed themselves as the world around them crumbled.

 READ JEREMIAH 5:3

B. ADDITIONAL COMMENTS FOR VERSE 3

God has been conducting a series of lengthy investigations in Jerusalem. But the leaders refuse to give up the truth. The fact is, they probably do not have the truth (within themselves) but maybe there is still some small hint of righteousness that has been hidden and tucked away so God is shaking them up and shaking them down.

ANSWER QUESTIONS FOR VERSE 3

B-1: When a body undergoes trauma from some serious injury or deadly disease, the only chance for survival is to keep the heart beating. I think that God sees Jerusalem as that important organ to the body of Judah (both of them being a fragment of all Israel). But God has some serious concerns about the heart too, so He tests it. God has discovered that the heart is not responding the way that it was created to. It is not suffering or showing any signs of distress as the rest of the body is being attacked. How is the heart reacting to the testing that the body is undergoing? (See the first part of verse 3.)

B-2: As the devastation from Israel is beginning to move into Judah, how are the people, inside the high walls of the city, described? (See the last part of verse 3.)

B-3 (OPTIONAL QUESTION): How do the people in your town react to all of the devastating events going on outside of your neighborhood, town, or county?

B-4: I am from one of the Midwestern states. When there is a hurricane to the south, an earthquake to the west, a devastating flood somewhere, or lack of food for hungry children in my country, I should be feeling some kind of pain for those fellow human beings who suffer. I know that I am just one human being but I should examine my life to see if I could do something to help change that situation.

These people in Jerusalem held the power to ease the pain of their fellow brothers and sisters as well as their own pain, which was quickly approaching with a vengeance; but they would not heed Jeremiah's messages from God. Turn to Judges 10:9-16. Read about the time when a true confession with sacrifice moved the heart and hand of God. What did the people confess and what did they sacrifice to ease the pain that was about to come upon them and their fellow countrymen?

 READ JEREMIAH 5:4-5

C. ADDITIONAL COMMENTS FOR VERSES 4-5

Jeremiah takes his tour through the streets of the city. He finds no hint of evidence that could lend salvation to the city.

ANSWER QUESTIONS FOR VERSES 4-5

C-1: Though Jeremiah has been on every square, he does not find the precious evidence that will save the city; but he has, what he thinks, is a perfectly good explanation for coming up empty handed. He says that these on the streets are only the poor and have no sense. It's true, the poor were at a disadvantage, not thought highly of, and not much time or money was spent on them; but Jeremiah thinks he can find someone who is just and seeks the truth among the rich. What does he find out when he speaks to the rich?

C-2: Jeremiah had the idea that the rich were better informed. In those days, the rich did seem to have an advantage when it came to unrevealed things. Gather some information from the following verses and tell why the rich did have an advantage when it came to spiritual matters.

(Judges 18:3-4 NRSV): While they were at Micah's house, they recognized the voice of the young Levite; so they went over and asked him, "Who brought you here? What are you doing in this place? What is your business here?" He said to them, "Micah did such and such for me, and he *hired* me, and I have become his priest."

(1Samuel 9:6-10 NRSV): But he said to him, "There is a man of God in this town; he is a man held in honor. Whatever he says always comes true. Let us go there now; perhaps he will tell us about the journey on which we have set out." Then Saul replied to the boy, "But if we go, what can we bring the man? For the bread in our sacks is gone, and there is no present to bring to the man of God. What have we?" The boy answered Saul again, "Here, I have with me a quarter shekel of silver; I will give it to the man of God, to tell us our way." (Formerly in Israel, anyone who went to inquire of God would say, "Come, let us go to the seer"; for the one who is now called a prophet was formerly called a seer.)

(2Kings 8:7-9 NRSV): Elisha went to Damascus while King Ben-hadad of Aram was ill. When it was told him, "The man of God has come here," the king said to Hazael, "Take a present with you and go to meet the man of God. Inquire of the Lord through him, whether I shall recover from this illness." So Hazael went to meet him, taking a present with him, all kinds of goods of Damascus, forty camel loads….

(Micah 3:11 NRSV): Its rulers give judgment for a bribe, its priests teach for a price, its prophets give oracles for money; …

(Numbers 22:7 NRSV): So the elders of Moab and the elders of Midian departed with the fees for divination in their hand; …

C-3: God instructs Jeremiah to stand in many public places and deliver messages that reveal the future of the nation as well as its current condition. Jeremiah's special call from God has left me wondering how much of the public actually got to hear God as He revealed Himself through word. I am wondering if God's word was bound up in greedy hearts of *His people*. This may be just one of the reasons behind these words of God.

(Jeremiah 6:13 NRSV): For from the least to the greatest of them, everyone is greedy for unjust gain; and from the prophet to the priest, everyone deals falsely.

(Jeremiah 7:11 NRSV): Has this house, which is called by my name, become a den of robbers in your sight?

Hearing God speak may have been a miracle for most of the poor. Turn to Matthew 11:4-5. What does the last part of verse 5 say?

C-4: Staying faithfully devoted, to only the Lord, was not important to the leaders. They did not seem to care that God's ways were not being observed in their hearts, in the capitol, or in their flailing cities. When the leaders from Israel did not allow God to sit on the throne and be Ruler (in their heart and in their land), people suffered. Go to 1Chronicles 21:1-17. How did King David end up feeling when the people, during his reign as king, were struck by the curses of the covenant due to his personal unlawful acts?

C-5: This incident (referring to the last question) that happened in 1Chronicles 21 is the law-in-action. When the law is broken penalties must be paid to balance the scales. The Old Testament Law is hungry and demands payment when it is offended. It sues and takes everything it can get and it is perfectly legal and backed up by the court. Can you think of a time when someone brought up a law-suit and many people had to pay the price due to the negligence of one?

📖 **READ JEREMIAH 5:6**

D. ADDITIONAL COMMENTS FOR VERSE 6

No just, or truth seeking, person could be found inside the city of Jerusalem. God has proof that these leaders are neither capable or worthy of being chosen. So God warns the people about the danger. Animals from the desert and forest are waiting to tear them to pieces. The animals are already ravaging the territory outside the walls.

ANSWER QUESTIONS FOR VERSE 6

D-1: What is the difference between the lion-in-the-thicket in Jeremiah 4:7 and the lion, the wolf, and the leopard in Jeremiah 5:6?

D-2: What reaction might God be expecting from these people, who are safe inside the walls, when He tells them about the wild animals?

D-3: This lion, wolf, and leopard could represent physical danger in the form of pestilence, famine, warring armies, etc. But as these physical dangers ravage the whole kingdom of Judah, whittling it down to the bone, what happens that could make these lions, wolves, and leopards, a real threat instead of just an allegory? See the following verse to find out what happens when a quick end comes to communities of people.

(Deuteronomy 7:22 NRSV): The Lord your God will clear away these nations before you little by little; you will not be able to make a quick end of them, otherwise the wild animals would become too numerous for you.

📖 **READ JEREMIAH 5:7-9**

E. ADDITIONAL COMMENTS FOR VERSES 7-9

Someone must answer and be held responsible for the lack of justice in the city.

ANSWER QUESTIONS FOR VERSES 7-9

E-1: In the United States, parents may be held liable for failing to exercise the control necessary to prevent their children from intentionally harming others. We know that the parents may be held responsible here in Jerusalem also. What does God ask that reveals this possibility?

E-2: But then those children do need to become accountable at some point. God asks a question indicating the children may be held responsible. What is it?

E-3: How do we know that the leaders, citizens, non-citizens, and aliens in the land could all be held responsible, what does God ask?

📖 **READ JEREMIAH 5:10-11**

F. ADDITIONAL COMMENTS FOR VERSES 10-11

What God does next, shows that the people may have gone through a short period of repentance.

The people in Jerusalem were like a finely planted vineyard that belonged to the Lord. He expected to gather choice grapes but at harvest time the produce did not meet up with expectations. All of the grapes on the vine were wild and rotten. But the vines get another chance to produce. The Lord sends in a vine dresser to attend to the wild vines. Maybe, just maybe, the vines can produce some choice fruit once the useless branches have been stripped away.

ANSWER QUESTIONS FOR VERSES 10-11

F-1: Instead of ordering justice, the Judge orders mercy. He calls in professionals to help, hoping for a turn around. The vinedressers are instructed to go in and strip away branches. Stripping away pride, selfish ambition, power, and vain thoughts could be what the vine dressers were stripping away. The leaders were losing a lot as the legal system stood behind and supported the conditions of the binding contract.

As God (the Judge) looked at His bleak and blighted harvest, what did the poor condition of the vines prove to the Court? (See verse 11 in this chapter.)

📖 **READ JEREMIAH 5:12-13**

G. ADDITIONAL COMMENTS FOR VERSES 12-13

When God's mercy was handed down, it did not take long for Jerusalem's pride to rejuvenate itself. The word on the street about God was: "…He will do nothing. No evil will come upon us, and we shall not see the sword or famine." But these words found in Jeremiah 5:12 (and also in the mouths of the people) were lies. The leaders and the people in Jerusalem believed the lies. Maybe they felt that they had good reason to believe those lies. Maybe they believed what they heard because, at the current time, they were living safe and unharmed inside God's city of choice, Jerusalem. Maybe they believed because their forefather was Abraham and we know that God made some pretty big promises to their grandpa concerning his offspring. Or maybe the promises that God made to King David gave them some reason to feel safe (1Chronicles 17:11-15); and the promises to Solomon could not be forgotten (2Chronicles 7:12-16). They thought they had connections in high places and these connections were personal friends with the Lord. All they had to do was 'drop' the powerful names and they felt safe. But who-they-know would no longer save them or keep them out of trouble. Even though the fiery and out of control overflow, from the pot, gets closer and closer to Jerusalem every day, these 'unjust' will continue to trust merely in who-they-know for protection. They are not preparing for the catastrophe that current national events are predicting.

ANSWER QUESTIONS FOR VERSES 12-13

G-1: There is a powerful name that Christians 'drop' when they want to be rescued from unwanted circumstances. What is the name?

G-2: You might be asking: Why were the people said to 'believe lies' when they were trusting, standing firmly, and counting on what God said? This next allegory is a little messy but so is this situation in Jerusalem. Though I do not intend any disrespect, I would like to compare God's promises to a peanutbutter-and-jelly sandwich that He (as a Father) gave to His children. When they got the peanutbutter-and-jelly sandwich (the truth), they tried to separate the sandwich, keeping only half. They kept the peanutbutter side of the sandwich, ripped off the jelly side, but yet continued calling it by its whole name, peanutbutter-and-jelly sandwich (which was lie). They lied about what they had.

Just one example: first God spreads the peanutbutter on the bread when He says to Solomon:… I will establish your royal throne, as I made covenant with your father David saying, 'You shall never lack a successor to rule over Israel' (2Chronicles 7:18 NRSV).

Then He spreads the jelly. It is the one and only thing that can justify the name of the sandwich. See 2Chronicles 7:19-20 for the jelly.

G-3: Even if Israel's greatest intercessors, saviors, and pillars, (those who, by their righteousness, had been able to retain grace from God previously) stood before God to defend these people, the acting-lawyers would not win their case as they had in the past. Read about a few of these intercessors below:

(Exodus 32:11-14 NRSV): But Moses implored the Lord his God, and said, "O Lord, why does your wrath burn hot against your people, whom you brought out of the land of Egypt with great power and with a mighty hand? Why should the Egyptians say, 'It was with evil intent that he brought them out to kill them in the mountains, and to consume them from the face of the earth'? Turn from your fierce wrath; change your mind and do not bring disaster on your people. Remember Abraham, Isaac, and Israel, your servants, how you swore to them by your own self, saying to them, 'I will multiply your descendants like the stars of heaven, and all this land that I have promised I will give to your descendants, and they shall inherit it forever.'" And the Lord changed his mind about the disaster that he planned to bring on his people.

(Numbers 25:10-13 NRSV): The Lord spoke to Moses, saying: "Phinehas son of Eleazar, son of Aaron the priest, has turned back my wrath from the Israelites by manifesting such zeal among them on my behalf that in my jealousy I did not consume the Israelites. Therefore say, 'I hereby grant him my covenant of peace. It shall be for him and for his descendants after him a covenant of perpetual priesthood, because he was zealous for his God, and made atonement for the Israelites.' "

(1Samuel 12:19-23 NRSV): All the people said to Samuel, "Pray to the Lord your God for your servants, so that we may not die; for we have added to all our sins the evil of demanding a king for ourselves." And Samuel said to the people, "Do not be afraid; you have done all this evil, yet do not turn aside from following the Lord, but serve the Lord with all your heart; and do not turn aside after useless things that cannot profit or save, for they are useless. For the Lord will not cast away his people, for his great name's sake, because it has pleased the Lord to make you a people for himself. Moreover as for me, far be it from me that I should sin against the Lord by ceasing to pray for you; and I will instruct you in the good and the right way.

(Numbers 21:7 NRSV): The people came to Moses and said, "We have sinned by speaking against the Lord and against you; pray to the Lord to take away the serpents from us." So Moses prayed for the people.

Turn ahead to Jeremiah 15:1 and Ezekiel 14:20. What does God say about the intercessors of Israel?

G-4: It is easy for me to imagine the intercessors standing semi-circle before God's throne. Their righteousness has been able to stand in the stead of all Israel. But the noise that comes from Jerusalem can no longer be ignored. "Move out of the way" says God to the righteous ones. When they moved, God looked and this is what He said: … the prophets are nothing but wind, for the word is not in them! (Jeremiah 5:13 NRSV.)

Who is being blown around by the false winds? (See Jeremiah 5:12.)

📖 **READ JEREMIAH 5:14**

H. ADDITIONAL COMMENTS FOR VERSE 14

Jeremiah approaches the throne where the righteous once stood.

ANSWER QUESTIONS FOR VERSE 14

H-1: What does Jeremiah hear God say?

📖 **READ JEREMIAH 5:15-17**

I. ADDITIONAL COMMENTS FOR VERSES 15-17

In verses 15-17, it seems that God brings His words of fire to life, revealing them in the form of a nation. These words of fire will be workers for God just like His words have always been workers with a mission and great purpose.

For example when Genesis 1:1 says: In the beginning when God created the heavens and the earth... (NRSV); we know that God did not use handheld tools, like chisels and hammers to carve out the valleys and mountains. He did not have to set night after night with great minds and go through a series of mathematic equations to get the sun and moon on schedule. He did not have to find able muscles to build any physical walls to keep the waters contained. He did not have to bring in artists to draw and paint everything on earth to give it definition. But He did have an army of workers and those workers were His words.

ANSWER QUESTIONS FOR VERSES 15-17

I-1: Our study now takes us away from the safe walls of Jerusalem, which is in Judah. We are going just over the border to northern sister Israel. We find her suffering but this suffering, brought on by her unfriendly relationship with the covenant/contract, is just the beginning. She is about to be caught in the middle of an all-out war. The Lord is doing everything possible. Somehow, someway, He will save some part of this family from that which destroys them. God is out to destroy the lion that hides in-the-thicket (hides in the heart). As Judah sits inside her jail cell (Jerusalem) being guarded by the animals under contract (Jeremiah 5:6), what does God say to Israel in the first part of verse 15?

I-2: A military draft is when a government selects (withdraws) young men (masculine) or women (feminine) from within a country for the specific duty of defending that nation. There has been a draft within the Word of God; and He is supplying power and support to those (words) defending that for which they stand. What does God reveal about the soldiers from this far away nation, to Israel, in verses 15-16?

I-3: Israel had a debt to pay. Though Israel's sentence had been announced and activated, God told her back in Jeremiah 3:12-13 that He would not be angry forever; but first, according to His words, she had to acknowledge her guilt. When and if she ever decided to acknowledge the truth about herself, that decision to face the truth would not change her sentence but it would change something. What do you think would be changed, in Israel's life?

I-4 (OPTIONAL QUESTION): Once you have finally worked your way to the bottom (like Israel), you may decide that it's time to acknowledge your sin and turn to God. As you turn to God, what do you expect from Him? Do you, as the offender, deserve to expect anything? What outcome would be acceptable for you? Will a Close Friend who disperses truth, strength, and direction (to change your heart) while you continue to suffer and serve a well-deserved sentence satisfy you?

I-5: (Back to the soldiers in verse 17) God describes what this military presence will do to those who have opposed, defied, and disrespected their government. What does God say?

I-6: How do you interpret the words *eat up* in these verses?

I-7: These are not sneak attacks and should not have come as a surprise to anyone. God has been preparing these people for what is coming. This far away nation will use a sword to destroy the *fortified cities* in which Israel trusts. What do you think these *fortified cities* are? Read the following verse before answering

(Jeremiah 1:18 NRSV): And I for my part have made you today a fortified city, an iron pillar, and a bronze wall, against the whole land— against the kings of Judah, its princes, its priests, and the people of the land.

I-8: These dispersed people may have had a lot of ancestors who were close to God and God may have shown Israel favor in the past because of that. The history between God and many of their great ancestors made them feel powerful and maybe that is where they were looking to gain strength. Their ancestors, as well as the acts of the ancestors, were highly honored within their society. But while the human ancestors were receiving much recognition and honor for their righteousness, the people, who honored them, had no righteousness to be found. What will this ancient nation do to the fortified institutions that protect the unjust who do not seek the truth?

📖READ JEREMIAH 5:18-19

J. ADDITIONAL COMMENTS FOR VERSES 18-19

A shepherd was absolved of blame, for loss of livestock, if even small remains were recovered from a predator's attack, such as a leg or piece of ear (Amos 3:12 talks about recovering some parts). The Lord (the Shepherd) has been doing everything that He can to get these people from the jaws of their attacking predator. He will not make a full end, walk away, or give up on this body of Abraham's offspring that seems to have very little hope of survival without Him.

ANSWER QUESTIONS FOR VERSES 18-19

J-1: As Israel suffers, God is yelling out toward Judah (she is just across the border): Get ready! You're next! Another round of curses, that you have not yet experienced, are coming for you too! When it comes to facing the truth and that all of this destruction was caused by their own acts, God's people are blind and deaf.. When the misguided, misinformed, and confused people ask why all of these things (curses that are just the beginning of birth pains) are happening to, and around, them; what are the words that the confused people should speak loudly? God gives the people words of truth. They are found in the last part of verse 19 and these words should also be found in their mouths. (Even when you are in trouble with God, He gives you a route to find your salvation.)

J-2: The trial and sentencing for Israel (the northern kingdom) has thus far been dramatic. Though we have not witnessed Judah's day in court, there was one and it also took place in the city of Jerusalem. Turn to Ezekiel 16:1-63 to see God-v-Judah. See that God often works in ways that are odd to us.

She was found unworthy. All strength and power was stripped from her. She was no longer a comforting presence within the Promised Land. But God will still use Jerusalem. He made room for her. Though loyalty to God, concern for others, and justice could never gain her a place, her weakness did. She will still bring comfort to her area (her sisters). But the comfort is delivered in a strange way. How will the weak and lowly Jerusalem do a great work for God now that she has lost everything? (See Ezekiel 16:52.)

📖 READ JEREMIAH 5:20-22

K. ADDITIONAL COMMENTS FOR VERSES 20-22

God makes an announcement for all of the inhabitants living in the Promised Land.

ANSWER QUESTIONS FOR VERSES 20-22

K-1: Declare it in the house of Jacob, proclaim it in Judah (Jeremiah 5:20 NRSV). It seems that God wants to address, and get the attention of, two different groups. The first group is the house of Jacob. It may be the blood-line, but the second group (Judah) may not be. God may be wanting to get the attention of a diverse group of people who had settled in Judah. The following verses reveal a reoccurring pattern in the land of promise. What happened?

(Joshua 13:13 NRSV): Yet the Israelites did not drive out the Geshurites or the Maacathites; but Geshur and Maacath live within Israel to this day.

(Joshua 16:10 NRSV): They did not, however, drive out the Canaanites who lived in Gezer: so the Canaanites have lived within Ephraim to this day but have been made to do forced labor.

(Judges 1:21 NRSV): But the Benjaminites did not drive out the Jebusites who lived in Jerusalem; so the Jebusites have lived in Jerusalem among the Benjaminites to this day.

(Judges 1:27-36 NRSV): Manasseh did not drive out the inhabitants of Beth-shean and its villages, or Taanach and its villages, or the inhabitants of Dor and its villages, or the inhabitants of Ibleam and its villages, or the inhabitants of Megiddo and its villages; but the Canaanites continued to live in that land. When Israel grew strong, they put the Canaanites to forced labor, but did not in fact drive them out. And Ephraim did not drive out the Canaanites who lived in Gezer; but the Canaanites lived among them in Gezer. Zebulun did not drive out the inhabitants of … (and so on).

(1Kings 9:20-21 NRSV): All the people who were left of the Amorites, the Hittites, the Perizzites, the Hivites, and the Jebusites, who were not of the people of Israel— their descendants who were still left in the land, whom the Israelites were unable to destroy completely— these Solomon conscripted for slave labor, and so they are to this day.

K-2 (OPTIONAL QUESTION): Turn to the book of 1Peter in the New Testament. Read this whole book (five short chapters) with the notion that it was written to the exiled remnant. Take any notes that support this notion. Knowing when God is speaking to you or someone else can be helpful in your goal to be obedient to His Word.

K-3 (OPTIONAL QUESTION): Turn to the book of 2Peter in the New Testament. Read this whole book (three short chapters) with the notion that it was written to the Gentiles. Take any notes that support this notion. Again, knowing if God is speaking to you or someone else can clarify what you must do in order to be obedient to the Lord.

📖READ JEREMIAH 5:23-25

L. ADDITIONAL COMMENTS FOR VERSES 23-25

All of those who live in the land only gaze briefly at God's majesty while the destructive power in their heart rules.

ANSWER QUESTIONS FOR VERSES 23-25

L-1: Do you think that most people, whether they believe in God or not, would like to know the truth about all of the tragedy and why bad things are happening in this world? Well God wants all of Judah to know the truth about what is going on all around them. What truth is heard in Judah?

L-2: You could say that the aliens and noncitizens residing in the Promised Land have been under God's welfare system. They have been receiving free assistance due to the showers of blessings that God sent to *His people*. But God wants all of Judah to know that the assistance will stop. What will be affected due to sins and iniquities (fraudulent activity) going on in the land?

L-3 (OPTIONAL QUESTION): If blessings, as well as curses (from God), flow through those known as the people Israel, (and that may include more than bloodline, Exodus 12:44-49 may be a clue that the door was open), what actions from foreigners and non-citizens would have proved to be advantageous to everyone dwelling there?

L-4: Who, besides Israel, did Solomon intercede for, in the following verses?

(2Chronicles 6:29-31 NRSV): whatever prayer, whatever plea from any individual or from all your people Israel, all knowing their own suffering and their own sorrows so that they stretch out their hands toward this house; may you hear from heaven, your dwelling place, forgive, and render to all whose heart you know, according to all their ways, for only you know the human heart. Thus may they fear you and walk in your ways all the days that they live in the land that you gave to our ancestors.

📖READ JEREMIAH 5:26-28

M. ADDITIONAL COMMENTS FOR VERSES 26-28

God makes it clear. He is aware of the mismanagement at the top.

ANSWER QUESTIONS FOR VERSES 26-28

M-1: God compares these scoundrels to those who set traps in order to catch birds. But they are not trapping birds. What are they setting their traps to catch?

M-2: What did the scoundrels gain for themselves through their wicked deeds?

M-3: What did the people loose through the wicked deeds of the scoundrels?

M-4 (OPTIONAL QUESTION): Turn to 1Kings 21:5-14. This is just one example of the scoundrels who sat in the seats of power and the kinds of things that they did. Who were they and what did they do?

M-5 (OPTIONAL QUESTION): 2Kings 4:1-2 gives another example of the oppression in the land due to uncaring scoundrels. What happened?

📖READ JEREMIAH 5:29-31

N. ADDITIONAL COMMENTS FOR VERSES 29-31

You may be a resident alien. You may be a citizen. Know the law and how it affects you.

ANSWER QUESTIONS FOR VERSES 29-31

N-1: Back in verses 7-9, the Judge was looking for the responsible party in order to bring the scales of justice into balance. It seems that the blame did not go to only the parents and it did not go to only the children because now there is only one question that God poses. What is the question and who, seemingly, is going to be held responsible for the lack of justice that is found? (See verse 29.)

N-2: Why will all be charged? (See verse 31.)

N-3: Even though the leaders in Jerusalem still claim innocence all of the evidence points to guilt. God has spoken to them. He has taken things away from them. He has grounded them. He has hurt them. He has hurt the ones they love. He has prospered their enemies and torn down their defenses. Though their warnings have been many they refused to turn back.

Now the sin debt is so high that all of Judah will have to contribute. But many still refuse to accept responsibility and pay the price. Instead they are running from the law. Not only is the evil in their hearts on the Most-Wanted poster but now, as aiders and abettors, they too are on the Most-Wanted poster. The avenger is coming after them. So since they believe they are innocent, they had better run! They need to reach a city of refuge!

Read the following legal process and answer the questions that follow.

(Joshua 20:1-6 NRSV): Then the Lord spoke to Joshua, saying, "Say to the Israelites, 'Appoint the cities of refuge, of which I spoke to you through Moses, so that anyone who kills a person without intent or by mistake may flee there; they shall be for you a refuge from the avenger of blood. The slayer shall flee to one of these cities and shall stand at the entrance of the gate of the city, and explain the case to the elders of the city; then the fugitive shall be taken into the city, and given a place, and shall remain with them. And if the avenger of blood is in pursuit, they shall not give up the slayer, because the neighbor was killed by mistake, there having been no enmity between them before. The slayer shall remain in that city until there is a trial before the congregation, until the death of the one who is high priest at the time: then the slayer may return home, to the town in which the deed was done.' "

Apply these questions to the situation we are studying. Who are the slayers? Who is the avenger of blood? What or who has been killed?

N-4: What is the name of the city that the Lord appointed for those who must run? (See the following verse.)

(Isaiah 14:32 NRSV): ..."The Lord has founded Zion, and the needy among his people will find refuge in her."

N-5: When God speaks of Zion, where will the leaders run to get away from the avenger?

N-6: There are about 613 laws 'on the books' for these people but here are the commands that were written in stone by God (taken from Deuteronomy 5:6-21). Check the ones that have been broken thus far in chapters 1-5 and give the chapter and verse that reveals that they were broken.

> ➢ 1 You shall have no other gods before me.
> ➢ 2 You shall not make for yourself an idol.
> ➢ 3 You shall not make wrongful use of the name of the Lord your God.
> ➢ 4 Remember the Sabbath Day and keep it holy.

➤ 5 Honor your father and mother.
➤ 6 You shall not murder.
➤ 7 You shall not commit adultery.
➤ 8 You shall not steal.
➤ 9 You shall not bear false witness against your neighbor.
➤ 10 You shall not covet anything that belongs to your neighbor.

N-7: As Jeremiah continues his task of plucking up, pulling down, destroying, overthrowing, building, and planting; has he affected your life? Explain.

Chapter 5 Tag-A-Long

A Name That Makes Things Happen

All of my life, I heard it in church. Now I say it myself. Whenever done praying I end the prayer by saying "In Jesus name I pray". But this study has caused me to question myself about a lot of spiritual habits. I now wonder if I am misusing the name of Jesus.

I thought about a family in my home town that recently lost their young son due to a tragic car accident. It seems like the whole community showed up in one way or another to support the family. How powerful the death of this young man had become in our town. I was thinking that just by using his name, great things could be accomplished.

For instance, if someone went from door to door right now and said they were collecting money for suffering families in the name of Michael (using the deceased's name), they would collect a lot of money for that cause. Or if there was a sign up for volunteers to console teens who had lost friends in car crashes, in the name of Michael, the sign-up sheet would be full.

But what if someone were to take advantage of his name, take advantage of his death? What if some used the name of Michael in order to obtain some sort of 'gain' for themselves or get a-boost for their business at hand? I don't think his father or his mother would be happy with that or support the person using their son's name to reach personal goals.

Is that how I use the name of Jesus? How unjust is that, to try to use the death and the power of the name of God's Son to get my needs met? I really need to be careful and take a close look at that. I hope I never take advantage of the power of Jesus' name but instead use it in memory of the things He started but didn't get to finish (in an earthly body). If I do that, as I use His name, His Father will support me. He will listen. He will hear. He will take exceptional note of when I pray.

✂ Scrapbook Page For Chapter 5

The Standard has Been Raised toward Zion

It bore the emblem of the nation, planted high and erect on one of the hills. If you had not seen the standard (the flag), before it was erected, if you had not seen it in your town during the campaigning of the reorganization of its government, you would have at least heard and been familiar with what it stood for, what it meant, and what it was.

There was no wind that day so the standard (the flag), just lies lifelessly against the pole. The message on the standard is hidden because of its unusual limp form. I wait and wait for the wind so I can see the face of my national emblem before I go home. I want to hear it whip through the wind as the trumpet sounds. I want to see its glory. That glory is what bonded us troops. Our allegiance was powerful as we rallied together at its sight. But it doesn't seem to be much of a rallying point, at least today, for loyal soldiers like me under its command.

There had been a lot of suffering and sacrifices made before the standard (my flag), took its place way up there. It had been through a lot and you could tell. There were rips and tears throughout the whole fabric. All the repulsive stains served as evidence that the standard had been greatly burdened. Its ground-in stains reflected the bloodthirsty, inhumane, and lawless places it had conquered, survived, and come out of. It had been trampled on and drug through the dirt and mud, but that just caused me to adore it even more. As the standard went from battle to battle, the flowing message that it carried as it rippled through the wind will never be forgotten by those who stood by and witnessed the work that was accomplished under its powerful monarchy.

In its glory days, people lined up to see the standard if they knew it was coming to, coming through, or close to their town. They cheered and shouted. They loved it in its lively motion and wanted to be a part of what it represented and the strength that it promised to bring to the nation.

As I see it up there, I know it is a victory, but it doesn't seem like one. I know that was the goal of the whole mission, to defeat the wild savage enemy and provide safety for every man, woman, and child. Today this battle is over and I heard no cheers when the base of its pole was driven into the ground high on the hill, forever to remind everyone of the presence and the reorganization that the new movement brings. Even though we knew that the planting of the standard on the hill was the sign we were waiting for, it seemed all wrong. But by the leader, we knew it was all right. He told us that once the standard is finally up, that's when we could know for sure that the highly covert mission had been successful.

As I started to walk home, I kept looking back, I couldn't help it. I was deeply distressed about what was high on the hill. I wasn't quite sure about its power any more. By the looks of everything in this town, the mission seems unsuccessful, as Jesus, my standard, my flag, the One I pledged allegiance to, died like a treasonous thief. And those he came to save look on, waiting for something to happen, looking for a sign....

In this snapshot Jesus (the Word made flesh) is the Standard (the flag) from ancient days.

(Isaiah 18:3 NRSV): All you inhabitants of the world, you who live on the earth, when a signal is raised on the mountains, look! When a trumpet is blown, listen!

Compare Answers For Chapter 5

A-1: He may be looking for someone who has put on sackcloth to lament, mourn, and wail; or those who have lost their appetite due to unrighteousness that surrounds them. He may be looking for tears falling on robes that are torn and those on their knees covered with dust.

A-2: "As the Lord lives!" Jeremiah must have heard it everywhere as he scoured the streets but the actions of the people did not reflect it. They did not acknowledge that God was even alive. They did not recognize what God was doing and how He was trying to get their attention to turn back to Him. They continued to allow idols to live in the land that was God's.

A-3: one

A-4: ...she and her daughters had pride, excess of food, and prosperous ease, but did not aid the poor and needy. They were haughty, and did abominable things before me; therefore I removed them when I saw it (Ezekiel 16:49-50 NRSV).

A-5: As a well keeps its water fresh, so she keeps fresh her wickedness; violence and destruction are heard within her; sickness and wounds are ever before me (Jeremiah 6:7 NRSV).

A-6: The Lord had made promises to David about Jerusalem.

A-7: David, Abraham, Isaac, and Jacob

A-8: I think they thought that God had handed it 'all' to them because they believed that the others were not righteous and if they thought that they got it 'all', they must have considered themselves to be righteous in God's sight.

B-1: God (by recourse of covenant) has struck the body and God (by recourse of covenant) has consumed the body, but the heart will not change its pattern.

B-2: They have made their faces harder than rock

B-3 (OPTIONAL QUESTION): Usually too busy with life's demands to notice the pain in the world around

B-4: They confessed that they had sinned. They were able to put it (the sinful acts) far away by accepting the consequences (they admitted that they deserved punishment) and their God of mercy could no longer bear to see them suffer.

C-1: they too like the poor had no bond with the Lord

C-2: Divine information came with a price. Getting answers and time with prophets (seers) apparently came with a price and the rich had the money. The poor could not afford to know about spiritual things. The poor were in-the-dark while the rich could have their own personal religious professionals.

C-3: the poor have good news brought to them

C-4: (1Chronicles 21:17 NRSV): And David said to God, "Was it not I who gave the command to count the people? It is I who have sinned and done very wickedly. But these sheep, what have they done? Let your hand, I pray, O Lord my God, be against me and against my father's house; but do not let your people be plagued!"

C-5: When a city or state is sued, taxpayer dollars usually take the hit and people might suffer when lack of funds are needed for other projects or programs.

D-1: The lion is the spiritual attacker. The other beasts may be representing the physical harm.

D-2: Justice and righteousness, maybe in the form of: remorse, admission of guilt, confession, repentance due to concern for those suffering outside the walls

D-3: wild animals grow rapidly in the area where no humans live.

E-1: How can I pardon you? Your children have forsaken me, and have sworn by those who are no gods.

E-2: The Lord says: shall I not punish them for these things? (*them,* in the first part of verse 9, indicates the children)

E-3: Shall I not bring retribution on a nation such as this? (See last part of verse 9.)

F-1: The house of Israel and the house of Judah have been utterly faithless to the Lord.

G-1: Jesus

G-2: (2Chronicles 7:19-20): "But if you turn aside and forsake my statues and my commandments that I have set before you, and go and serve other gods and worship them, then I will pluck you up from the land that I have given you; and this house, which I have consecrated for my name, I will cast out of my sight…"

G-3: Pillars of society and good friends of the Judge could no longer step in and save their troublesome and rebellious children. (Ezekiel 14:20 NRSV): even if Noah, Daniel, and Job were in it, as I live, says the Lord God, they would save neither son nor daughter; they would save only their own lives by their righteousness.

G-4: the priests and the people who are safe and sound

H-1: Therefore thus says the Lord, the God of hosts: Because they have spoken this word, I am now making my words in your mouth a fire, and this people wood, and the fire shall devour them (Jeremiah 5:14 NRSV).

I-1: I am going to bring upon you a nation from far away, O House of Israel,…(Jeremiah 5:15 NRSV).

I-2: …It is an enduring nation, it is an ancient nation, a nation whose language you do not know, nor can you understand what they say. Their quiver is like an open tomb; all of them are mighty warriors (Jeremiah 5:15-16 NRSV).

I-3: her heart and her relationship with the Lord

I-4 (OPTIONAL QUESTION): I used to expect easy sailing but I can see that is not how God makes me (the vessel of a rebellious heart) stronger, useful, or productive for the good.

I-5: They shall eat up your harvest and your food; they shall eat up your sons and your daughters; they shall eat up your flocks and your herds; they shall eat up your vines and your fig trees; they shall destroy with the sword your fortified cities in which you trust (Jeremiah 5:17 NRSV).

I-6: To affect something by gradual destruction or consumption

I-7: They depended on the 'great names' in their society, on the reputation and mighty names like Moses and Samuel to save them. But dropping those names will no longer bring favor or mercy when they want to get out of trouble.

I-8: destroy them with the sword

J-1: They should say something like this: Just as we have forsaken God and served foreign gods in the land so we shall serve strangers in a land that is not ours.

J-2: Her sisters will find comfort in knowing that even though they were bad, they were not as bad as sister Jerusalem; and God *still* chooses her for His purposes.

K-1: They could not drive out the inhabiting nations.

K-2: (OPTIONAL QUESTION): 1:1 to the exiles; 1:2 chosen and destined; 1:18 you know that you were ransomed from the futile ways inherited from your ancestors; 2:5 a holy priesthood; 2:9 you are a chosen race, a royal priesthood, a holy nation, God's own people, 2:11 I urge you as aliens and exiles; 2:12 conduct yourself honorably among Gentiles 2:25 you were going astray like sheep, but now you have returned; first part of chapter 3 may deal with Jewish/

Gentile marriage; 4:3 you have spent enough time in doing what the Gentiles like to do; 4:17 judgment to begin with the household of God; 5:1 as an elder… I exhort the elders; 5:9 your brothers and sisters in all the world are undergoing the same kinds of suffering

K-3 (OPTIONAL QUESTION): 1:1 to those who have received a faith as precious as ours; 1:4 and may become participants; 1:10 confirm your call and election; 1:12 the truth that has come to you; 1:16 devised myths; 1:20-21 explains prophets and this is something that the exiles already know; 2:18 they entice people who have just (currently?) escaped those who live in error; 2:22 referred to as dogs and sows; 3:15 Paul wrote to you (Paul was sent for Gentiles)

L-1: But this people has a stubborn and rebellious heart; they have turned aside and gone away (Jeremiah 5:23 NRSV).

L-2: rain appointed for harvest (survival)

L-3 (OPTIONAL QUESTION): encourage and support the relationship between God and Israel in whatever ways are available

L-4: It sounds as if Solomon prays for *any* individual who calls out toward God's house.

M-1: human beings

M-2: The scoundrels gained greatness, riches, weight, and ability to slip out of trouble.

M-3: The people lost prosperity and their rights.

M-4 (OPTIONAL QUESTION): Elders and nobles of the city were among the scoundrels and they were instructed to frame an innocent man of a crime that he did not commit. The innocent man was then stoned so the king of Israel could now get what he wanted while his (the king's) hands still seemed to be clean of shedding innocent blood.

M-5 (OPTIONAL QUESTION): A woman's husband died and she was left with only debt and children. The government was going to take her children for the debt she owed.

N-1: It seems the whole nation will suffer for the wrongs committed as the question now is: Shall I not punish them for these things and shall I not bring retribution on a *nation* such as this?

N-2: the prophets prophecy falsely, and the priests rule as the prophets direct; my people love to have it so (Jeremiah 5:31 NRSV).

N-3: The leaders and the people are slayers who need to run to the city of refuge. The curses of the law are the avengers. That which was slain: God's word along with the prophets of God who carried it.

N-4: Zion

N-5: Jerusalem

N-6: This is a running list from the previous chapter.

Number 1: You shall have no other gods before me (broken law according to Jeremiah 1:16)

Number 2: You shall not make for yourself an idol (broken law according to Jeremiah 1:16)

Number 5: Honor your father and mother (broken law according to Jeremiah 2:27)

Number 6: You shall not murder (broken law according to Jeremiah 2:30b and 34)

Number 4: Remember the Sabbath day and keep it holy (broken law according to Jeremiah 2:32)

Number 7: You shall not commit adultery (broken law according to Jeremiah 3:6)

Number 3: You shall not make wrongful use of my name (broken law according to Jeremiah 5:2)

Number 10: You shall not covet anything that belongs to your neighbor (broken, see Jeremiah 5:8)

N-7: Jeremiah has planted a seed in my heart to tear down the walls that keep me from knowing the pain of others. I know that I, being one, can make a difference. God looked for *one* in all Jerusalem. I will strive to be what He looks for.

Chapter 6

Chapter 6 Prelude

The Replica

Kerry was so excited. It was time for the whole family to start that big project that Dad announced at the dinner table a few nights ago. They were going to build a miniature model house and everyone's input was important because this miniature house will be an exact replica of the life-size house in which they live.

It will have three floors (including the basement), two fireplaces and three bathrooms. The living room walls in this replica will be the same shade of blue as the life sized walls in their real house. From hard-wood floors to vaulted ceilings, the house would be identical! And when that was done, they were going to continue with the outside. There would be tall trees, green grass, and rose bushes all around the house. Even the wooden gate between the hedges that led to the neighbor's yard would be part of the replica. This would be the perfect miniature house because they, as the builders, knew every nook and cranny of the real one. Kerry thought it would be great if they could replicate the whole town. Dad thought that would be great too but said that it was probably not humanly possible!

When God said "…Let us make humankind in our image, according to our likeness;" in Genesis 1:26 (NRSV), I wonder if there was child-like excitement in heaven (like that of Kerry's); but more than that, I wonder if "in our image" and "according to our likeness" included more than just what human beings look like and how the human body is formed? What if God's creative plan included everything from man's ways of governing to his common everyday ways of life? The following verses might help us to understand God's overall plan a little better.

In Job 38:33 (NRSV) God asks: "Do you know the ordinances of the heavens? Can you establish their rule on the earth?" This verse may present evidence that man's physical appearance was not at the forefront of God's plan. And in Matthew 6:10 it seems that Jesus reveals support for this plan when He told us to pray: "Your kingdom come. Your will be done, on earth as it is in heaven." And in Jeremiah 33:2 we read that the Lord formed the earth to establish it. But it seems that establishing a kingdom on this earth that reflects His kingdom in heaven is not going to be an easy task.

King Solomon, like God, was also mindful to build a kingdom of magnificent proportion. King

Solomon, like the builder in Luke 14:28-29 must have sat down to estimate the cost before he started this project. But cash flow was probably not what Solomon was counting. His major concern, from his actions, seems to be manpower and the way that he had to spend it. Would his manpower be spent on the building project or would it have to be spent on war efforts with hostiles that did not welcome the expansion of competing powers?

At the time of this building project, the king of Egypt seems to be the greatest threat to Solomon's plan. But Solomon, like many other kings, found a way to pull the threat of this prickly thorn from his side. 1Kings 3:1 (NRSV) says: Solomon made a marriage alliance with Pharaoh king of Egypt; he took Pharaoh's daughter and brought her into the city of David, until he had finished building his own house and the house of the Lord and the wall around Jerusalem.

Maybe that was part of God's reason for making a covenant with a chosen group of people too. Maybe He wanted to form some sort of marriage alliance and create friendly relationships. Maybe He wanted to secure peaceful surroundings and gain some allies as His kingdom was being established. Maybe that's why God chose her (Israel) and sat her right in the middle of it all (Ezekiel 5:5). He made sure that she lacked nothing and the neighboring nations couldn't help but watch as God blessed her, one of their own kind. But her devotion, to Him, was called for and her obedience, to Him, was a critical factor in keeping the neighboring tools of destruction away from the new kingdom. As it turned out, the Lord needed a second plan because the greatest threat to God's kingdom did not come from the neighboring nations outside. The greatest threat came from the bride that He had purchased and sat inside.

Chapter 6 Study

The Art of Warfare

CHAPTER 6 READING, COMMENTS, AND QUESTIONS

The geographical area that I live in is not flatland. There are hills, hollows, and large trees but I can still see some very tall towering structures. As I drive from town to town I am able see three different water towers. I always try to calculate just how far those towers are from where I am. I have determined that they are anywhere from five to seven miles away. If someone were to put a warning flag or a flaming fire atop those tall towers I would be able to see the signal very clearly.

There is a particular reason that I wonder about this. People in the days of old did the best they could to alert all of the citizens of approaching dangers. Sentinels (tall towers) were set at regular intervals so messages could be sent from one town, to the next town in line. Signals may have been smoke by day, fire by night, flags of different colors, or flashes of light with shining shields. If one town was under attacked (or soon to be), that town would raise a signal. The towns that could see the signal were, more than likely, next in line to be attacked.

When the warning signal went up I wonder what the other town, next in line, did. I wonder how much time they had before the enemy was upon them. The enemy army would have been on horses, so those preparing *for* or *to avoid* the attack, did have time to do something. Maybe they grabbed their kids and ran for their lives trying to find a hiding place or if they did live near a fortified city, maybe the men all gathered at the iron gates of that city and got ready to fight as their families went further inside. If you lived close to a fortified city like Jerusalem, inside its fortified walls would be your place of refuge.

📖READ JEREMIAH 6:1

A. ADDITIONAL COMMENTS FOR VERSE 1

The Judge has arrived for yet another trial at the city gates and as usual an entourage accompanies Him. (Jeremiah 6:2-5 can be added to the eclectic list of entourages that was given in the chapter 1 tag-a-long.) All of the suspects for the next trial have been rounded up (one way or another) and are now inside Jerusalem. But there is a problem. The Judge (God) can't get in and the suspects won't come out. They have locked themselves inside.

ANSWER QUESTIONS FOR VERSE 1

A-1: Harboring a murderer is not acceptable in our country and it was not acceptable in Israel either. (See Deuteronomy 19:11-12 to confirm.) Corporately, God's people have been charged with murder and Jerusalem is harboring fugitives that, by law, must be handed over to the avenger. Innocent blood was spilled and truthful restitution had not been made. Whose blood was spilled? (See the following verses for clues.)

(Lamentations 4:13 NRSV): It was for the sins of her prophets and the iniquities of her priests, who shed the blood of the righteous in the midst of her.

(Revelation 19:2 NRSV): "for his judgments are true and just; he has judged the great whore who corrupted the earth with her fornication, and he has avenged on her the blood of his servants."

(Jeremiah 26:15 NRSV): "Only know for certain that if you put me to death, you will be bringing innocent blood upon yourselves and upon this city and its inhabitants, for in truth the Lord sent me to you to speak all these words in your ears" (says Jeremiah).

(Matthew 23:30-32 NRSV): and you say, 'If we had lived in the days of our ancestors, we would not have taken part with them in shedding the blood of the prophets.'

(Jeremiah 2:30 and 34 NRSV): …Your own sword devoured your prophets like a ravening lion….on your skirts is found the lifeblood of the innocent poor, though you did not catch them breaking in.

(Ezekiel 9:9-10 NRSV): … "The guilt of the house of Israel and Judah is exceedingly great; the land is full of bloodshed and the city full of perversity; for they say, 'The Lord has forsaken the land, and the Lord does not see.' As for me, my eye will not spare, nor will I have pity, but I will bring down their deeds upon their heads."

A-2: From the spiritual eye, *something else* (other than the answer to the last question) was being murdered. It was because of this, *something else*, that blood was truly shed. What was the *something else*? What did the murderers really want to silence? (See Jeremiah 1:9.)

A-3: When God first arrived at Jerusalem (we can still compare Jerusalem to the heart), I would think that He tried to enter on the east side. This is where the king's gate is located (1Chronicles 9:18). It was only logical that this would be His place to enter, He was (supposed to be) the King of this great city. But when no one would let Him in, He tried another entrance. The Lord went to another gate and knocked. He also yelled in a warning: Flee for safety! At what (heart) gate did the Lord stand? (See Jeremiah 6:1 and 37:13.)

A-4: Wars and rumors of wars, danger is on every side! Though warnings to take cover and get into the fortified cites (see Jeremiah 4:5-7 and 5:6) have been issued, Benjamin is warned to flee from the midst of their current stronghold, Jerusalem. The danger outside the city is nothing compared to what is going to be happening inside those city walls. When God calls Benjamin out, obeying His voice may not be an easy task. There is a reason that Benjamin might find it hard to walk away from the midst of the city and leave it all behind. The answer may be hidden in the following verses. What stands between Benjamin and God as God knocks at his gate (heart)?

(Joshua 18:21-28 NRSV): Now the towns of the tribe of Benjamin according to their families were Jericho, Beth-hoglah, Emek-keziz, Beth-arabah, Zemaraim, Bethel, Avvim, Parah, Ophrah, Chephar-ammoni, Ophni, and Geba— twelve towns with their villages: Gibeon, Ramah, Beeroth, Mizpeh, Chephirah, Mozah, Rekem, Irpeel, Taralah, Zela, Haeleph, Jebus (that is Jerusalem), Gibeah and Kiriathjearim—fourteen towns with their villages. This is the inheritance of the tribe of Benjamin according to their families.

A-5 (OPTIONAL QUESTION): This city of Jerusalem was not always in the hands of Israel's offspring. They had to move in and take possession. What do, you think the following verses reveal about Jerusalem's previous land owners (or inhabitants)?

(Joshua 15:63 NRSV): But the people of Judah could not drive out the Jebusites, the inhabitants of Jerusalem; so the Jebusites live with the people of Judah in Jerusalem to this day.

(Judges 1:21 NRSV): But the Benjaminites did not drive out the Jebusites who lived in Jerusalem; so the Jebusites have lived in Jerusalem among the Benjaminites to this day.

A-6 (OPTIONAL QUESTION): How did the city of Jerusalem finally come into the hands of Judah, according to the following verses?

(1Chronicles 11:4-6 NRSV): David and all Israel marched to Jerusalem, that is Jebus, where the Jebusites were, the inhabitants of the land. The inhabitants of Jebus said to David, "You will not come in here." Nevertheless David took the stronghold of Zion, now the city of David. David had said, "Whoever attacks the Jebusites first shall be chief and commander." And Joab son of Zeruiah went up first, so he became chief.

A-7: The sentinels are commanded. What is the command for Tekoa and what is the command for Beth-haccherem?

A-8: A warning is ordered to go out from Tekoa and Beth-heccherem. The warning is to alert everyone that: evil looms out of the *north* and great destruction. Since Jerusalem is *north* of Tekoa and Beth-heccherem, could this be a dual warning? What is coming out of Jerusalem? Look ahead to verse 7. What is inside of this city?

📖READ JEREMIAH 6:2-5

B. ADDITIONAL COMMENTS FOR VERSES 2-5

Though they bring instruction, the shepherds (God's entourage in this chapter who diligently press forward with their flocks and pitch their tents in the pasture, all in their places, that surrounds Zion) are not welcomed by the inhabitants of Jerusalem. The city gate is closed tight. God is unable to enter the place declared, by Him, to be the place of His presence and throne (Jeremiah 3:17). This city of Jerusalem, which has locked God out, is a reflection of the uncircumcised heart. But Jerusalem's little scheme will not halt the Righteous Judgment that showed up on the front steps of her city. He is knocking at the door of the city (of her heart).

ANSWER QUESTIONS FOR VERSES 2-5

B-1: The suspects, inside Jerusalem, are holding hostages. The hostages are overjoyed to hear the knock of Salvation at the door. Earlier, God had a conversation with those who are hostage. He spoke to them about the help that He would send. The hostages are His offspring (His seedlings that are trapped in the heart). How did God describe the 'helpers' to those who were stranded in the dangerous and unwelcoming hearts of men? (See Jeremiah 3:15.)

B-2: Turn to Jeremiah 12:10. These verses describe what the previous shepherds did. What did they do?

B-3: When Jerusalem looks out at the shepherds, and their flocks, (who want to enter their city, enter their heart) their eyes are deceived. Because of previous instruction from previous shepherds, they see something far different.

This living contract/covenant between God and His people could be seen as a raving wild beast or a gracious domestic animal. How the covenant revealed itself at the doorstep of God's people was dependent upon their obedience toward It and/or Its composer. I believe that Isaiah 11:6-9 could be a description of the covenant when His people become obedient and accept the ways of the Covenant.

(Isaiah 11:6-9 NRSV): The wolf shall live with the lamb, the leopard shall lie down with the kid, the calf and the lion and the fatling together, and a little child shall lead them. The cow and the bear shall graze, their young shall lie down together; and the lion shall eat straw like the ox. The nursing child shall play over the hole of the asp, and the weaned child shall put its hand on the adder's den. They will not hurt or destroy on all my holy mountain; for the earth will be full of the knowledge of the Lord as the waters cover the sea.

When the people of Jerusalem look outside the city walls, do they see covenant blessings (a field full of lambs, kids, calves, fatlings, cows, oxen) or covenant curses (a field full of wolves, leopards, lions, bears asps, and adders)? Go to Jeremiah 4:16-17 and Jeremiah 5:6 for clues.

B-4: A shepherd had a few tools for his trade. The sheep were very familiar with two of them. He carried a long rod with a knob on the end. He also had a staff that looked like a walking cane, usually with a crook on one end. Though the sheep did not know it, these pieces of equipment that the shepherds used (on them) was for their own protection. When one of the sheep got too close to the edge of a cliff, the shepherd would use his crooked staff and grab that sheep by the neck. He might have to pull back hard sometimes if the sheep was moving at a fast momentum or refused to turn around. And if one of the sheep tended to wander out where wolves and wild animals were, the shepherd would have to smack their sides, with the rod, coaxing them in the direction that they needed to go, back to the safety of his fold. The sheep may have received bruises, bumps, and even breaks from that rod and staff. They probably hated as well as feared those *tools of the trade* that the shepherd carried. But once they reached the safety of "green pastures" and "still running waters" they may have looked at the rod and staff a little differently.

Once the shepherd unhanded them (the rod and staff) and set them up against the tree as he and his sheep rested, the tools took on a whole new meaning. The sheep could understand why the rod and the staff were so important to them and the shepherd. If it was not for those weapons which they feared and sometimes hated, they would have been dinner, a long time ago, for the wild animals. It was at times like these (times of rest) that the sheep learned to love the rod and staff. The (often times) cruel equipment, was the very thing that brought them to "green pastures and still running waters".

God has now called in 'rod and staff' in numerous force. They (the shepherds with their flocks) have pitched their tents around her, in her pastures, in all of her places. God orders the trumpet sound that means: "Prepare for war!" What is the plan for attack? (See verse 4.)

B-5: Describe the type of person that God needs behind the 'rod and staff' according to the following verses.

(Isaiah 28:27-28 NRSV): Dill is not threshed with a threshing sledge, nor is a cart wheel rolled over cummin; but dill is beaten out with a stick, and cummin with a rod. Grain is crushed for bread, but one does not thresh it forever; one drives the cart wheel and horses over it, but does not pulverize it.

📖READ JEREMIAH 6:6-7

C. ADDITIONAL COMMENTS FOR VERSES 6-7

Though the Lord knocks, He cannot enter so orders to begin a siege are released. The orders that were released by the Judge, and lawfully carried out, were written long ago in the legal contract between God and Israel: "cut down her trees". The trees outside of the city walls will be used to build the siege ramps to get inside.

ANSWER QUESTIONS FOR VERSES 6-7

C-1: A siege ramp was piled earth and rubble strengthened with wood. It was built in a ramp like fashion against the walls of the city under attack. The ramp allowed the attacker to scale the wall and enter. Joel 2:7-9 (NRSV) describes what happens after the ramp is completed and in fact it may just be describing what will happen here: Like warriors they charge, like soldiers they scale the wall. Each keeps to its own course, they do not swerve from their paths. They do not jostle one another, each keeps to its own track; they burst through the weapons and are not halted. They leap upon the city, they run upon the walls; they climb up into the houses, they enter through the windows like a thief.

Scan over Ezekiel, chapter 4 to see what a siege against a fortified city like Jerusalem would be like. Then look at the final verses, 16 and 17, of that chapter. What would be happening inside these city walls over the days, months, and sometimes years, while the siege was taking place?

C-2: It seems likely that the order and act of 'Cutting down the trees' could be another analogy. The cutting down of trees could be the curses (plagues, pestilence and war) in action. The curses, by legal contract follow recourse and must now cut down human lives. Though Jerusalem continues to be safe, those outside the walls of Jerusalem suffer. The disobedient leaders inside Jerusalem have the power to save the trees (human lives) from being cut down. But the leaders inside the walls don't seem to care. They will not comply or adhere to the power of the Court. Unlike the words of the covenant, the leaders do not act in obedience to their contractual obligations. Seeing all of those fallen trees (fallen human lives) in a nation would cause a caring leader to stop, look, and listen. How could the leaders stop all of the trees (human lives) from being cut down and destroyed?

📖 READ JEREMIAH 6:8-9

D. ADDITIONAL COMMENTS FOR VERSE 8-9

God's warning trumpets and signals have had no rest. God has been warning Judah and the inhabitants of Jerusalem about this disaster for a long time now. Jerusalem has received many chances (like back in Jeremiah 5:10) to come clean. A soldier, from a special operations unit, infiltrates for one last check. Remorse and repentance would speak loudly to the Judge; but it seems doubtful that the under-cover operation will find any of that inside of Jerusalem.

ANSWER QUESTIONS FOR VERSES 8-9

D-1: God sends one of His soldiers to do a meticulous ground search inside the city under siege. What are the orders to the one He sends in? (See verse 9.)

D-2: What is the difference between this gleaning ordered for Jerusalem, here in Jeremiah 6, and the type of gleaning in Jeremiah 5:10?

D-3: What does God call those, in this chapter, who will be gleaned? It is a clue that not many of His people are left.

📖 **READ JEREMIAH 6:10-12**

E. ADDITIONAL COMMENTS FOR VERSES 10-12

The gleaning reveals that Jerusalem has no plans to open the gate and corporately accept the instruction that has come to them through the shepherds who wait outside with their flocks.

ANSWER QUESTIONS FOR VERSES 10-12

E-1: God has been bombarding Jerusalem with fiery warnings. The danger gets closer and closer but they cannot feel the heat. What is going to continue to happen to the inhabitants of the land as the calloused, uncaring, and unconcerned leaders remain barricaded inside Jerusalem?

E-2: Jeremiah, the walking, talking refinery (Jeremiah 5:14) is meeting up with a lot of resistance. In order for silver to become separated from the dross or impurities, it must go through a refining process. It must be heated to one thousand two hundred degrees in a special furnace before there is a reaction that produces the pure silver. God is expecting to get some certain results from this fire. What are the results that God wants as His people (who should be acting and feeling as one body with many parts) go through the harsh process of purification? (See the following verses.)

(Isaiah 1:24-26 NRSV): Therefore says the Sovereign, the Lord of hosts, the Mighty One of Israel: Ah, I will pour out my wrath on my enemies, and avenge myself on my foes! I will turn my hand against you; I will smelt away your dross as with lye and remove all your alloy. And I will restore your judges as at the first, and your counselors as at the beginning. Afterward you shall be called the city of righteousness, the faithful city.

E-3: Referring to the verses (Isaiah 1:24-26) in the previous question: What would be the difference within the governmental system once that the judges are restored as at first and counselors as at the beginning? Turn to 1Samuel 8:4-9. You may find a clue in verse 7 of what God's intentions were.

📖 **READ JEREMIAH 6:13-15**

F. ADDITIONAL COMMENTS FOR VERSES 13-15

The messages going into this city, through Jeremiah, from God are meeting up with interference. God once again backtracks, rechecks, and retraces the communication lines. There is evidence that leads, once more, straight to the leaders who have shirked their responsibilities. They are interrupting the lines of communication.

ANSWER QUESTIONS FOR VERSES 13-15

F-1: God is sounding the trumpets and raising warning flags in order to get the attention of people inside the walls of Jerusalem but the leaders of the city are just as busy as God. They are distracting all of the attention away from God's warnings. How are they doing that? (See verse 14.)

F-2: 'Wars and rumors of wars', Jerusalem was all too familiar with that way of life from behind the majestic walls. This City of David (Jerusalem) had escaped capture time and time again. The leaders must be feeling safe and secure while claiming to be blessed and favored with knowledge in pleasing God. They were saying: "Peace, Peace" and "The Lord lives!" They thought that they knew God. They thought that everything was 'good' between them and their Lord. But what does God say about them in verse 15 of this chapter?

📖 **READ JEREMIAH 6:16-17**

G. ADDITIONAL COMMENTS FOR VERSES 16-17

The people will not open up and let God in. They do not know His voice.

ANSWER QUESTIONS FOR VERSES 16-17

G-1: The tools of the shepherd have been overly gentle with Jerusalem. How has God used His rod and staff on these wild sheep in Jerusalem and how did they react to the nudges from the rod and the hook of the staff? (See verses 16-17.)

📖 **READ JEREMIAH 6:18-19**

H. ADDITIONAL COMMENTS FOR VERSES 18-19

God announces His verdict for Jerusalem (the place that He chose for His presence and throne).

ANSWER QUESTIONS FOR VERSES 18-19

H-1: The devastation from the curses has hit Judah. As the reports of destruction continue to roll into Jerusalem, the leaders seem to have no emotional attachment to their land or the people who live there; but God continues to issue the warnings anyway. Maybe someone will open up their eyes and unplug their ears: I am going to bring disaster on this people, the fruit of their schemes, because they have not given heed to my words; and as for my teaching, they have rejected it (Jeremiah 6:19 NRSV).

Who is God talking about when He says 'this people' and who are the 'fruit of their schemes'?

H-2: The people inside do not know God's voice and will not let Him in. God's leaders will not deliver His urgent message to the general population, so God does it Himself. He addresses those who need to be taking immediate cover. Who are they?

📖 **READ JEREMIAH 6:20-21**

I. ADDITIONAL COMMENTS FOR VERSES 20-21

As God declares His verdict, the people inside of Jerusalem do not hear. They are too busy doing what they have always done. They are busy at rejecting God's word and listening to their hearts that have been filled with ill instruction.

ANSWER QUESTIONS FOR VERSES 20-21

I-1: As the siege ramps were being built outside the majestic walls, the blood in the temple must have been knee-deep. Those at the temple (the priests) thought they could pay their way out of this problem. Bringing God all of the best that they had to offer would surely gain His favor.

If all of the people in Jerusalem had cars, all of them would be guilty of ignoring the road signs and exceeding the legal speed limit. No one paid attention to the signs. The speed limit signs did not work as a warning. The signs did not work as a reminder. The signs did not work as a threat. No one even slowed down to read the signs (signs of famine, pestilence, war). Everyone thought they could just pay the required price to get the law off of their back and continue to speed through the streets of the city just as they had always done. The high price being paid by the nation (through loss of lives and land) was not causing them to change. Since this penalty system is not working, (the people were not slowing down) God will lay stumbling blocks. What is going to happen because of these stumbling blocks?

I-2: Stumbling blocks might not sound so bad but the condition of the people causes a stumbling stone to be very deadly for everyone. What condition are the Lord's people in? Their condition makes the stumbling blocks even more dangerous. (See Isaiah 42:18-19.)

I-3: … "Can a blind person guide a blind person? Will not both fall into a pit?" (Luke 6:39 NRSV). When all the blind fall into a pit, the result will be double-trouble for the leaders. What does Ezekiel 33:5-6 say?

I-4: The foretold stumbling blocks may flourish from Israel's own planting. Look ahead to verse 24 in this chapter. What do the people compare themselves to?

📖READ JEREMIAH 6:22-25

J. ADDITIONAL COMMENTS FOR VERSES 22-25

God may not get into Jerusalem but He has a message for the hostages.

ANSWER QUESTIONS FOR VERSES 22-25

J-1: Jeremiah may be describing more than one army. If that is so, who are the two groups (armies), where are the two groups (armies) coming from and who is named as one of the targets?

J-2: This may be a dual warning. The message that God sends may also serve to warn His offspring inside the heart. (The spiritual battle is real and His word is living.) These forces that God describes as being "cruel and have(ing) no mercy" are not only coming against Jerusalem but God warns that they come against Zion. What will (at least one of) these armies be attacking, crippling, and disarming? (The following verse will tell you what is inside Zion.)

(Isaiah 2:3 NRSV): …For out of Zion shall go forth instruction, and the word of the Lord from Jerusalem.

J-3: "…anguish has taken hold of us, pain as of a woman in labor" (Jeremiah 6:24 NRSV). Why is Israel's pain or sorrow compared to a woman in labor (in your opinion)?

📖 READ JEREMIAH 6:26

K. ADDITIONAL COMMENTS FOR VERSE 26

Even though the people mourn and lament, there is still a problem.

ANSWER QUESTIONS FOR VERSE 26

K-1: "I will love you forever, for the rest of my life." When a man or woman says those words on their wedding day, that is the heart speaking. Those are words from the heart. But months and years later the heart can take an abrupt turn. Jeremiah 17:9 (NRSV) says: The heart is devious above all else; it is perverse— who can understand it?

The heart…even God cannot understand it. What does He do in order to know what is in our hearts? (See Jeremiah 17:10.)

K-2: It is very disheartening to realize that a person does not and cannot know what is hiding-out and lurking in his or her very own heart; and that it can take a long, long time to know the truth about what is really inside the heart. Turn to Deuteronomy 8:2-10. Those verses speak about a test. How long did it take to get the results of that testing of the heart?

📖 READ JEREMIAH 6:27-30

L. ADDITIONAL COMMENTS FOR VERSES 27-30

In order to find the truth, the testing will continue. It is the only way God can know what is truly in the hearts of His people.

ANSWER QUESTIONS FOR VERSES 27-30

L-1: God says "The bellows blow fiercely…" (Jeremiah 6:29 NRSV). His strong arm is fanning the fiery words that He has put in Jeremiah's mouth. His words are fire and the people are wood. (See Jeremiah 5:14.) Look up the word— backfire. This may be the strategy that God in using here as He comes against the lion-in-the-thicket. After looking up the definition, explain how this hurtful strategy is also beneficial.

L-2: But through all of this, the bride is still not pure. What do you think God means by "rejected silver" in verse 30? The following verses may give an answer.

(Matthew 23:25-28 NRSV): "Woe to you, scribes and Pharisees, hypocrites! For you clean the outside of the cup and of the plate, but inside they are full of greed and selfish-indulgence. You blind Pharisee! First clean the inside of the cup, so that the outside also may become clean. "Woe to you, scribes and Pharisees, hypocrites! For you are like whitewashed tombs, which on the outside look beautiful, but inside they are full of the bones of the dead and of all kinds of filth. So you also on the *outside look righteous to others*, but inside you are full of hypocrisy and lawlessness.

L-3: What is it that God wants through all of this refining? (See the following verse.)

(Proverbs 25:4 NRSV): Take away the dross from the silver, and the smith has material for a vessel.

L-4: What did God tell Ezekiel about this whole situation? (See Ezekiel 22:18-20 NRSV.)

L-5: Even though there are about 613 laws in the Old Testament, here is a list of the ten laws that were written in stone for the people of God. Check the ones that have been broken and give the reference (from chapters 1-6) to indicate why you placed the check.

- ➢ 1 You shall have no other gods before me.
- ➢ 2 You shall not make for yourself any idols.
- ➢ 3 You shall not make wrongful use of the name of the Lord your God.
- ➢ 4 Remember the Sabbath Day and keep it holy.
- ➢ 5 Honor your father and mother.
- ➢ 6 You shall not murder.
- ➢ 7 You shall not commit adultery.
- ➢ 8 You shall not steal.
- ➢ 9 You shall not bear false witness against your neighbor.
- ➢ 10 You shall not covet anything that belongs to your neighbor.

L-6: Is there a message just for you, from Jeremiah, in chapter six?

Chapter 6 Tag-A-Long
The 'I Do' To-Do-List

When a couple gets married, one of the things on the To-Do-List is to have children. I would suppose every couple's dream is to have children that they can be proud of. I know that my hope for our kids is that they are always productive in this world, in a good way, and that their offering in this world is one that can bring positive things to the lives of others.

I suppose God had that in mind when He chose Israel for His bride. He and His bride would make a difference in this world through their little family. But Israel was not quality bride material. She was not the one you would want to 'bring home' to meet the family. She would not be a good mother for your offspring.

Jeremiah 6:26 (NRSV) says: 'O my poor people; put on sackcloth, and roll in ashes; make mourning as for an only child...'

It was definitely going to happen, the death of the one and only son, on the cross. How else could it end? What chance did their son have? God's bride was not a good wife and she was not a good mother. She rejected her son and paid no attention to Him. He should have been treated like a king but she treated Him the same way she treated His Father. She failed to hold Him close to her heart. She failed to provide what He needed for healthy growth. She failed to protect Him. She did nothing to try to stop His death.

Maybe that's a good message for us today. Lament and wail O nation. How many of our sons and daughters are we losing due to our negligence? As the warning signs are being sent out, how do the future generations see us respond to them? Do our reactions cause our sons and daughters to fear only the sign or do our reactions cause them to fear God?

When my dad was a young boy, he was in a hurricane/tornado. The hurricane took the lives of some of his relatives and friends. He had experienced and actually lived through great devastation. I heard him tell the story (more than once) of what may have been one of his greatest fears. As I continued to grow, from toddler to teen, I witnessed his fear. I saw that fear that he had for wind-storms, time and time again. I remember 'tornado warnings' scrolling across the bottom of the TV screen and that fear always returned to my dad. And guess what? I learned that fear. I too became fearful when tornado warnings were broadcast over the radio or TV. I saw that fear in my dad enough times, to know that it was something serious and whenever there were storm warnings, I prayed. I wrung my hands. I repented. I fretted. I made promises to the Lord.

And at that time, I could only say the same as God's people in verse 24. "I have heard news of them (the disaster warnings) my hands fall helpless and anguish has taken a hold of me." My heart turned at that moment toward God. But once the storm passed, it was the storm that I still feared, not God. I am not saying that you should not fear dangerous storms but I am saying that the best time to wring your hands, fret, repent, and make promises to the Lord, is not in the middle of one. Doing something because you feel threatened or forced is just not the same as doing something because you want to. I'm glad to say that I kind of know what is going on and where God stands in the whole storm situation. I want to allow God's everyday word to motivate me…not the storms.

✂ Scrapbook Page For Chapter 6

I Am Nothing without God

I created the heavens, I created the earth, yet I am Word.

I am powerful, yet nothing without God.

He is my only hope, but I feel that he has abandoned me.

My God, my God, why hast thou forsaken me?

THE LONGINGS OF THE WORD, FOR DAYS GONE BY

"…O that I were as in the months of old, as in the days when God watched over me; when his lamp shone over my head, and by his light I walked through darkness; when I was in my prime, when the friendship of God was upon my tent; when the Almighty was still with me, when my children were around me; when my steps were washed with milk, and the rock poured out for me streams of oil!

When I went out to the gate of the city, when I took my seat in the square, the young men saw me and withdrew, and the aged rose up and stood; the nobles refrained from talking, and laid their hands on their mouths; the voices of the princes were hushed, and their tongues stuck to the roofs of their mouths.

When the ear heard, it commended me, and when the eye saw, it approved; because I delivered the poor who cried, and the orphan who had no helper. The blessing of the wretched came upon me, and I caused the widows heart to sing for joy. I put on righteousness, and it clothed me; my justice was like a robe and a turban.

I was eyes to the blind, and feet to the lame. I was a father to the needy, and I championed the cause of the stranger. I broke the fangs of the unrighteous, and made them drop their prey from their teeth.

Then I thought, 'I shall die in my nest, and I shall multiply my days like the phoenix; my roots spread out to the waters, with the dew all night on my branches; my glory was fresh with me, and my bow ever new in my hand.'

"They listened to me, and waited, and kept silent for my counsel. After I spoke they did not speak again, and my word dropped upon them like dew. They waited for me as for the rain; they opened their mouths as for the spring rain. I smiled on them when they had no confidence; and the light of my countenance they did not extinguish. I chose their way, and sat as chief, and I lived like a king among his troops, like one who comforts mourners.

THE WORD FEELS PERSECTION FROM ITS FOLLOWERS

But now they make sport of me.

And now they mock me in song; I am a byword to them. They abhor me, they keep aloof from me; they do not hesitate to spit at the sight of me. Because God has loosed my bowstring and humbled me, they have cast off restraint in my presence.

On my right hand the rabble rise up; they send me sprawling, and build roads for my ruin. They break up my path, they promote my calamity; no one restrains them. As through a wide breach they come; amid the crash they roll on. Terrors are turned upon me; my honor is pursued as by the wind, and my prosperity has passed away like a cloud.

THE WORD FEELS PERSECUTION FROM GOD

With violence he seizes my garment; he grasps me by the collar of my tunic. He has cast me into the mire, and I have become like dust and ashes. I cry to you and you do not answer me; I stand, and you merely look at me. You have turned cruel to me; with the might of your hand you persecute me.

You lift me up on the wind, you make me ride on it, and you toss me about in the roar of the storm. I know that you will bring me to death, and to the house appointed for all living.

"Surely one does not turn against the needy, when in disaster they cry for help. Did I not weep for those whose day was hard? Was not my soul grieved for the poor? But when I looked for good, evil came; and when I waited for light, darkness came. My inward parts are in turmoil, and are never still; days of affliction come to meet me. I go about in sunless gloom; I stand up in the assembly and cry for help.

I am a brother of jackals, and a companion of ostriches. My skin turns black and falls from me, and my bones burn with heat. My lyre is turned to mourning, and my pipe to the voice of those who weep.

O that I had one to hear me! (Here is my signature! Let the Almighty answer me!) O, that I had the indictment written by my adversary! Surely I would carry it on my shoulder; and I would bind it on me like a crown; I would give him an account of all my steps; like a prince I would approach him.

All of this has been taken from the book of Job (Job 29:2-30:1; 30:9-15; 30:18-31; 31:35-37 NRSV). Though the book depicts Job's trouble, I could not help it; I saw the troubles of the Word and then at last I recognized it as Jesus. We can see in this snapshot the He is nothing without God.

Compare Answers For Chapter 6

A-1: They killed God's servants. The innocent blood flowed from prophets of God.

A-2: God's word, it was inside the vessel-prophets

A-3: gate of Benjamin

A-4: Jerusalem was Benjamin's legal inheritance. It was a great city called the City of David. It was the place that God chose for His presence.

A-5 (OPTIONAL QUESTION): They were probably numerous and strong.

A-6 (OPTIONAL QUESTION): under the command of King David

A-7: Blow the trumpet in Tekoa. Raise a signal on Beth-haccherem.

A-8: Violence and destruction are heard within her, sickness and wounds are ever before God.

B-1: God describes their help as shepherds. These shepherds are 'after God's own heart' and they will bring knowledge and understanding.

B-2: destroyed God's vineyard, trampled down His portion, made His pleasant portion desolate

B-3: Besiegers, lions, wolves and leopards, they see curses

B-4: They will attack at noon. They will attack at night.

B-5: The person must be very attentive to the prize. He must be patient because he does not want to destroy the prize. This threshing is a tedious assignment that sounds as if the prize comes in very small quantities over a long period of time.

C-1: no food or water, sickness, many die causing disease

C-2: Listen and obey God's word; concede, surrender

D-1: Thus says the Lord of hosts: Glean thoroughly as a vine the remnant of Israel; like a grape-gatherer, pass your hand again over its branches (Jeremiah 6:9 NRSV).

D-2: Chapter five strips away the bad. Chapter six is looking for any good and gathering.

D-3: remnant

E-1: All inhabitants shall be taken, their houses and fields turned over to others.

E-2: He wants to restore the judges and counselors so that Jerusalem will be a city of righteousness.

E-3: Man will no longer be the king. God will be the king.

F-1: The leaders were proclaiming peace, peace when there is no peace

F-2: They acted shamefully, they committed abomination; yet they were not ashamed, they did not know how to blush. Therefore they shall fall among those who fall; at the time that I punish them, they shall be overthrown, says the Lord (Jeremiah 6:15 NRSV).

G-1: God tried to speak to them. God told them to stand at the crossroads, and look, and ask for the ancient paths, where the good way lies; and walk in it, and find rest for your souls. But they said "We will not walk in it." He says: Also I raised up sentinels for you: "Give heed to the sound of the trumpet!" But they said: "We will not give heed." (This message was probably communicated to God through their actions of refusal.)

H-1: I think it is the leaders and the people in the land.

H-2: nations, congregation, earth

I-1: They shall stumble; parents and children together, neighbor and friend, shall perish

I-2: They are deaf and blind.

I-3: They heard the sound of the trumpet and did not take warning; their blood shall be upon themselves. But if they had taken warning, they would have saved their lives. But if the sentinel sees the sword coming and does not blow the trumpet, so that the people are not warned, and the sword comes and takes any of them, they are taken away in their iniquity, but their blood I will require at the sentinel's hand (Ezekiel 33:5-6 NRSV).

I-4: a woman in labor

J-1: there is 'a people' coming from the land of the north and there is a 'nation' stirring from the farthest parts of the earth; and they are coming against daughter Zion.

J-2: They may be coming to destroy instruction.

J-3: Her sorrow comes from no other place than herself. She conceived it herself and now she must give birth. No one dropped all of this trouble off on her doorstep, she has been carrying it around for a long time.

K-1: I the Lord test the mind and search the heart, … (Jeremiah 17:10NRSV).

K-2: 40 years

L-1: backfire- a fire started to check an advancing forest or prairie fire by clearing the area or to have the reverse of the desired or expected effect— if you start your own fire and make a clearing, the approaching fire will not reach you. This backfire gives you an opportunity to save some of your own land from destruction (though some will be sacrificed, that which you set fire to).

L-2: Outside in appearance they are sparkling clean but inside, at the heart, they are filthy dirty.

L-3: material for the making of a vessel.

L-4: (Ezekiel 22:18-20 NRSV): Mortal, the house of Israel has become dross to me; all of them, silver, bronze, tin, iron, and lead. In the smelter they have become dross. Therefore thus says the Lord God: Because you have all become dross, I will gather you into the midst of Jerusalem. As one gathers silver, bronze, iron, lead, and tin into a smelter, to blow the fire upon them in order to melt them; so I will gather you in my anger and in my wrath, and I will put you in and melt you.

L-5: This is a running list from the previous chapter.

   Number 1: You shall have no other gods before me (broken law according to Jeremiah 1:16)

   Number 2: You shall not make for yourself an idol (broken law according to Jeremiah 1:16)

   Number 5: Honor your father and mother (broken law according to Jeremiah 2:27)

   Number 6: You shall not murder (broken law according to Jeremiah 2:30b and 34)

   Number 4: Remember the Sabbath day and keep it holy (broken law according to Jeremiah 2:32)

   Number 7: You shall not commit adultery (broken law according to Jeremiah 3:6)

   Number 3: You shall not make wrongful use of my name (broken law according to Jeremiah 5:2)

   Number 10: You shall not covet anything that belongs to your neighbor (broken, see Jeremiah 5:8)

L-6: Letting God into my heart (my personal city) can be painful as He cleans up and gets rid of all the undesirable counsel that has been living there. In order to become clean my city (heart) must be tested like silver and gold. It must undergo a refining fire. It must also bring new birth (produce) after the clean-up is done.

Chapter 7

Chapter 7 Prelude

The Car from Dad

His dad finally gave it to him. He was now the owner and he could hardly believe it! From torque and horsepower to body and build this was the car that every car-lover can only dream about! It was a high performance model that came with five on the floor and it was tuned to perfection. It had only two seats and little to no cargo space. This pearl blue, fuel powered machine didn't allow the owner to haul much baggage around. And talk about getting you somewhere, it could go from zero to seventy in no time flat.

Although he had never gotten the opportunity to sit behind the wheel of the car and experience its power on the open road, he believed everything his dad said. Many times, down at his dad's garage, he heard all of the guys talk about the things this machine could do. Anyone who had seen it in action would have given their right foot to have it. That was a joke down at the garage because you need your right foot to operate it…right?

There are benefits to owning a car like this. You gain a sense of confidence that you never had before. You feel taller when you hold those keys in your hand. And that's a fact. Just ask anybody who has seen you holding those keys as you stand next to the car and talk to your friends. Other car owners can't help but stop to notice when they see you washing it, checking under the hood, or putting gas in it. Your prow serves your appearance well. And it doesn't matter if you are a dirty mess. You still look good and command respect when you are in, beside, or around your awesome car.

But as the giddy title holder there is something that you need to remember. This car can make anyone look good. But you happen to be the privileged one. So showing respect to the high performance machine is a must. When you see the warning lights on the dashboard flashing, address the issue. And if you don't know what the warning light means, find out! If you don't heed the warnings this powerful machine is going to let you down. It is not going to do all the things that your dad said it would. You won't get the same respect form the other car owners if you have to push-n-pull your car around. You and your high performance car will become a joke.

The house of the Lord in Jerusalem is just like a high performance car that needs immediate attention. The warning lights are flashing. But when God's people see the warning lights they just turn away. They neglect to fix and change the things that God tells them to. So now God tells them that they can no longer trust in or depend upon the power of the vehicle that they sit in. They may think that they look good sitting in the house of the Lord but the power that this vehicle once held is just about gone. If they trust in this place, they are deceived.

Chapter 7 Study

Bells, Flashing Lights, Sirens, and Whistles

CHAPTER 7 READING, COMMENTS, AND QUESTIONS

📖READ JEREMIAH 7:1-4

A. ADDITIONAL COMMENTS FOR VERSES 1-4

God once again gives Jeremiah instructions, telling him how to use the words that were put in his mouth (Jeremiah 1:9). Jeremiah is to stand at the gate of the Lord's house and speak to those who come to worship.

ANSWER QUESTIONS FOR VERSES 1-4

A-1: As Jeremiah represents God, what better place is there to stand than outside the temple? The evil acts of the people have reached the limit and God is getting ready to leave this place. He will make that perfectly clear in this message. Turn to Jeremiah 36:5. What may be the most likely reason that God is no longer speaking from inside the temple?

A-2: I imagine myself in the crowd that arrives at the temple scene. I see Jeremiah at the gate of the Lord's house. Coming from the temple behind him I hear a beautiful song being sung by Levi. Praising God through music was just one of their many duties. The choir of Levi sings: This is the temple of the Lord… This is the temple of the Lord…This is the temple of the Lord…The words of the song are ironic. Why?

A-3: In chapter 2, the Lord instructed Jeremiah to go speak the anointed word to the leaders but the leaders would not listen. In chapter 5, Jeremiah was instructed to take the anointed word of the Lord to the streets (to the rich and poor alike) but they would not listen. Now he is instructed to go to the house of the Lord. This is where true followers of God are suspected to be found. But what does God say will happen when Jeremiah speaks to the worshippers? Look ahead to verse 27.

A-4: Travel by foot was probably the most popular form of transportation. The journey to the temple may have lasted for many days or weeks. Going to the house of God to attend worship services, like we do today, was not a real option for the ordinary people in this society. Even though the men were required to appear before the Lord three times a year (see Exodus 23:17 or Deuteronomy 16:16), approximately how often did the family get to go to the temple according to the following scenarios?

(1Samuel 1:1-5 NRSV): There was a certain man of Ramathaim, a Zuphite from the hill country of Ephraim, whose name was Elkanah son of Jeroham son of Elihu son of Tohu son of Zuph, an Ephraimite. He had two wives; the name of the one was Hannah, and the name of the other Peninnah. Peninnah had children, but Hannah had no children. Now this man used to go up year by year from his town to worship and to sacrifice to the Lord of hosts at Shiloh, where the two sons of Eli, Hophni and Phinehas, were priests of the Lord. On the day when Elkanah sacrificed, he would give portions to his wife Peninnah and to all her sons and daughters; but to Hannah he gave a double portion, because he loved her, though the Lord had closed her womb.

(Luke 2:41-45 NRSV): Now every year his parents went to Jerusalem for the festival of the Passover. And when he was twelve years old, they went up as usual for the festival. When the festival was ended and they started to return, the boy Jesus stayed behind in Jerusalem, but his parents did not know it. Assuming that he was in the group of travelers, they went a day's journey. Then they started to look for him among their relatives and friends. When they did not find him,....

A-5: How did those who were far away, from the temple, pray to God? (See the following verses.)

(1Kings 8:29-30 NRSV): that your eyes may be open night and day toward this house, the place of which you said, 'My name shall be there,' that you may heed the prayer that your servant prays toward this place. Hear the plea of your servant and of your people Israel when they pray toward this place; O hear in heaven your dwelling place; heed and forgive.

(1Kings 8:44-45 NRSV): "If your people go out to battle against their enemy, by whatever way you shall send them, and they pray to the Lord toward the city that you have chosen and the house that I have built for your name, then hear in heaven their prayer and their plea, and maintain their cause.

(Daniel 6:10 NRSV): Although Daniel knew that the document had been signed, he continued to go to his house, which had windows in its upper room open toward Jerusalem, and to get down on his knees three times a day to pray to his God and praise him, just as he had done previously.

A-6: What provoked God's anger in the following verses? (See the following verses that have been selected from the books of Ezekiel and Jeremiah.)

(Ezekiel 8:16-17 NRSV): And he brought me into the inner court of the house of the Lord; there, at the entrance of the temple of the Lord, between the porch and the altar, were about twenty-five men, with their backs to the temple of the Lord, and their faces toward the east, prostrating themselves to the sun toward the east. Then he said to me, "Have you seen this,

O mortal? Is it not bad enough that the House of Judah commits the abominations done here? Must they fill the land with violence, and provoke my anger still further? See, they are putting the branch to their nose!"

(Jeremiah 2:27 NRSV): …For they have turned their backs to me, and not their faces…..

A-7: Through Jeremiah, God let the people know His plans. He was fed-up and about to move-on. What had to happen if they, the worshippers, wanted to see God stay in His chosen place? (See verse 3.)

📖READ JEREMIAH 7:5-7

B. ADDITIONAL COMMENTS FOR VERSES 5-7

The worshippers receive a direct ultimatum from God:

- Truly amend your ways (conversations, customs) and doings (acts, works)
- Truly act justly with one another
- Do not oppress the alien, orphan and the widow, or shed innocent blood in this place
- Do not go after other gods to your own hurt

ANSWER QUESTIONS FOR VERSES 5-7

B-1: What will be the end result *if* the people accept the conditions that God has presented? (See verse 7.)

B-2: The benefits were great if God's people were obedient. (See Leviticus 26:1-13.) But when the people were offensive, penalties occurred. The penalties were continuing to escalate. Leviticus 26:14-33 gives legal reasons for escalation. What was the legal process?

B-3 (OPTIONAL QUESTION): At what penalty stage does Jerusalem seem to be in?

B-4: What would happen to a five-time repeat offender in our modern-day court system?

B-5: True worshippers may have a certain power. What was the power in Numbers 25:10-11?

📖READ JEREMIAH 7:8-11

C. ADDITIONAL COMMENTS FOR VERSES 8-11

It was true. The leaders were treating the wound of *God's people* carelessly. The most popular antidotes being prescribed by the leaders:

- Peace, peace
- We shall not see sword or famine
- The Lord lives!
- This is the house of the Lord

These antidotal words were careless lies. The prescriptions only brought painful death to the nation.

ANSWER QUESTIONS FOR VERSES 8-11

C-1: The people who have come to worship at the temple feel safe. But lights are flashing and bells are dinging. Why can't they trust in these words: "This is the temple of the Lord, the temple of the Lord, the temple of the Lord", the house which is called by His name?

C-2: "It has been a long journey for you and me, oh precious one, but I see the temple! I see the temple of the Lord! My salvation is near! I can't wait to get rid of this guilt. It is just about to kill me. I am soon to be a new and clean man because of you and your flowing blood." said the man to the sacrificial lamb that he was leading to the temple. "At this time tomorrow I will be free from this sin thanks to the temple of the Lord. I 'see' my sanctuary. I 'see' my rest." (This man is a repeat offender. He has come to the temple to have his record wiped clean for the same abominable sin for the last five years, three times a year.)

It is gracious that God has always made a way for sin to be removed from the record that He keeps but God seems to be the only one doing the erasing. The legal record of the law will be changed but this man will not. The people here at the temple unload their wrongs on God, just to go out and do all of the things that are abominable to God, again and again and again. They keep dragging, soon to be, dead animals in and leaving them in God's house. God gets the dead carcass with the smell of burnt flesh while they get a clean record.

Those who continue to do wrong even though they have been warned, 'see' the house of the Lord as a safe place to acquire security (at a price) but God sees something else when He watches the flurry of activity as His children come home to visit. What does God see when He looks at His house?

C-3: Look up the word— den. What is its purpose for the predatory animal?

C-4: God calls these mortals 'robbers'. What do you think they are stealing and who are they stealing it from?

📖 **READ JEREMIAH 7:12-15**

D. ADDITIONAL COMMENTS FOR VERSES 12-15

About Ephraim

Jacob had twelve sons. Joseph was one of them.

Because of hatred and rivalry, Joseph was sold by his brothers for 20 pieces of silver.

The traders who bought Joseph took him to Egypt where he fell on much hardship.

But he possessed the gift of interpreting dreams. Due to this gift from God,

Joseph gained authority over Egypt and there was only one in the land being more superior than he;

that superior of Joseph was Pharaoh, the King of Egypt. (See Genesis 41:39-40.)

Many years later the rest of his family came to Egypt in search of food during a great famine

and unbeknownst to them, Joseph was alive, large, and in charge.

Joseph had married the daughter of a priest (of Egypt) and they had two sons. (See Genesis 46:20.)

Manasseh was the oldest son and Ephraim was the youngest.

Upon the death of Joseph's father (Israel) Joseph's two sons were blessed and counted

among the sons of Israel.

Manasseh and Ephraim took their place among the names of the 12 tribes,

See Genesis 48 for the restructure.

Ephraim became dominant and powerful in the land of Israel.

When Ephraim spoke, there was trembling; he was exalted in Israel; (Hosea 13:1 NRSV).

But the dominant power stumbled.

Now Ephraim must lead out his children for slaughter (Hosea 9:13NRSV).

Why?

Those worshippers coming and going from Shiloh

would not listen to God or answer His calls.

ANSWER QUESTIONS FOR VERSES 12-15

D-1: The break-up with Israel was painful. The move was difficult and the journey was especially long as God had to witness all of the ill and damaged fruit, along the way, that Israel had produced. The land was littered, ugly, and unfriendly. The route God took, which started in Shiloh, went south through Ephraim. As He stayed on the south-bound course to exit Israel, no one in all northern kingdom did anything to keep Him in His place. He was not wanted or recognized in the land that was His own.

He went to the southern kingdom, into Judah, and into Jerusalem. If you wanted to be in God's presence, you now had to go there. But God has a message of warning for the people who have come to His house. What is the message? (See verses 12-15.)

D-2: God desired one thing from His people. What was it? (See the verses below.)

(Hosea 6:4-6 NRSV): What shall I do with you, O Ephraim? What shall I do with you, O Judah? Your love is like a morning cloud, like the dew that goes away early. Therefore I have hewn them by the prophets, I have killed them by the words of my mouth, and my judgment goes forth as the light. For I desire steadfast love and not sacrifice, the knowledge of God rather than burnt offerings.

📖READ JEREMIAH 7:16-20

E. ADDITIONAL COMMENTS FOR VERSES 16-20

Intercession (before it even begins) is put to a stop.

ANSWER QUESTIONS FOR VERSES 16-20

E-1: While alarms were going off and warning lights were flashing inside the vehicle, the outside of the vehicle was no different. Danger! Caution! Slow down! The lights and alarms could be seen and heard everywhere. No matter where you were, it was clear, God's ways were not being enforced in His land, in His city, or in His house. What were the people, seemingly as a family affair, still doing without any interference (from law enforcement) throughout the towns of Judah and in the streets of Jerusalem after all that God had spoken?

E-2: That is *your* vehicle that is on fire! The people hear the words of the (spiritual) warning but continue to throw fuel into the flames. The fire that once served as a light in the dark and chased away the cold now serves to harm! Jeremiah describes something that apparently no one else can see. What will be the results as they continue to feed this fire?

E-3 (OPTIONAL QUESTION): As for you, do not pray for this people, do not raise a cry or prayer on their behalf, and do not intercede with me, for I will not hear you (Jeremiah 7:16 NRSV). Those were God's words to an interceder. Do you think that it is possible for God to say those words when intercession is made on behalf of you, your town, your neighborhood or your place of worship? What would cause Him to say those words to the One who intercedes (Romans 8:34) on behalf you and yours?

📖READ JEREMIAH 7:21-26

F. ADDITIONAL COMMENTS FOR VERSES 21-26

God must have had high hopes when He first brought the ancestors out of Egypt. He gave them one command (law) and it was not backed up by threats (penalties). He could not imagine this little girl, of His (Israel), ever doing anything wrong.

ANSWER QUESTIONS FOR VERSES 21-26

F-1: What was the command when the ancestors came out of Egypt? (See verse 23.)

F-2: How did God's people hear His voice? (See Daniel 9:10.)

F-3: Passing a new law, or revising one, in the U.S. is no easy task. How did the leaders in Jerusalem show their veto power when God spoke His words of reform and change, throughout time, within the Promised Land?

F-4: God tells the worshippers the truth about their ancestors. He tells them how their grandmas and grandpas from long ago quickly became law-breakers. They had an evil will and walked in their own counsels. They kept looking back (at where they came from) instead of ahead (where God was leading them). Even though God persistently sent His servants, the prophets, to speak to their grandmas and grandpas, they did not listen. And as hard as that must have been to hear, the message from God got worse. What was the real shocking news that day at the temple?

F-5 (OPTIONAL QUESTION): The people in Jerusalem have received numerous warnings, fines, and citations. The penalties that were put in place to lead and guide them will now have to chase them down or back them in a corner. How do imposed penalties affect you? Do they work as watchdogs in your life or do you view them as counselors (like seeing-eye dogs, that lead the blind)?

📖READ JEREMIAH 7:27-29

G. ADDITIONAL COMMENTS FOR VERSES 27-29

The actions of this generation have stirred up a riot in another realm. The words of God's wrath have been aroused and are now raging mad: "Destruction to our destroyer! Destruction to our destroyer!" is heard in the streets and written on the picket signs in a place unseen and far away. God's word is tired of being rejected, trampled on, and treated with no respect!

ANSWER QUESTIONS FOR VERSES 27-29

G-1: Compare this generation to a girl who is running straight into big trouble. God's Word has called her, chased her, and struck her down but she will not quit running. What will she not willingly accept from God? (See verse 28.)

G-2: What do her run-a-way actions reveal? (See the last part of verse 28.)

G-3: God is definitely sending punishment. The people can bend and accept it or stand stiff, try to reject it, and be broken. Either way, it is going to hurt. But what advantage is there for those who continue to bend to God? Your personal answer is required here.

G-4: Cut off your hair and throw it away; raise a lamentation on the bare heights, for the Lord has rejected and forsaken the generation that provoked His wrath (Jeremiah 7:29 NRSV). Sometimes you just have to take your punishment. At first you will probably cry a lot. But weather your punishment is short lived or lasts a lifetime, do not suffer in vain. Work hard on changing your heart to be obedient to God. Live in obedience. Die in obedience. What other generation did the Lord reject and who was a part of that generation that felt the Lord's rejection? (See Numbers 32:11-13 and Deuteronomy 1:34-37; 34:1-8. You may want to look up the meaning of the word reject in order to receive fuller understanding.)

READ JEREMIAH 7:30-31

H. ADDITIONAL COMMENTS FOR VERSES 30-31

Repeat offenders! Repeat offenders! No one will change!

ANSWER QUESTIONS FOR VERSES 30-31

H-1: The people were doing two things that were evil in God's sight. What were the two evil acts at that time, on that day? (See verses 30-31.)

H-2: God's people may have been sacrificing their children by throwing them into a real fire but in the following verses God speaks of and warns the people against another fire that would be kindled due to evil acts of parents.

(Deuteronomy 7:1-4 NRSV): When the Lord your God brings you into the land that you are about to enter and occupy, and he clears away many nations before you...and when the Lord your God gives them over to you and you defeat them, then you must utterly destroy them. Make no covenant with them and show them no mercy. Do not intermarry with them, giving your daughters to their sons or taking their daughters for your sons, for that would turn away your children from following me, to serve other gods. Then the anger of the Lord would be kindled against you, and he would destroy you quickly.

Look ahead to verse 34 in this chapter. It could support the theory that something other than -sacrifice by actual fire- was going on in this valley. What does verse 34 say here in chapter 7?

READ JEREMIAH 7:32-34

I. ADDITIONAL COMMENTS FOR VERSES 32-34

Here in the United States, some of our cities have been given nick-names. Nick-names may indicate what that city is best known for. For instance, Las Vegas is called 'Sin City'. Detroit is known as the 'Motor City'. Chicago is 'The Windy City'. Topheth which is in the valley of the son of Hinnom will also get a nick-name. It will be known as the 'Valley of Slaughter'.

ANSWER QUESTIONS FOR VERSES 32-34

I-1: What will happen at Topheth that causes the nick-name, Valley of Slaughter, to come about?

I-2: Can you think of any negative, modern day clichés about marriage that could have very well originated in the 'Valley of Slaughter'?

I-3: Read Numbers 25:1-9 and Deuteronomy 21:10-14. New women are *brought into the house* in both sets of selected verses. Why, in your opinion, is God angry in one instance but not the other?

I-4: Here are the 10 laws that God wrote in stone for His people (even though there are about 613 laws altogether). Check mark the ones that have been broken and continue to keep track of the verses that support your answer.

- ➤ 1 You shall have no other gods before me.
- ➤ 2 You shall not make for yourself any idols.
- ➤ 3 You shall not make wrongful use of the name of the Lord your God.
- ➤ 4 Remember the Sabbath Day and keep it holy.
- ➤ 5 Honor your father and mother.
- ➤ 6 You shall not murder.
- ➤ 7 You shall not commit adultery.
- ➤ 8 You shall not steal.
- ➤ 9 You shall not bear false witness against your neighbor.
- ➤ 10. You shall not covet anything that is your neighbors.

I-5: Pluck up and pull down, destroy and overthrow, build and plant; that is what Jeremiah was called to do. Has Jeremiah done any of that in your life through chapter seven?

Chapter 7 Tag-A-Long

Sermon on the Mount Check-up

As I worked on this chapter I really began to wonder about where I stand with God when I worship. Is my trust in the 'name of Jesus' comparable to the worshipper's trust in the 'temple of the Lord'? I had a lot of questions to answer.

- ✓ When I say "in the name of Jesus" here… and "in the name of Jesus" there… here in His name… there in His name… everywhere in His name… am I deceived?
- ✓ As I use it and say it, is the 'name of Jesus' giving me a sense of false security?
- ✓ Am I really a lot like the people of Judah?
- ✓ Is there something about me that I should fix or change?
- ✓ Am I really listening to and obeying God or do I lie to myself?
- ✓ Do I hear correctly when God speaks or do I just hear what I want to hear?
- ✓ Do I trust in His promises and the power of the name but neglect His commands and warnings?

Well I thought the 'Sermon on the Mount' might be a good place to do a quick check-up.

- Do I rejoice when others demean my belief in Christ?
- When I do good works for the Lord, do I think I am the one who deserves the praise, thanks and adoration (once the 'work' is brought to light or mentioned)?
- How long will it take me to remember that my anger against someone is like murder?
- Do I reconcile with someone who is angry with me before I pray and worship or do I stand before God and ask Him to exact revenge?
- When will I remember that it's adultery when I look at others with the eyes (thoughts) that are for my spouse only?
- Have I divorced on unlawful grounds?
- Do I swear and make promises when I do not even have control over the next moment of my life?
- Do I love my enemies?
- Do I pray for those who persecute me?
- My right hand always seems to know what my left hand is doing, giving gifts with my right and then writing down the amount of every gift given so I can claim it on my 1040.

- Do I pray powerfully, sing loud, and cry hard hoping that others will recognize that I am spiritual?
- Do I love profit?
- Do I strive to gain, for my own personal satisfaction?
- Do I worry about what I will eat, what I will drink, and what I will wear?
- Do I judge unjustly?
- When someone asks me to do something, do I go the extra mile and do even more?

Well I can now say that if I were in Jerusalem the day that Jeremiah was searching for someone who acts justly and seeks the truth, back in chapter 5, the outcome would have been no different. My presence in the city would not have provided support for the unbalanced scales. I could not have been (the one) responsible for the pardoning of the city. I am not so different from those in Jerusalem who believed and put their trust in 'the temple of the Lord' because I too believe and put my trust in the 'temple of the Lord' but the temple that houses my Lord is 'Jesus'.

Jeremiah's message is still relevant for me today. My trust is not what causes God to dwell with me; it is my actions that beckon Him to stay.

✂ Scrapbook Page For Chapter 7

God's Original Signature

For seven years my mother made me take piano lessons but I hated to practice and well, I didn't. If I would have faithfully practiced back when I had the opportunity, I would be able to (at the least) recognize some of the classical pieces today. But because I hated to practice I barely know the difference between Beethoven and Chopsticks when I hear them being played! That is how it seems to be with *God's people*. When they hear God, they do not know who He is. Because, being just like me, they hated to practice.

You have to practice God in order to recognize His voice when He speaks. He speaks to us in many ways so work on becoming a master in the arts of God. You can know His Voice when you hear it. You can know His Work when you see it. You will rejoice when you hear and see His Original Signature.

Compare Answers For Chapter 7

A-1: Jeremiah was prevented from going into the house of the Lord.

A-2: God says: Do not trust in these deceptive words: "This is the temple of the Lord, the temple of the Lord, the temple of the Lord" (Jeremiah 7:4 NRSV). These words cannot be counted on and at this point the words are not truth.

A-3: ...they will not listen to you. You shall call them, but they will not answer you (Jeremiah 7:27 NRSV).

A-4: once a year

A-5: If you could not go to Jerusalem, you prayed toward the city.

A-6: when the people turned their backs to the Lord

A-7: For if you truly amend your ways and your doings, if you truly act justly one with another, if you do not oppress the alien, the orphan, and the widow, or shed innocent blood in this place, and if you do not go after other gods to your own hurt, then I will dwell with you in this place, in the land that I gave of old to your ancestors forever and ever (Jeremiah 7:5-7 NRSV).

B-1: God will dwell with them in this place in the land that He gave to their ancestors forever.

B-2: First offense: ....I will bring terror on you; consumption and fever that waste the eyes and cause life to pine away. You shall sow your seed in vain, for your enemies shall eat it. I will set my face against you, and you shall be struck down by your enemies; your foes shall rule over you, and you shall flee though no one pursues you (Leviticus 26:16-17 NRSV).

Second offense: ....I will continue to punish you sevenfold for your sins. I will break your proud glory, and I will make your sky like iron and your earth like copper. Your strength shall be spent to no purpose; your land shall not yield its produce, and the trees of the land shall not yield their fruit (Leviticus 26:18-20 NRSV).

Third offense: If you continue hostile to me, and will not obey me, I will continue to plague you sevenfold for your sins. I will let loose wild animals against you, and they shall bereave you of your children and destroy your livestock; they shall make you few in number, and your roads shall be deserted (Leviticus 26: 21-22 NRSV).

Fourth offense: If in spite of these punishments you have not turned back to me, but continue hostile to me, then I too will continue hostile to you: I myself will strike you sevenfold for your sins. *I will bring the sword against you, executing vengeance for the covenant*; and if you withdraw within your cities, I will send pestilence among you, and you shall be delivered into enemy hands. When I break your staff of bread, ten women shall bake your bread in a single oven, and they shall dole out your bread by weight; and though you eat, you shall not be satisfied (Leviticus 26:23-26 NRSV).

Fifth offense: But if, despite this, you disobey me, and continue hostile to me, I will continue hostile to you in fury; I in turn will punish you myself sevenfold for your sins. You shall eat the flesh of your sons, and you shall eat the flesh of your daughters. I will destroy your high places and cut down your incense altars: I will heap your carcasses on the carcasses of your idols. I will abhor you. I will lay your cities waste, will make your sanctuaries desolate, and I will not smell your pleasing odors. I will devastate the land, so that your enemies who come to settle in it shall be appalled at it. And you I will scatter among the nations, and I will unsheathe the sword against you; your land shall be a desolation, and your cities a waste (Leviticus 26:27-33).

B-3 (OPTIONAL QUESTION): between 3 and 4

B-4: They would be thrown in jail and the key thrown away.

B-5: They can turn God's wrath back by their zeal.

C-1: They steal, murder, commit adultery, swear falsely, make offerings to Baal and go after gods they have not known.

C-2: den of robbers

C-3: it is a cavern used as a hide-out for predatory animals or a center of secret activity

C-4: They are gaining forgiveness and righteousness under false pretenses. They are robbing from God.

D-1: Go now to my place that was in Shiloh, where I made my name dwell at first, and see what I did to it for the wickedness of my people Israel. And now, because you have done all these things, says the Lord, and when I spoke to you persistently, you did not listen, and when I called you, you did not answer, therefore I will do to the house that is called by my name, in which you trust, and to the place that I gave to you and to your ancestors, just what I did to Shiloh. And I will cast you out of my sight, just as I cast out all your kinsfolk, all of the offspring of Ephraim (Jeremiah 7:12-15 NRSV).

D-2: steadfast love

E-1: The children gather wood, the fathers kindle fire, and the women knead dough, to make cakes for the queen of heaven; and they pour our drink offerings to other gods…. (Jeremiah 7:18 NRSV).

E-2: God says: My anger and my wrath shall be poured out on this place, on human beings and animals, on the trees of the field and the fruit of the ground; it will burn and not be quenched (Jeremiah 7:20 NRSV).

E-3 (OPTIONAL QUESTION): When Jesus intercedes on our behalf at the throne, I am sure that our actions do not go unnoticed. We may be saying: Peace, Peace and Jesus lives! But I am not so sure that the lives of His people reflect that today either. Willful disobedience (even the smallest) on our part would be reason, good enough, for God to not listen to anyone who calls on Him when we are in need.

F-1: "…Obey my voice, and I will be your God, and you shall be my people; and walk only in the way that I command you, so that it may be well with you" (Jeremiah 7:23 NRSV).

F-2: through His servants, the prophets

F-3: killed His servants, the prophets

F-4: They were doing worse than their ancestors.

F-5 (OPTIONAL QUESTION): I can see both aspects (watchdog and counselor) when I view the penalties that are set in place. Even though I am affected by them and they change my actions the penalties cannot make me perfect. Even when I try to be perfect, I can't. I know. I have really tried.

G-1: discipline

G-2: truth has perished; it is cut off from their lips

G-3: bear the burdens with inner peace as God gives you the strength to carry them

G-4: the generation that came out of Egypt along with Moses

H-1: set their abominations in Gods house and build a high place to burn their sons and daughters

H-2: And I will bring to an end the sound of mirth and gladness, the voice of the bride and the bridegroom in the cities of Judah and in the streets of Jerusalem; for the land shall become a waste (Jeremiah 7:34 NRSV).

I-1: …for they will bury in Topheth until there is no room. The corpses of this people will be food for the birds of the air, and for the animals of the earth; and no one will frighten them away (Jeremiah 7:32-33 NRSV).

I-2: Signing your wedding certificate may be referred to as signing your death certificate or "He or she is wearing the ball and chain now"

I-3: Some marriages caused them to turn their hearts to other gods.

I-4: This is a running list from the previous chapter.

Number 1: You shall have no other gods before me (broken law according to Jeremiah 1:16)

Number 2: You shall not make for yourself an idol (broken law according to Jeremiah 1:16)

Number 5: Honor your father and mother (broken law according to Jeremiah 2:27)

Number 6: You shall not murder (broken law according to Jeremiah 2:30b and 34)

Number 4: Remember the Sabbath day and keep it holy (broken law according to Jeremiah 2:32)

Number 7: You shall not commit adultery (broken law according to Jeremiah 3:6)

Number 3: You shall not make wrongful use of my name (broken law according to Jeremiah 5:2)

Number 10: You shall not covet anything that belongs to your neighbor (broken, see Jeremiah 5:8)

Number 8: You shall not steal (broken law according to Jeremiah 7:11)

I-5: If I am a true worshiper of God my actions as a *worshiper in truth* should be far greater than the actions of those who are believers in God. A lot of people believe in God and acknowledge that He is real. As I see warning lights inside and outside of the vehicle, I ask the Lord to have mercy and teach me how to handle all of the signals. The signs are warnings that should not be ignored but my actions for the warnings must be correct if I want to be effective for change. I pray for wisdom and love that would create the kind of change that causes men to open their hearts and allow God to be the Ruler and King, providing a great place for His presence and His throne, a place He calls home.

Chapter 8

Chapter 8 Prelude

At God's House

The bride tiptoes into the house. This is one of those times when she *doesn't want* God to hear her. But that will not happen..

God: Why do you continually keep wandering so far from home? Where have you been this time?

Bride: (a little startled) Over at the Euphrates, just getting something to drink. You know… I wanted something that is a little different from what we have around here.

God: I don't understand you. I have given you your own personal well. It's the best, the only one of its kind. The well in your own back yard offers something far better than anything you can get anywhere else.

Bride: But honestly God, I love it over there. Their drinks make me feel great. After I have had a few, I feel differently about myself! Just look at me. Are you telling me that you don't think the new-me is great? (She twirls herself around.) If you would drink what I drink, you would think I was perfect! (She confidently sits down and crosses one leg over the other. She thinks God will think she looks great too.)

God: (Without a word, God just looks at her. He tries to see what she sees.)

Bride: (answers in a sweet voice) I didn't do anything wrong... Everyone still knows… I make sure that I tell them… you are my God.

There were times when being God's girl came in handy. There was great power in the old name that she carried in her back pocket. No matter where she went, far and wide, the name was respected. When she wandered away from home, she loved to pull out her powerful ID. But for years, she has been, and still is, dirtying God's name up. The brash bride started bringing her godly (little 'g') friends back to the place she called home. Her friends eventually moved in! It wasn't long before the home, that God designed for Himself, His bride, and their (Godly) family, was refurnished. Many of the priceless, God-given treasures had been shamefully broken due to the new scheme and redesign of the home. But that did not bother her at all. She just hid all of the broken treasures (broken laws) in the closet.

Whenever God complained (and He did that often) about the condition of their house and her good-for-nothing, idle friends, that same dazed look and numb smile would cross her face; because by now her friends were her lovers. But as years passed, her body grew frail and weak. Her live-in friends did not have the strength that they claimed and she became real skittish and nervous about that. She can sense that something is different when God starts cleaning the old home place this time-around. He is personally reckoning the situation Himself.

God has tried everything to get this bride to come clean. If it wasn't for that contract, which offered His bride protection, it would be Sodom and Gomorrah all over again! His only contractual option, was to put her and her baggage out for the whole world to see. She, and everything hidden in her closets, would have to go. She could not live here any longer.

Chapter 8 Study

Dead Men Walking

CHAPTER 8 READING, COMMENTS, AND QUESTIONS

📖READ JEREMIAH 8:1-3

A. ADDITIONAL COMMENTS FOR VERSES 1-3

The remnant exposed: This bizarre revelation from Jeremiah was hard for the worshippers entering the temple to understand. (Jeremiah continues the message that he began back in chapter 7.)

ANSWER QUESTIONS FOR VERSES 1-3

A-1: When I think of people being buried in biblical times, I think of their resting places as caves or caverns that have been hewn out of rock. Verses like Genesis 23:9; 25:9; 49:29; Matthew 27:60; John 11:38 and 20:6 leave me with this notion. But when God speaks about *bones* and *tombs* in the first verse of this chapter, I don't think He is talking about places where the dead are laid to rest and I don't think that we are reading about skeletal remains.

Jeremiah's message from chapter 7 seems to flow over into chapter 8. Verse one continues: *At that time,* says the Lord, the bones of the kings of Judah, the bones of its officials, the bones of the priests, the bones of the prophets and the bones of the inhabitants of Jerusalem will be brought out of their tombs (Jeremiah 8:1 NRSV).

First of all, when God says '*At that time*'…, what '*time*' could God be talking about? (See 2Kings 24:10-25:8 for a possible answer.)

A-2: When walled cities like Jerusalem were under siege, the sieges sometimes lasted for years. Knowing that Judah had been dealing with drought (Jeremiah 5:24-25), I think we can safely say that demand for food and water, inside Jerusalem, was great while supply was not. The people (in a time of being under siege) will be facing death due to starvation and disease. They have no way in or out of the city that is under attack. What do the following verses reveal about the food situation during sieges? (See 2Kings 25:1-3 and Jeremiah 38:9.)

A-3: After months of being trapped inside the city, at the hand of Nebuchadnezzar's servants, the (starving) prisoners eventually will be brought out of the city gates. The people will (according to the Scripture) be nothing but bones (being nothing but skin and bone serves as evidence of starvation). What served as the tomb for these walking bones?

A-4: God says that they, being nothing but bone, will be spread before the sun and the moon and all the host of heaven, which they have loved and served, which they have followed, and which they have inquired of and worshipped. Turn to Deuteronomy 28:64 to see what the meaning of this could be. What does this verse say?

A-5: In a previous chapter, God says that He is making His 'word' (that comes forth from the mouth of Jeremiah) like fire. And with that fire, He will devour His people. They will be like wood. (See Jeremiah 5:14.)

Now here in this chapter, the bones (of the people who are like wood) shall be brought out of their tombs; and they shall be spread before the sun and the moon and all the host of heaven, which they have loved and served, which they have followed, and which they have inquired of and worshipped. God will disperse the woody-people, by His fiery words from one end of the earth to the other. What was the purpose of burning 'bones out of a tomb' in or over an area, according to the following verse?

(2Kings 23:16 NRSV): As Josiah turned, he saw the tombs there on the mount; and he sent and took the bones out of the tombs, and burned them on the altar, and defiled it, according...

A-6: What is the area that will become defiled by these bones (coming out of their tomb) that are scattered and burned by (according to Jeremiah 5:14) God's fiery words?

A-7(OPTIONAL QUESTION): When I think about the word holocaust my only thought is Germany, Hitler, and the Jews. We date the start of the Holocaust as 1939. But look up the word holocaust in the dictionary and write down the definition. It began (in a spiritual sense) long before 1939 and does not end in 1945.

A-8: Have you ever told your children a scary tale in order to get them to turn away from being bad or doing something that you know will hurt them? Have you ever seen a scary movie or show that had the moral of: 'this is what will happen if you are bad'? I am not trying to insinuate that this was just a scary tale; but go back and review Jeremiah 5:17. It would have served well as a warning that could scare some kid straight. God warned the people (his children) of a nation that would come. This nation would eat up their sons and daughters. But that did not scare them into changing their wild and rebellious ways. So now the horror episode continues and God tells them what will happen once they have been chewed up and how their lives will end up. What will they become after the scary nation has chewed them up?

A-9: Now, down to its last days, Jerusalem is frail, bent, and nothing but skin and bones. What will their feelings be about life after they are driven away from their home land?

A-10: What does God call the remains of this, what He refers to as, 'evil family' that will end up in all the places that He has driven them? (See verse 3.)

A-11 (OPTIONAL QUESTION): What is the common ground for Jeremiah 8:3 and the following verses?

(Revelation 9:3-6 NRSV): Then from the smoke came locusts on the earth, and they were given authority like the authority of scorpions of the earth. They were told not to damage the grass of the earth or any green growth or any tree, but only those people who do not have the seal of God on their foreheads. They were allowed to torture them for five months, but not to kill them, and their torture was like the torture of a scorpion when it stings someone. And in those days people will seek death but will not find it; they will long to die, but death will flee from them.

A-12: As exiles are being taken out of the city at this time, the captors take those who are useful or threatening. Who was taken according to the following verses?

(2Kings 24:14-17 NRSV): He carried away all Jerusalem, all the officials, all the warriors, ten thousand captives, all the artisans and the smiths; no one remained, except for the poorest people of the land. He carried away Jehoiachin to Babylon; the king's mother, the king's wives, his officials, and the elite of the land, he took into captivity from Jerusalem to Babylon. The king of Babylon brought captive to Babylon all the men of valor, seven thousand, the artisans and the smiths, one thousand, all of them strong and fit for war. The king of Babylon made Mattaniah, Jehoichin's uncle, king in his place, and changed his name to Zedekiah.

A-13: Who are the ones that are left behind according to the following verses?

(2Kings 24:14 NRSV): He carried away all Jerusalem......no one remained, except the poorest people of the land.

(2Kings 25:12 NRSV): But the captain of the guard left some of the poorest people of the land to be vinedressers and tillers of the soil.

(Jeremiah 40:7 NRSV): When all the leaders of the forces in the open country and their troops heard that the king of Babylon had appointed Gedaliah son of Ahikam governor in the land, and had committed to him men, women, and children, those of the poorest of the land who had not been taken into exile to Babylon,

A-14: Using your dictionary, find the definition of the word– bone. Choose the definition that best describes what you think God means when He uses the word: bones.

📖READ JEREMIAH 8:4-7

B. ADDITIONAL COMMENTS FOR VERSES 4-7

Even though the revelations are proclaimed and even though the curses continue to hit the land, God's chosen people continue to be victorious in the backsliding.

ANSWER QUESTIONS FOR VERSES 4-7

B-1: The curses, outlined in the contract, are very successful in carrying out their assigned mission but something has a power over God's people that the curses cannot defeat. What are the people holding on to?

B-2: A foreign power has taken over in Jerusalem. The strange power proves its victory to God when He hears what His people are saying and He sees what they are doing. They run wild with lies in their mouths. God finally finds a creature to compare His people to. What animal is God reminded of when He sees His people?

B-3: This wild war horse has bucked, kicked, and bitten God every time that He was able to get a little bit close. There was only one chance left of breaking this wild horse and get it to see the truth. And that was to get her in a coral. Once she was trapped inside (and Jerusalem serves as the corral) He will do everything that He can to apply the restraints.

I have read that once a wild horse is in the coral, the horse trainer will use a noisemaker to keep the horse's attention (on something other than the new head-dress that he must place on the horses head in order to get her used to the reigns). Jerusalem is the coral and Jeremiah is the noisemaker. The people hear the sound but they still buck and kick at the unnatural headdress. The noise is not working. They will continue to head straight into battle with a battle plan that was haphazardly constructed; and their battle weapon does not possess the power that they profusely believe. God is not truly with them.

Storks, turtle doves, swallows, and cranes all follow certain paths that they instinctively know. They know when to go and where to go. They know their place and fulfill their purpose on the earth and in the air. As monogamous pairs, they prepare for a new birth in a new season. Together the male and female take part in the birthing process and defending the territory of the newborn. They observe and follow their ways of preservation. But those who inhabit Jerusalem continue to stray from their predestined path. Jerusalem continually feeds her own destruction. What do the actions of the people in Jerusalem reveal? (See last part of verse 7.)

B-4: Have you ever watched a western show where cowboys are trying to break a wild horse? And when I say 'break', I don't mean breaking the horse's neck, legs, or back but it is conditioning the horse to accept the human as the dominant side in the relationship. And the wild horse in this chapter (the people in Jerusalem) will not be broken or allow God to be the one on the dominant side of this struggling relationship.

As I stated in the last question; trainers use noise to distract their horses. As the horse is distracted by a constant noise, the trainer keeps adding burdens to the horse. At first the burdens are light. First it may be part of the reign, then a blanket, then something else, and then more. And all of the time that the horse is distracted by the noise, the trainer keeps dressing the horse with the hope of riding. Finally after much hard work and a lot of noise, the horse is fully equipped and ready for the big burden, and that is, the one who rides and controls the reigns.

God has certainly been making noise for these people. The words from Jeremiah's mouth are like trumpets of warning as His words continue to come true. But the people seem to continually turn to the noise of something else. They will not be fully equipped with God's giddy-up gear. God is continually struggling and fighting to keep these people from destroying themselves (spiritually and physically). Different noises are fighting for your attention too. What noise do you most often follow or listen to and is it leading you (and those who follow you) to destruction?

B-5 (OPTIONAL QUESTION): Have you ever experienced a burden (duty or responsibility) that turned into a great blessing?

📖READ JEREMIAH 8:8

C. ADDITIONAL COMMENTS FOR VERSE 8

The war horses still run wildly around the corral as if they are ready to go into battle. The war cry from the wild herd is: "We are wise and the law of the Lord is with us! We are wise and the law of the Lord is with us!"

ANSWER QUESTIONS FOR VERSE 8

C-1: Even though those in charge of the written law continued to write and rewrite the laws on lifeless paper; their pen did not possess the power to transfer the law into the lives of the citizens. The words from the wet ink were useless once they were permanently dried. The words that should have been living in the hearts of the people were rolled up and put on a shelf while some other law was being inscribed on the hearts of God's people, instituted in His towns, and then called His law.

Do you proclaim to be living by some code of conduct? If some stranger from a distant land visited you and looked at your life and then looked at a written copy of your law or code of conduct, would they say: "There is a mistake in what is written here; in fact this paper tells lies" or would your life line up with what was written? There is outstanding historical evidence that your life, and the way you live it, speaks louder than any written word. Your life (at this time) has more power to create change in, and throughout, this world than what is written. Written words have no power unless you pick them up and give them power.

Here is a silly thought just to make a point: God walks in the courtroom and takes His place on the Judges seat. When He opens the book of the law, it is really you. Your life is opened in front of Him and He will use your life and your ways as the true and lawful benchmark that measures the defendant. He looks up from the law book (you) to addresses the defendant. The defendant is His word! (The roles are reversed.) If God used your day-to-day life to judge the His Word, what would happen? Would His word have to be charged with breaking the law (you)? Does your ways and God's ways look similar?

C-2 (OPTIONAL QUESTION): How many times can something be broken and continue to be useful? (Think of a cup, a car, a heart, or the law in Israel.)

📖**READ JEREMIAH 8:9-12**

D. ADDITIONAL COMMENTS FOR VERSES 9-12

The wise will be put to shame because they have rejected the word of the Lord.

ANSWER QUESTIONS FOR VERSES 9-12

D-1: Though Solomon had the reputation of being a wise king not all kings were wise, nor was wisdom a requirement for one who was a king. They usually received the crown because they were sons of the previous king or great warriors. What do leaders do when something is too difficult for them to figure out? (See selected verses below for answers.)

(Esther 1:13 NRSV): Then the king consulted the sages who knew the laws (for this was the king's procedure toward all who were versed in law and custom.)

(2Kings 3:10-11 NRSV): Then the king of Israel said, "Alas! The Lord has summoned us, three kings, only to be handed over to Moab." But Jehoshaphat said, "Is there no prophet of the Lord here, through whom we may inquire of the Lord?" Then one of the servants of the king of Israel answered, "Elisha son of Shaphat, who used to pour water on the hands of Elijah, is here."

(Genesis 41:8 NRSV): In the morning his spirit was troubled; so he sent and called for all the magicians of Egypt and all its wise men. Pharaoh told them his dreams, but there was no one who could interpret them to Pharaoh.

D-2: Back in Jeremiah 6:13-15, God outlined the problems that He had concerning His leaders. He let them know that due to this list of problems, the people in the land would suffer. So now here in Jeremiah 8:10-12, God returns. He has to outline the same problems again; nothing has changed and the list has not gotten any shorter and the people in the land still suffer. But this time when God confronts them with the to-do-list (that has not been touched) the fine that must be paid is different. Something of great value to the leaders will be taken away. What is it? (See verse 8-10.)

D-3: More steps will be taken to create change in Jerusalem. God is going to take the advice that we find in Proverbs 25:4-5. This next step will affect the leaders in a personal way. What is going to happen?

D-4: Israel was like an onion and God started peeling away the outer layers in order to get to the core (the leaders, the bone). After a lot of painful peeling, this suffering is going to hit a little closer to home. Hopefully, this time, the hearts of *the leaders* will feel-the-peeling as God takes yet one more layer.

This 'onion peeling' process may be the routine procedure that God follows when it comes to knowing and proving what is truly inside the human heart. Read the first two chapters of Job. Where did the peeling process for Job, start and then eventually lead?

D-5: Being one of *God's chosen leaders* as well as being human cannot be easy. There does seem to be evidence that God has a process in order to get to the core. Turn to Numbers chapter 12. How did God get to (touch) the heart of the priest in this chapter?

D-6: Turn to 1Chronicles chapter 21. How did God get to the heart of the king?

D-7: God compared *His* people to well-fed lusty stallions back in Jeremiah 5:7. In this chapter, in verse 6, He compares *His* people to a horse plunging head long into battle. Look ahead to verse 16 in this chapter. God speaks of snorting horses and neighing stallions. Who may be the real culprits devouring the land?

D-8: If these chosen leaders of Jerusalem are dangerous and out-of-control war horses, we may need to define them further. Turn back to Jeremiah 2:30 and 4:7. What words in those verses indicate that they may also be enemies of God?

D-9 (OPTIONAL QUESTION): Take another look at Genesis 49:9-10. Write the words on your own paper. Look up the words that you do not understand.

D-10: Before I start lowering my chin, showing my forehead and looking out over my rimmed glasses at those who have sat in leadership positions in Jerusalem, I thought I should look at this from a different perspective. God said that from the least to the greatest, they were greedy for unjust gain. Can God still say that today about me; I who claim to be one of His own sheep? I have gained life by the death of another, His son. That gain is unjust, but I still take it instead of demanding that He take the air that I breathe...and I cry peace, peace!

God said they deal falsely. Can God still say that today about me; I who claim to be one of His own sheep? I open my hand and take all His love and proclaim: 'I have peace, peace' and in turn give Him my polluted heart? I'm afraid I try (too often) to make God think that He got a good deal with that trade.

I too, who claim to be one of His own, can only be proven to be greedy for unjust gain and just taking lots of things that I don't deserve, I've acted shamefully, committing the very acts that God hates in order to save my own skin.

If I am among these that God speaks of, what should rightly happen to me according the word in the last part of verse 12?

📖READ JEREMIAH 8:13-15

E. ADDITIONAL COMMENTS FOR VERSES 13-15

When God speaks, you would think that He would draw great crowds. You would think that He would have the reputation of being the best 'how to' author concerning the earth. Since He is its creator He would be the authority on what it holds, how to control it and where to find any hidden treasures. God has scheduled many rallies (that come by way of His servants the prophets) for *His people*. He wanted them to know 'how to' achieve real peace but like always when He shows up (through the words spoken by His prophets), at these rallies to speak, no one is really there. What He finds is an empty auditorium. He says it like this: 'There were no grapes on the vine nor figs on the trees and the leaves are withered'.

ANSWER QUESTIONS FOR VERSES 13-15

E-1: Though they claimed to have it back in Jeremiah 6:14, what do they look for now that they are facing death? (See verse 15.)

E-2: The people continue to be blinded by their own words of deceit even as they consider death. They cannot quit speaking lies which are composed of personal feelings and human will. That which fills the heart pours out the mouth like a fountain. Their words of consolation and regret hold deceit. They start out with: "Why do we sit still?" They deceive themselves when they say these words. Why? What is going on in the following verses?

(Jeremiah 1:16 NRSV): …they have made offerings to other gods, and worshipped the works of their own hands.

(Jeremiah 2:13 NRSV): …and dug out cisterns for themselves, cracked cisterns that can hold no water.

(Jeremiah 2:27 NRSV): …who say to a tree, "You are my father," and to a stone, "You gave me birth," For they have turned their backs to me…

(Jeremiah 2:33 NRSV): …even to wicked women you have taught your ways.

(Jeremiah 3:6 NRSV): She went up on every high hill and under every green tree, and played….

E-3: What would be the truthful picture if they were sitting still? (See the following verses.)

(Jeremiah 4:8 NRSV): Because of this put on sackcloth, lament and wail: ….

(Jeremiah 6:26 NRSV): Oh my poor people, put on sackcloth, and roll in ashes; make mourning as for an only child, most bitter lamentation…

E-4: They continue deceiving themselves with the words they speak. In verse 14 they say: "the Lord our God has doomed us to perish." Why are those words out of line? (See Jeremiah 4:18.)

E-5: The lies in verse 14 continue: "God… has given us poisoned water to drink." Why is that slander? (See the following verses.)

(Jeremiah 2:13 NRSV): …and dug out cisterns for themselves…

(Jeremiah 2:17-18 NRSV): Have you not brought this upon yourself by forsaking the Lord your God, while he led you in the way? What then do you gain by going to Egypt, to drink waters of the Nile? Or what do you gain by going to Assyria, to drink the waters of the Euphrates?

E-6: In the last part of verse 14, they say: "because we have sinned against the Lord" (infringed upon the rights of the Lord). Who are they really sinning against (infringing upon) with all of their unlawful acts? (See Jeremiah 7:19.)

E-7: The deceitful words, that they believe, continue: We look for peace, but find no good, for a time of healing, but there is terror instead (Jeremiah 8:15 NRSV). Why would God just consider this whole statement nothing but 'a lot of hot air'? (See Jeremiah 6:16-17.)

E-8: (OPTIONAL QUESTION): When God looked, He saw that there were no grapes on the vine and no figs on the trees and the leaves were all withered, He made a statement. He said: "what I gave them has passed away from them". What gift from God had expired from this generation (according to the evidence in front of Him)?

E-9: I compare Judah to a terminally ill patient with a chronic disease. Sometimes chronic illnesses go into remission (or are brought under submission and controlled) if caught early enough and treated. But this illness that has a hold on Jerusalem has not been brought under submission. It has eaten up all of her vital organs. They (the vital organs) cannot function and keep the body alive. She can't hear. She speaks delusional thoughts and her heart (Jerusalem) is about to have a massive attack. She will become nothing but brittle bones as the disease takes over and destroys her. She is in pain. The only relief available, for her, is brought by death.

The leaders failed to promote what was needed for a good healthy life and now, as many victims discovered too late, they do not have the 'peace, peace' that was being proclaimed. How will the last measure of their lives be spent?

E-10: How do we know that *'at that time'* is now very near for these people? What are they going to do (in verse 14) that will begin the fulfillment of the bizarre revelation from verses 1-3 in this eighth chapter?

READ JEREMIAH 8:16-17

F. ADDITIONAL COMMENTS FOR VERSES 16-17

The snorting of their horses is heard from Dan; at the sound of the neighing of their stallions the whole land quakes... (Jeremiah 8:16)

ANSWER QUESTIONS FOR VERSES 16-17

F-1: As already stated back in chapter 4, Dan was the rear-guard for the military in the days of Moses. Back in Jeremiah 4:15, the warning voice could (spiritually) be heard from the rear.

(The rear-guard usually incurs heavy casualties due to their military position which was to act as a defense between the main body and the enemy). But at this point, it is not warning-voices that are coming from Dan's position. The voice of Dan is silent, which is a bad sign. What is heard from the rear-guard position instead of Dan's voice?

F-2: God cannot stop the beastly covenant that His people continue to feed but God does offer a place of safety for those who are willing to confess and face the Truth. But getting there, to surrender, will not be easy as there are wars and rumors of wars everywhere.

- The covenant, by way of curses, is at war with God's people while…
- God's people are at war with God (the Word) while…
- God is at war with the lion-in-the-thicket while…
- the lion-in-the-thicket is at war with those who he has not come in control of while…
- many earthly kings are coming and going. They are at war, hungry for power and control.

It will take open ears, open eyes, and open heart to survive the journey to the safe place that God provides. Even if God's people are running to Zion (the city of refuge) the scheme of the land remains the same. God is even gracious to the indecisive in times of war. He warns the world of the dangers that He imposes in these uncertain times:

SEE

I AM LETTING SNAKES LOOSE AMONG YOU

ADDERS THAT CANNOT BE CHARMED

AND THEY SHALL BITE YOU

In what form might the snakes and adders show themselves? (See the following verses.)

(Jeremiah 29:17-19 NRSV): Thus says the Lord of hosts, I am going to let loose on them sword, famine, and pestilence, and I will make them like rotten figs that are so bad they cannot be eaten. I will pursue them with the sword, with famine, and with pestilence, and will make them a horror to all the kingdoms of the earth, to be an object of cursing, and horror, and hissing, and a derision among all the nations where I have driven them, because they did not heed my words, says the Lord, when I persistently sent to you my servants the prophets, but they would not listen, says the Lord.

F-3: Back in C-2 it was stated that God's people were at war with God. What is a continual war strategy used by this brigade of enemies? (See the following verses.)

(Matthew 23:29-37 NRSV): "Woe to you, scribes and Pharisees, hypocrites! … You snakes, you brood of vipers! How can you escape being sentenced to hell? Therefore I send you prophets, sages, and scribes, some of whom you will kill and crucify, and some you will flog in your synagogues and pursue from town to town, so that upon you may come all the righteous blood shed on earth,… "Jerusalem, Jerusalem, the city that kills the prophets and stones those who are sent to it!"

F-4: God not only reveals the dangers that He imposes during the war but He offers hope for those who seek Him. See the following verses. Can you find words of consolation concerning the snakes that have been loosed?

(Mark 16:17-18 NRSV): "And these signs will accompany those who believe: by using my name they will cast out demons; they will speak in new tongues; they will pick up snakes in their hands, and if they drink any deadly thing, it will not hurt them; they will lay their hands on the sick, and they will recover."

F-5: Can you find words of consolation in those same verses, Mark 16:17-18, for the poisoned water that the people speak of in Jeremiah 8:14?

F-6: Can you find words of comfort in Mark 16:17-18 concerning the destructive nation (spoken of in Jeremiah 5:15) whose language cannot be understood?

F-7: Can you find words of comfort in Mark 16:17-18 concerning the lion-in-the-thicket (the evil seed that has taken root and lives in the heart)?

F-8: God's people should have known it all too well. God's word is like a two edged sword. The very thing that God's people were to serve and love could hurt them if they did not follow 'instructions for handling'. In 2Samuel 6:1-11, David gathered all the *chosen men* of Israel for a task. Though assembly of the ark was correct, handling was not. What happened?

READ JEREMIAH 8:18-21

G. ADDITIONAL COMMENTS FOR VERSES 18-21

The biggest battle is of the spiritual kind. Some of God's people are lost in the deep spiritual jungles. Some are wandering in the spiritual desert. Some are spiritually drowning. You will find them everywhere and most are ill-equipped for the battle of their lives as they are scattered throughout the earth full of danger.

ANSWER QUESTIONS FOR VERSES 18-21

G -1: What is the cry of *God's* people far and wide?

G-2: God gave warning that He was going to leave if the people did not change their ways. He gave the warning back in Jeremiah 7. Those who heard the words of warning, in that chapter, should have taken some action to prevent the ugly outcome. The social conditions may have been horrific in Judah but it seems that, according to Jeremiah 7:2, the obedience of *His worshippers* would have kept God at, or in, the place He desires to call home. Who, in this study, has been established as the worshippers at the tabernacle, chosen and called by God? (See Numbers 3:5-45 and 1Chronicles 6.)

G-3: God exists as, and is, 'Word'. But if His body is like the human body, it is made up of many parts. Though God's body is made up of elements unseen, He must have many different elements. The covenant (referred to as the contract in this study) is just one part of those many elements.

Have you ever heard someone say: "I am torn"? This feeling might arise because someone has more than one obligation to fulfill in their life. God might be a lot like that. He is obligated to the covenant (part of His own body), He is obligated to His imprisoned offspring (part of His own body), and He also has obligations to the children of Israel (part of His body by joint covenant). What is that question that comes from the body that must be, what we would call, torn? (See the third question in verse 19.)

G-4: What have they done! It seems that they have done *everything* possible. The leaders must have been very busy. They have been searching far and wide for help as well as making sacrifices day and night at the temple. They seem to be surprised because all of their works have not been noticed and the destruction that gets closer and closer is not being diverted. Their efforts have changed nothing. What do they say? (See verse 20.)

G-5: As God hears all the forms of hurt what does He do and what does He feel? (See verse 21.)

📖 READ JEREMIAH 8:22

H. ADDITIONAL COMMENTS FOR VERSE 22

Gilead became famous because of some of its exported products. Balm was one of the exports that put their town on the map (so to speak) because of its healing properties and medicinal use. Verse 22 insinuates that the people, who were looking for peace, went to the most reputable medicinal facility in the land but still found nothing to alleviate the suffering and pain that terror, which was spreading throughout all of the land, was bringing.

ANSWER QUESTIONS FOR VERSE 22

H-1: God asks, those whom He has loved, prodding questions. He asks three questions with a tear of concern rolling down His cheek. But He is speaking to those who have deep feelings for other gods while He (the only God) is not in their hearts. What are the questions that should make *the leaders* wake up and see that the answer to all of their problems is right in front of them?

H-2: Here is a shortened version of the Ten Commandments. Even though there are about 613 commands altogether, these were the ones written in stone and given to God's people. Check the ones that have been broken in the first eight chapters of Jeremiah.

➤ 1 You shall have no other gods before me.

➤ 2 You shall not make for yourself any idols.

➤ 3 You shall not wrongfully use the name of the Lord your God.

➤ 4 Remember the Sabbath Day and keep it holy.

➤ 5 Honor your father and mother.

➤ 6 You shall not murder.

➤ 7 You shall not commit adultery.

➤ 8 You shall not steal.

➤ 9 You shall not bear false witness against your neighbor.

➤ 10 You shall not covet anything that belongs to your neighbor.

H-3: Has Jeremiah planted any seeds or torn down any strongholds in your life?

Chapter 8 Tag-A-Long

The Trade-in

God walked through His house and like always, no one was there but the place was a mess. I guess His bride has taken off again and who knows when she will be back this time? But when she does return, you can be sure she will not be able to walk in empty handed. She will have a bull or a goat or some innocent animal at the other end of her hanging rope. Today she offered the sacrifice for her sin but even as she was cutting the throat of the innocent animal, she could not wait until she could go and commit her evil acts again. She did not shed a tear over the blood flow. And all of the innocent blood in the world would not cause her to change. Her heart was calloused and their (her and God's) life together was nothing but total chaos.

This had to stop so God started to clean up the mess Himself. He goes through the house with a broom and gets a big empty box. It's time that He just packs up everything that He gave her. All the riches He has given her mean nothing. If it isn't dusty or grungy, it's broken. A lot of things are even missing, completely gone! Ah! There's something that she broke, thrown over there in the corner. God picks it up and knows that it was just another 'stupid law' to her.

So God gathers up all of these unappreciated and abused treasures. As He swept, He wept. He wrapped all of the precious items into one perfect package. When He was done, He simply wrote 'sacrifice' on the front of the box. There, in front of Him, altogether in one place, was everything that would have made their union perfect. To Him it was precious, to her, it was trash. The riches in the goodwill package will be given freely for whoever wants it.

As He carries the box out of the place that He and the bride were to share, He comes up with an idea. He thinks there is one more thing that might bring her back. He often dreamed of the day that He could sweep her off her feet and this idea just might work. Even though He was not materialistic God was willing to trade the precious box in for something different… a new set of wheels, a shiny new ride would be the answer for His material girl! That might catch her eye when she sees Him driving around town, sitting inside of a new vehicle! It would be just 'perfect'.

But her ways come back to His mind and He imagines Himself inside of the new set of wheels. He drives slowly, with the passenger's window down, pleading with the lost bride, who is walking by the roadside. He calls out to her. "Come on honey, hop in, let's go home", but He knows she won't get in. She'll just shake her head 'no' as she prefers to walk down the long and rocky road.

The new set of wheels didn't turn her head. The make and model of the expensive vehicle, the new Jesus LS, was not appealing to her. She definitely does not like the way the body is built, it looks too much like a car that only foreigners could appreciate. "Come on Izzy, (that's what He used to call her when she was faithful and whole) I traded everything in, that was ours, for this. You may not like it but it is your only way back home."

✄ Scrapbook Page For Chapter 8

Prodigy

God wanted her to wear His wedding ring and talk highly of Him. He called her holy. She would be greatly adorned and blessed for being His faithful bride. She would be beautiful and He would make her famous. She would be renowned in all the earth. All people would see her crown of wisdom, knowledge, mercy, and grace that her God gave her. The whole world would know that there was no other God in the heavens like Him. God promised her all of that and He put it in writing in a covenant. As the covenanter, God was bound to perform the duties expressed in the covenant. She would never have to doubt His devotion to her. She would never, as the covenant-ee, ever have to look at Him in a suspicious way.

But at this point in the relationship, being the covenanter was not a happy place to be. God's obligations, as outlined in the covenant, take a turn for the worse; because, she didn't wear anything that identified her as God's bride. She told lies about Him and gave Him no respect. She was unrighteous and disobedient. And the worst part of it all, she cheated on Him. God warned her in every generation but she just got worse.

In reading, I imagine that God was at war with Himself. From a human point of view, His emotions must have been going crazy! I suspect, there were many times, that He did not want to do what He was obligated, by law, to do. He kept warning her to come back. He chased after her, ferociously, and this was for her own good, because at this point she probably looked pretty disgusting to the Lord. In Jeremiah 6:8, God goes straight to the top (again) and addresses the backbone of Judah. He confronts the 'big wigs' in the capitol and He says: Take warning O Jerusalem or I will turn from you in disgust.

I would imagine that God hoped He would never have to go to this particular clause in the binding agreement. Deuteronomy 28:45-46: All these curses shall come upon you, pursuing and overtaking you until you are destroyed, because you did not obey the Lord your God, by observing the commandments and the decrees that he commanded you. They shall be among you and your descendants as a sign and a portent forever.

This above text may *sound like* a decree from a bitter divorce settlement. It *sounds as if* the legal order will be forever present, requiring an eternal alimony payment for the scandalous acts of God's (now) ex-bride. It's *as if* she will never be free and *as if* all generations will remember her and be burdened by her infidelities. But if you focus in, you will see something else that sheds a different light on this tattered relationship. Something inside those very words ('They, the curses, shall be among you and your descendant as a sign and a portent forever') offers hope to make this odd relationship work.

It seems that God, by way of the cross, re-evaluated the properties, attributes, and the very essence of Israel. (Colossians 2:14-17) He made a public example of those things and nailed them to the cross. Someday God's bride will look at Jesus and know that He became the curses and rose to be the *portent* forever. When she looks at what is 'forever present', she will think of mercy and she will be glad. The curses will surely be among her and all of her descendants as a sign and a portent forever!

Compare Answers For Chapter 8

A-1: when King Nebuchadnezzar comes to besiege the city of Jerusalem

A-2: there is no bread left in the city

A-3: the walled Jerusalem

A-4: The Lord will scatter you among all peoples, from one end of the earth to the other; and there you shall serve other gods, of wood and stone, which neither you nor your ancestors have known (Deuteronomy 28:64 NRSV).

A-5: It seems that burning bones over a space defiled the space on which they were burnt.

A-6: the whole earth from one end to the other

A-7 (OPTIONAL QUESTION): holocaust-a sacrifice consumed by fire; a thorough destruction especially by fire

A-8: They shall be like dung on the surface of the ground.

A-9: death will be preferred to life

A-10: remnant

A-11 (OPTIONAL QUESTION): In both sets of selected verses the people seek death but cannot find it. They will long to die but death will flee from them.

A-12: the king, the king's mother, the king's wives, his officials, the elite of the land, all the men of valor (7,000), the artisans and smiths (1,000), verse 14 says there were 10,000 captives.

A-13: the poor

A-14: essence; core; the most deeply ingrained part; heart; the basic design or framework

B-1: deceit

B-2: a horse plunging headlong into battle

B-3: God's people do not know the ordinance of the Lord

B-4: There is a lot of noise that fights for my attention; the radio, the TV, listening to (and adding to) idle talk and my own idle thoughts in my head, I had to ask myself who is winning the 'battle of the saddle'? I must admit, I try to do better now that I am aware of my circumstances (I am not the leader of my own life; that which drives me is). I am aware that there are a lot of noises that fight for my attention. Maybe I should start stopping myself, from all of my business, during the day and night and look to see who is in the saddle.

B-5 (OPTIONAL QUESTION): the responsibilities of home, family, and workplace could, at times fall under this category of burdensome, as well as the responsibility of living righteously but at some point it is recognized as joy

C-1: His Word would be guilty of not living (down) to my standards. The pen that wrote the word would have to be proclaimed 'a lie' if I was the (low) bar that it had to match.

C-2 (OPTIONAL QUESTION): There seems to always come a time when it must be replaced or it dies or it has so much glue and tape that it's useless and collects dust.

D-1: call on those wise men having a reputation for knowing what to do

D-2: The wise, they will be put to shame, they will be dismayed and taken, their wives will be given to others, and their fields will go to conquerors.

D-3: Take away the dross from the silver, and the smith has material for a vessel; take away the wicked from the presence of the king, and his throne will be established in righteousness (Proverbs 25:4-5 NRSV).

D-4: It started with peeling away his family and possessions and then it hit him personally. As I continued reading, he also loses the respect and honor due him from his wife and that place of honor where his friends once placed him.

D-5: God afflicted someone else who was near and dear to the heart.

D-6: God afflicted the people that David cared for and watched over.

D-7: *God's leaders*

D-8: ravening lion, lion gone up from his thicket

D-9 (OPTIONAL QUESTION): Judah is a lion's whelp; from the prey, my son, you have gone up. He crouches down, he stretches out like a lion, like a lioness— who dares rouse him up? The scepter shall not depart from Judah, nor the ruler's staff from between his feet, until tribute comes to him; and the obedience of the peoples is his (Genesis 49:9-10 NRSV).

D-10: I should be punished.

E-1: peace

E-2: They run to other gods and idols and then teach others the same.

E-3: put on sackcloth, roll in ashes, mourn, lament and wail

E-4: They doomed themselves.

E-5: They dug out their own wells and drank from foreign pools

E-6: They sin against themselves and their future generations.

E-7: God told them how and where to find peace (rest for their souls) but they did not listen to Him or follow His instructions.

E-8 (OPTIONAL QUESTION): They lost peace (which comes from knowing God). They were like plants and trees whose fruit was being eaten alive by blight. The plants and trees were suffering and dying a painful death through continual blight.

E-9: in terror

E-10: They are making plans to go to the fortified cities which serve as the tombs that they will be brought out of.

F-1: The snorting of horses and the neighing of stallions

F-2: could be in the form of curses

F-3: they kill God's instruction by killing the one who brings it

F-4: The snakes can be picked up

F-5: and if they drink any deadly thing it will not hurt them

F-6: they will speak in new tongues

F-7: they will cast out demons

F-8: Someone was struck dead

G-1: Is the Lord not in Zion? Is her King not in her?"

G-2: Levi

G-3: (Jeremiah 8:19 NRSV)...("Why have they provoked me to anger with their images, with their foreign idols?")

G-4: "The harvest is past, the summer is ended, and we are not saved" (Jeremiah 8:20 NRSV).

G-5: ....I am hurt, I mourn, and dismay has taken hold of me" (Jeremiah 8:21 NRSV).

H-1: Is there no balm in Gilead? Is there no physician there? Why then has the health of my poor people not been restored?

H-2: This is a running list from the previous chapter.

Number 1: You shall have no other gods before me (broken law according to Jeremiah 1:16)

Number 2: You shall not make for yourself an idol (broken law according to Jeremiah 1:16)

Number 5: Honor your father and mother (broken law according to Jeremiah 2:27)

Number 6: You shall not murder (broken law according to Jeremiah 2:30b and 34)

Number 4: Remember the Sabbath day and keep it holy (broken law according to Jeremiah 2:32)

Number 7: You shall not commit adultery (broken law according to Jeremiah 3:6)

Number 3: You shall not make wrongful use of my name (broken law according to Jeremiah 5:2)

Number 10: You shall not covet anything that belongs to your neighbor (broken, see Jeremiah 5:8)

Number 8: You shall not steal (broken law according to Jeremiah 7:11)

H-3: Jeremiah has planted a thought that causes fear and humility. If I am like His people in Jerusalem, it is possible for me to go boldly into the face of death believing that I will be saved. I must open my eyes wider and listen harder for messages from the Lord.

Chapter 9

Chapter 9 Prelude

Tell the Truth

When you tell a hungry, and in-need, neighbor that you have no bread to give but there are really three loaves in your cupboard, you told a lie. When one of your relatives says "I am behind you one hundred percent" but anxiously waits for the day that you fall flat on your face, your relative lied to you. When someone has a horse for sale and classifies it as 'a mighty fine horse' while knowing the horse is sick, that someone told a lie. Although God's people are credited here in this chapter for telling lies, I don't believe that these are the kinds of lies that brought them to their fall. This is what God says: They all deceive their neighbors, and no one speaks the truth; they have taught their tongues to speak lies; …They refuse to know me…. (Jeremiah 9:5-6 NRSV).

When you hear these words: "…speak the truth to one another…" (Zechariah 8:16 NRSV), how do you interpret that? What exactly will you have to do in order to follow through? First of all don't let all of your personal, embarrassing, and hidden secrets stop you from taking that step. This command has little to do with placing yourself under a microscope and it is not a command that permits you to place anyone else there either. Speaking the truth to one another has a bigger and more powerful subject behind it than you, me, or your neighbor. And that bigger subject is God.

There were lies going around about God. When the people of Judah heard all of the lies, they believed what they heard and passed it on. And why wouldn't they? Most of the untruths were coming from their leaders. Jeremiah seems to be the only one intercepting and interrupting the deceitful words that were being passed off as the truth. Here are some of the lies that God lived with due to His people:

- "He will do nothing. No evil will come upon us, and we shall not see sword or famine" (Jeremiah 5:12 NRSV). In saying this, they may be trying to present themselves as righteous and blameless in God's sight. Or on the other hand, they may be trying to present God as inattentive.
- …"Peace! Peace! … (Jeremiah 8:11 NRSV) was another deep-seated lie even though God warned them that these were not times of peace.
- …"We are free"… (Jeremiah 2:31 NRSV). These words remained upon their lips

while the working curses of the covenant continued to prove that proclamation of independence and freedom to be false.

- Last though no-way least on this list, two of the biggest lies were told when they said to trees: …"You are my father," and to a stone: "You gave me birth"… (Jeremiah 2:27 NRSV).

The lies prevailed in Judah. One person told two people the lie. Those two repeated it by telling two. And those two told two. It went on and on until it came back around and started again. The repetition gave the lies strength. The lies became dominant forces in the minds and hearts of the people. The standing lies brought a false hope into the lives of God's people.

Chapter 9 Study

There Goes the Neighborhood

CHAPTER 9 READING, COMMENTS, AND QUESTIONS

📖 **READ JEREMIAH 9:1-2**

A. ADDITIONAL COMMENTS FOR VERSES 1-2

The cries of God's people are heard from far and wide and God mourns over their suffering; but the top leaders, who still feel safe behind the walls of Jerusalem, do not mourn. Levi, the lower echelon of leadership (those who have already fulfilled their scheduled and appointed duties at the temple, see 1Chronicles 23:6 and 27:1) can be found far and wide among those who cry.

ANSWER QUESTIONS FOR VERSES 1-2

A-1: We know, by God's comments, that the number of *God's people* being slain throughout the land is remarkable in magnitude and never halting. God describes His degree of mourning through an analogy. What is the analogy?

A-2: As the cries were coming from far and wide, God must have heard many familiar voices. They were familiar voices because they had inhabited Jerusalem, time and time again, serving in and around the temple that housed His name, even guarding it. As God hears the distressed voices that were once joyful, He thinks of 'what could have been'… There was one group of Israel's children that God was partial to. They were closer, than all of the rest. What group might God be most distraught over?

A-3: When someone that you love, more than yourself, is dying; you experience a pain that cannot be described. You can speak no words, only a deep moaning from your soul escapes. The grief that you feel is even greater when you hear the dying loved one say: *"It would have been better*, if I would have never been born." Maybe God heard those words coming from *His suffering chosen people*.

At this point, it sounds like the Lord is exhausted. It must be painful, especially from His all-knowing view that misses nothing, to see all of the non-stop wickedness, violence, destruction, sickness, death, and pain. He has supported all acts of the law. Justice was, and is being, served; and correction (for the purpose of reform) administered. But there is a big problem, the administration of justice was not bringing reform. God must be wondering if this mess can ever be fixed.

When I read God's words: O that my head were a spring of water, and my eyes a fountain of tears, so that I might weep day and night for the slain of my poor people! (Jeremiah 9:1 NRSV), I wondered if He was having a flashback and if He had any regrets about Genesis 6. *Would it have been better* if He would not have spoken to Noah at all? Maybe He should have let the springs (from His head) and fountains (from His tears) claim everything the last time…..

(Genesis 6:5-6 NRSV): The Lord saw that the wickedness of humankind was great in the earth, and that every inclination of the thoughts of their hearts was only evil continually. And the Lord was sorry that he had made humankind on the earth, and it grieved him to his heart.

There was a great cleansing in Genesis 6 but we do not call it a cleansing. What do we call it?

A-4: May my teaching drop like the rain, my speech condense like the dew; like gentle rain on grass, like showers on new growth (Deuteronomy 32:2 NRSV). That was the gentle cleansing. But there was a problem with this form of cleansing. What was it? (See the following verses.)

(Matthew 23:25-28 NRSV): "Woe to you, scribes and Pharisees, hypocrites! For you clean the outside of the cup and of the plate, but inside they are full of greed and self-indulgence. You blind Pharisee! First clean the inside of the cup, so that the outside also may become clean. "Woe to you, scribes and Pharisees, hypocrites! For you are like whitewashed tombs, which on the outside look beautiful, but inside they are full of the bones of the dead and of all kinds of filth. So you also on the outside look righteous to others, but inside you are full of hypocrisy and lawlessness.

A-5: Even though cleansed, to a sparkling clean, on the outside *God's people* have continually refused to give Him any room on the inside. So they were warned of a change in the weather pattern. What does Jeremiah 4:11-14 say.

A-6: It seems that God wants to take a break from this relationship that is only skin deep. If He could remove Himself for a just while, it would give Him, as well as His loved one(s), a break from all the pain. But the covenant does not allow Him to walk out when things get tough. He is bound by contractual agreement. A payment of one type or another must be delivered. Both parties entered into this legal and binding agreement back in the days of desert-living. He must stand by His legal word in good times and in bad times. What brought the good times for the, now, unhappy pair according to the following verse?

Deuteronomy 28:1 (NRSV): If you will only obey the Lord your God, by diligently observing all his commandments that I am commanding you today, the Lord your God will set you high above all the nations of the earth.

A-7: What brought the bad times according to the following verse?

(Deuteronomy 28:15 NRSV): But if you will not obey the Lord your God by diligently observing all his commandments and decrees, which I am commanding you today, then all these curses shall come upon you and overtake you.

A-8: God calls *His people* adulterers. Why does He call them adulterers? (See verses below.)

(Jeremiah 3:6-9 NRSV): …Have you seen what she did, the faithless one, Israel, how she went up on every high hill and under every green tree, and played the whore there? And I thought, "After she had done all this she will return to me"; but she did not return, and her false sister Judah saw it. She saw that for all the adulteries of that faithless one, Israel, I had sent her away with a decree of divorce; yet her false sister Judah did not fear, but she too went and played the whore. Because she took her whoredom so lightly, she polluted the land, committing adultery with stone and tree.

A-9: God also calls *His people* a *band* of traitors. A *band* is a group of persons joined together to serve a purpose. Who do you think is in this *band*?

📖READ JEREMIAH 9:3

B. ADDITIONAL COMMENTS FOR VERSE 3

There is proof. His people do not know Him. He does not live in their hearts.

ANSWER QUESTIONS FOR VERSE 3

B-1: Why won't the contention in Jerusalem stop? God's chosen leaders are God's contenders. They are like boxers and each will take a turn inside the ring with God. They all practice their punches in the air as they wait in line. Even though everyone who comes into the ring must be carried out, no one backs down. The lame and broken are all around, outside the ring. As they call for someone to attend to their injuries, they do not know that their only help comes from the One that they are busy fighting against. And as for those still in line, they see the condition of the others who have been inside the ring but continue to stand, planted firmly, in line.

"Just stop fighting against me and I will help you!" But the people cannot see the real Truth and they cannot hear the real Truth. They are deaf and blind, full of false wisdom that guides them. They do not know Him, the One on whom they were commanded to found their towns and cities. They have built their towns and cities (hearts) on lies and not on God's Truth. In what form are the punches as they are thrown at God?

B-2: What word indicates that these people (*God's people*) are moving right along, without a break, continuing on the wrong course? (See last part of verse 3.)

📖 **READ JEREMIAH 9:4-6**

C. ADDITIONAL COMMENTS FOR VERSES 4-6:

Jeremiah has been everywhere, all over God's city, but the people of Jerusalem will not listen to the message that God sends. Jeremiah went to the leaders of Jerusalem (see chapter 2). Jeremiah went to the streets of Jerusalem (see chapter 5). He went to the temple in Jerusalem (see chapter 7). No one will heed God's message that is full of warnings.

ANSWER QUESTIONS FOR VERSES 4-6

C-1: Since Jeremiah has been everywhere inside the (supposed to be) leader-city, and no one will listen to the message from God, there is only one thing for God, (the city's true Leader), to do. In order for God to maintain His reputation, the truth must be heard.

It was well publicized that Jerusalem was the city that God had chosen for His presence and His name to dwell. (His people made sure to spread that bit of information to the world.) But things are different now, what has been heard, and accepted as truth, is no longer true. Imagine Jeremiah as he goes outside the city walls. First he walks to the east side and yells out a message. Then he walks to the south side and yells out a message. He goes to the west side and north side. He yells out the same message of warning. What does God want the world to know?

C-2: What was God's plan for Jerusalem according to the following verses?

(Isaiah 1:26 NRSV): …you shall be called the city of righteousness, the faithful city.

(Jeremiah 3:17 NRSV): …Jerusalem shall be called the throne of the Lord, and all nations shall gather to it, to the presence of the Lord, in Jerusalem….

C-3: What does God say in 2Kings 23:27?

C-4: From the looks of things, at this point in time, it seems that God's plan will never come to fruition. His people are busy supplanting. What does supplant mean?

C-5: What statement reveals the vigorous energy that God's people share as they continue to plant, cultivate, and harvest deceit? (See the last part of verse 5.)

C-6: What causes weariness according to the following verse?

(Isaiah 57:10 NRSV): You grew weary from your many wanderings, but you did not say, "It is useless." You found your desire rekindled, and so you did not weaken.

C-7: The buffed words of slander and deceit that continually roll from the tongue are like runners in training. With each practice-run they grow stronger and stronger. The people believe, live by, and live on, the words that run throughout their cities. (Just as blood runs through the heart giving life so the lying words run through the cities giving life.) As the deceit and oppression continue to be what the people use to fortify their cities with, it not only proves that the people do not know the Lord (verse 3) but it proves more. What makes their problem even bigger than it already is? (See the last part of verse 6.)

📖READ JEREMIAH 9:7-9

D. ADDITIONAL COMMENTS FOR VERSES 7-9

God will refine those who have been a part of the coup d état.

ANSWER QUESTIONS FOR VERSES 7-9

D-1: What is the definition of coup d état?

D-2: God sees that *His people* have become great masters of deceit. What do they now have the capability to do?

D-3: Their acts are evil in God's sight but the people cannot accept the truth. They do not believe these words (what they call false accusations) that are coming from Jeremiah. So God has something else in mind for them. How will God try to get their attention and wake them up? (See verse 9.)

📖READ JEREMIAH 9:10-11

E. ADDITIONAL COMMENTS FOR VERSES 10-11

During the Vietnam War a toxic chemical was sprayed in enemy territory. By doing this the forested and rural battlegrounds would be defoliated, giving the embedded enemy no place to hide from US military forces. It also gave the local commoners, in that area, no other choice but to seek refuge elsewhere. This was surely a strategy of war, copy-catted, from long ago. In fact maybe it was copied right from this battle between God and the-lion-in-the-thicket.

ANSWER QUESTIONS FOR VERSES 10-11

E-1: God says: I will make Jerusalem a heap of ruins, a lair of jackals; and I will make the towns of Judah a desolation, without inhabitant (Jeremiah 9:11 NRSV). What is the only thing that God's people can do at this point as God reveals the devastation that He will leave behind? (See Jeremiah 9:10.)

E-2: God is at work. He is moving the people right where He needs them to be. They will go to the fortified cities as they run for their lives. What sound will be heard and what will those who have made it to the safety of the fortified cities say when they reach their place of refuge? (See verse 19.)

E-3: When the people run to the safe cities, what is eventually in store for them? (See Jeremiah 1:15-16.)

📖 **READ JEREMIAH 9:12-16**

F. ADDITIONAL COMMENTS FOR VERSES 12-16

The people who are (what they believe to be) safe in the capitol of Jerusalem can see the signs of destruction outside the walls but they do not understand that the devastation originated inside the walls. This is something that God's people cannot comprehend.

ANSWER QUESTIONS FOR VERSES 12-16

F-1: Is there anyone who will understand? Is there anyone who will speak understanding? After all of the current and continuous on-going disasters, surely someone in Jerusalem knows the answer to this riddle: Why is the land ruined and laid waste like a wilderness, so that no one passes through?

F-2: When I was in grade school and my class, as a whole, got a good score on a test, we were rewarded. Bringing in fun food and playing games, instead of studying, was the ideal reward for the team-achievement. How will God's people know that their class had a failing score? What will they get? (See verse 15.)

F-3: As God hands the people what their scores have earned, what will they really have to swallow and live with? (See verse 16.)

F-4: …and at the end of your life you will groan, when your flesh and body are consumed, and you say, "Oh how I hated discipline, and my heart despised reproof! I did not listen to the voice of my teachers or incline my ear to my instructors. Now I am at the point of utter ruin in the public assembly" (Proverbs 5:11-14 NRSV). Who or what are the forsaken teachers and instructors? (See Jeremiah 9:13.)

📖 **READ JEREMIAH 9:17-19**

G. ADDITIONAL COMMENTS FOR VERSES 17-19

God's people, especially His leaders, do not know how to be remorseful over the devastation that their actions, of neglect, have contributed to. They do not know how to be ashamed and they do not know how to blush according to Jeremiah 8:12. God tries to get these people started on the *right track*. He suggests professional help for those who are full of false hope, oppression, and deceit. If they are not automatically moved to grieving by the truth, maybe some professionals can get the job done.

ANSWER QUESTIONS FOR VERSES 17-19

G-1: Some movies make us cry, some make us angry, and some make us laugh. Words put to music can also persuade our moods. If you have ever stood in a worship service or rock concert and looked around, you may have seen or even experienced this for yourself. There are certain people (human vessels) that are trained, skilled, and gifted in this area of persuasion.

They have the ability to bring different emotions out of their audience. In verse 17 God says that His people should consider calling these professionals in. What should the skilled professionals be able to do once they have been called in and what will be the response that these skilled professionals draw from the audience?

G-2: Destruction and death are everywhere. It is urgent that God's people (His leaders) come to the point of lamenting, mourning, and grieving. It is the only thing that will save the nation. What is going on that should make them stop dead in their tracks and say: What have we done!? (See verse 19.)

📖READ JEREMIAH 9:20-22

H. ADDITIONAL COMMENTS FOR VERSES 20-22

God's people have to face the truth. It is evident that the final day of destruction is close at hand. And things are not looking good for God's imprisoned word (the seed He has planted in the heart) either. The good and the bad, whether physical or spiritual, will suffer because of the devastation that war brings.

God, like a physician, has been trying to tell His people that their lives are in serious danger because of their fatal disease. The lion-in-the-thicket, that lives in their hearts and rules their lives, is like a cancer that destroys the body. God wants them to know that this will not be easy but He, as their physician will administer the only treatment that will bring hope. The treatment is dangerous. He explains it as fire. The treatment that He must use in order to rid the bad (cancerous cells) will, unfortunately, also affect and kill some of the good (useful cells) too. All that anyone can do now: lament and wail.

ANSWER QUESTIONS FOR VERSES 20-22

H-1: Though this treatment has started it is far from over. How do we know, by God's word, that the disease is still present and dangerous today? (See Matthew 13:27-30.)

H-2: God proceeds to set up the professional mourners. He tries to help His people get ready for the worst. The mourning women do not know the words to the truth so God gives the professionals the dirge that will tell the truth. They are to teach this prophetical and truthful lament to their daughters and to their neighbors. This procession will go down in history as a funeral for someone of royalty, with much outward mourning to reflect the great loss. What are the words to the dirge that God teaches the women?

H-3 (OPTIONAL QUESTION): These professionals may have been teaching something else before all of this devastation. What type of professional and destructive work might they have been doing before? (See Jeremiah 2:33.)

H-4: Even if the city gates (hearts) are locked tight, death will not be stopped. It will enter the windows like a thief. Death is no respecter of persons. It will not take the poor and leave the rich. It will take the good and bad alike. Death will have no specific instructions like it did in Egypt (Exodus 11:4-7). The seed (word) in the heart will feel the effects of death too. It is not immune to the coming invasion. The useful and useless are all in danger. No one is safe. What illustration does God use to get that message across? (See verse 22.)

H-5: Does anyone have a promise of being kept safe in troubled times? (See 2Chronicles 15:1-7.)

H-6: There will be nothing to do but lament and wail when death enters their *palaces* like a thief. What is the thief taking from the women who deliver the dirge? What could the *palaces* represent?

H-7: There will be nothing to do but lament and wail when death cuts the *children* off the streets. What is the thief taking from the women who deliver the dirge? What could the *children* represent?

H-8: There will be nothing to do but lament and wail when death takes the *young men from the squares*. What is the thief really taking from these women who deliver the dirge? What could the *young men in standing in the squares* represent?

H-9 (OPTIONAL QUESTION): Though death has no specific instructions this time, sometimes it does. Turn to Ezekiel 9. What prevented death during this battle-round in Ezekiel 9:4?

📖READ JEREMIAH 9:23-24

I. ADDITIONAL COMMENTS FOR VERSES 23-24

Omission of the truth (not telling the whole story) helps man to see himself as something that he is truly not. He hurts himself and others by not accepting the whole truth.

ANSWER QUESTIONS FOR VERSES 23-24

I-1: Jerusalem has been stripped of all the things that they could boast about. Their iconic leaders, their wisdom, their strong government, their military strength, their future; everything was taken away. But instead of turning around, mourning, lamenting, and asking for mercy, they found something else to fall back on. The covenant between God and Abraham gave them another hope for eternal claim. Even in New Testament times, they held on tight. What weak and material evidence is presented, by the people, as they continue to demand 'their rights' from God? They believe that something else will ensure their salvation. See the following verses. In these verses you will find what insurance they still use against the deadly disease that has come to all.

(Philippians 3:2-6 NRSV): Beware of the dogs, beware of the evil workers, beware of those who mutilate the flesh! For it is we who are the circumcision, who worship in the Spirit of God and boast in Christ Jesus and have no confidence in the flesh— even though I, too, have reason for confidence in the flesh. If anyone else has reason to be confident in the flesh, I have more: circumcised on the eighth day, a member of the people of Israel, of the tribe of Benjamin, a Hebrew born of Hebrews; as to the law, a Pharisee; as to zeal, a persecutor of the church; *as to righteousness under the law, blameless.*

I-2: God allows one boast and that boast contains words of truth. There are some words we can say with confidence every time that we say them, with no questions of doubt. What are the words of truth that we can say with all confidence? (See verse 24.)

READ JEREMIAH 9:25-26

J. ADDITIONAL COMMENTS FOR VERSES 25-26

God promised to bless Abram and make his name great. God followed through with that promise. But unfortunately being a *child of Abraham* was a bigger boast, among the nations, than being a *child of God*.

ANSWER QUESTIONS FOR VERSES 25-26

J-1: ..."To your descendants I give this land, from the river of Egypt to the great river, the river Euphrates," (Genesis 15:18 NRSV); that was another promise that Abraham received from the Lord. It seems that those whom God will attend to, in verse 26, fall in this area, between those two named boundaries. Many in that area claimed to be children of Abraham. Name those who God will attend to?

J-2: Have you ever signed a contract without really reading the content or fully understanding it? Maybe the children of Abraham did. Courts will stand behind the contract if your signature is on the line. Those who wanted to be a part of Abraham's promised blessings gave their signatures. How did they sign? See Genesis 17:11.

J-3: Did you have to be a blood relative to sign? (See the following selected verse.)

(Genesis 17:12 NRSV): Throughout your generations every male among you shall be circumcised when he is eight days old, including the slave born in your house and the one bought with your money from any foreigner who is not of your offspring.

J-4: Were you automatically signed-up if you were a blood relative? (See the following selected verse.)

(Genesis 17:14 NRSV): "Any uncircumcised male who is not circumcised in the flesh of his foreskin shall be cut off from his people; he has broken my covenant."

J-5: God's people were slow about fulfilling their responsibilities and duties. In the following verses they are confronted. In the days of Joshua, this is how their obedience is put to the test.

(Joshua 5:2-9 NRSV): At that time the Lord said to Joshua, "Make flint knives and circumcise the Israelites a second time." So Joshua made flint knives, and circumcised the Israelites at Gibeath-haaraloth. This is the reason why Joshua circumcised them: all the males of the people who came out of Egypt, all the warriors, had died during the journey through the wilderness after they had come out of Egypt. Although all the people who came out had been circumcised, yet all the people born on the journey through the wilderness after they had come out of Egypt had not been circumcised. For the Israelites traveled forty years in the wilderness, until all the nation, the warriors who came out of Egypt, perished, not having listened to the voice of the Lord. To them the Lord swore that he would not let them see the land that he had sworn to their ancestors to give us, a land flowing with milk and honey. So it was their children, whom he raised up in their place, that Joshua circumcised; for they were uncircumcised, because they had not been circumcised on the way. When the circumcising of all the nation was done, they remained in their places in the camp until they were healed. The Lord said to Joshua, "Today I have rolled away from you the disgrace of Egypt." And so that place is called Gilgal to this day.

This seems like an act of direct disobedience, though not presented as one. What had not happened for forty years in the nation of Israel?

J-6: How does God test your obedience today?

J-7: Read Jeremiah 4:4. What does God say to Judah? What type of circumcision are these people falling short of?

J-8: When you read verse 25 and 26, here in chapter 9 of Jeremiah, you see that Judah is among those whom God will attend to. Do you understand those named nations to be uncircumcised in the skin or circumcised in the skin?

J-9: God has made it very clear throughout this study that a circumcised heart is what He wants. That type of circumcision allows God's power and truth to enter into the heart to live with man and through man. It is the only power that man can depend upon and boast about.

I used to be a Sunday school teacher. I tried to be very careful as I chose words of discipline. Because I noticed that if I showed any disapproval toward the actions of one student, a lot of the other kids found it to be their personal duty to rally behind me. Some would whisper, laugh, and point at the student who had managed to get into trouble. They must have felt safe thinking that they and the teacher (the disciplinarian) were on the same team. But the actions of those kids (the teacher's fan-club and supporters), who were feeling safe, also needed discipline. I have found that children misunderstand the true purpose of discipline. According to some verses that we are going to be looking at, those who God says He will "*attend to*" act a lot like children in the classroom who formed a fan-club (a bunch of teacher's fans with clubs in hand) that was not appropriate or teacher-approved.

Israel (the one receiving the discipline right now) was spiritually blind. Due to her blind condition, her discipline was doubly hard. Israel and all of those in verses 26 may have been Abraham's offspring but there was little resemblance. Those listed in verse 26 should have felt some sympathy for, not only Israel but, all of their fellow countrymen. If the near-kin would have had the kind of heart that it took to come and lift their near kin and neighbors up, encourage those under oppression, and serve as a companion on the long walk of shame, they may not have been on the list of those God will 'attend to'.

While their fellow countrymen were being raided, killed, taken captive, and carried to all four corners of the earth, not one of those named in verse 26 had the heart to help Jacob (aka Israel). As the following verses will show, they just kept pointing at each other, laughing at each other, and kicking each other instead of helping each other up during times of struggle.

Turn Ezekiel 29:6-7 to see why God will attend to Egypt.

Turn to Ezekiel 11:14-16 to see why God will attend to Judah.

Turn to Ezekiel 25:3-7 to see why God will attend to the Ammonites.

Turn to Ezekiel 25:8-10 to see why God will attend to Moab.

While God was working on Israel, she was under His fire and hammer. But others were coming along and placing dents and dings where God did not want them. These previous verses show that God expected more from Jacob's neighbors and Abraham's kin. They did have some kind of responsibility toward her as she was going through trouble. Being close to the wrath-and-draft of the fire and swinging hammer may have brought some personal improvement to these neighbors and "children of Abraham". What kind of neighbor and near-kin are you? What would God write about you?

J-10: The Old Testament has some evidence that God interacted with the other offspring of Abraham and that leaders out of Israel are not the only leaders that God spoke to. Jeremiah records God's steps to communicate with the leaders of those who are mentioned here in verse 26. See the following verse and then answer these three questions: What is the message? How does He send it? Who exactly does He send it to?

(Jeremiah 27:3-7 NRSV): Send word to the king of Edom, the king of Moab, the king of the Ammonites, the king of Tyre, and the king of Sidon by the hand of the envoys who have come to Jerusalem to King Zedekiah of Judah. Give them this charge for their masters: Thus says the Lord of hosts, the God of Israel: This is what you shall say to your masters: It is I who by my great power and my outstretched arm have made the earth, with the people and the animals that are on the earth, and I give it to whomever I please. Now I have given all these lands into the hand of King Nebuchadnezzar of Babylon, my servant, and I have given him even the wild animals of the field to serve him. All the nations shall serve him and his son and his grandson, until the time of his own land comes; then many nations and great kings shall make him their slave.

J-11: Even though God does not seem to have a direct open line (from Israel) into Egypt, He still tries to get a message of warning to the leader. Maybe the leader will hear 'through the grapevine'. What does Jeremiah 44:30 say?

J-12: Go back to Jeremiah 1:10 and be reminded of what Jeremiah was called to do. What was it?

J-13 (OPTIONAL QUESTION): What other way might God speak to leaders? (See Genesis 41; Daniel 2 and 4; Matthew 27:19.)

J-14: Here is a shortened version of the Ten Commandments. Even though there are about 613 commands altogether, these were the ones (taken from Deuteronomy 5:6-21) written in stone and given to God's people. Check the ones that have been broken in the first nine chapters of Jeremiah.

- ➢ 1 You shall have no other gods before me.
- ➢ 2 You shall not make for yourself any idols.
- ➢ 3 You shall not wrongfully use the name of the Lord your God.
- ➢ 4 Remember the Sabbath Day and keep it holy.
- ➢ 5 Honor your father and mother.
- ➢ 6 You shall not murder.
- ➢ 7 You shall not commit adultery.
- ➢ 8 You shall not steal.
- ➢ 9 You shall not bear false witness against your neighbor.
- ➢ 10 You shall not covet anything that belongs to your neighbor.

J-15: How has Jeremiah affected your life with his message in chapter nine?

Chapter 9 Tag-A-Long

Making Funeral Arrangements

Today I started thinking about funerals fit-for-a-king (or queen). I then did a computer search on royal-funerals. There were many pictures of the casket being carried or transported. These pictures reminded me of the many pictures I had seen, in Bible stories, of the Levites carrying the ark of the covenant. In fact one of those memorable pictures of the Levites, carrying the ark of the covenant, would have blended in perfectly with all of the other funeral procession pictures on the computer screen.

In Exodus 25 God gives precise instructions for building the ark of the covenant. If you would happen to read those instructions without being told that they were specific instructions for constructing the ark of the covenant; you just might think that these were instructions for a very lavish casket. Though lavish, the dimensions of the casket are small, so you might think that it was ordered by a king who had tragically lost his most beloved young son.

(Exodus 25:10-16 NRSV): They shall make an ark of acacia wood; it shall be two and a half cubits long, a cubit and a half wide, and a cubit and a half high. You shall overlay it with pure gold, inside and outside you shall overlay it, and you shall make a molding of gold upon it all around. You shall cast four rings of gold for it and put them on its four feet, two rings on the one side of it, and two rings on the other side. You shall make poles of acacia wood, and overlay them with gold. And you shall put the poles into the rings on the sides of the ark, by which to carry the ark. The poles shall remain in the rings of the ark; they shall not be taken from it. You shall put into the ark of the covenant that I shall give you.

The way I see it; God started making funeral arrangements for His 'word' (a part of His offspring) early on. And now here in chapter nine of Jeremiah, He is lining up the professional mourners. They will sing the truthful song. Though the truth has never changed things, up to this point, maybe the words of the song will bring tears to the eye and draw a groaning from, deep inside, the soul. It is the very least that could be expected from those who lied about, defiled, and destroyed His word.

✂ Scrapbook Page For Chapter 9

Trial of the Unborn

"I had just finished writing the curses and washed them off into the water of bitterness, when I heard the shuffle of feet outside. I walked out and met the couple. I was expecting them. The man handed me that required amount of barley flour while she, young and beautiful, stood at his side. She was under his authority and that's why they were here.

Many of these cases come to the priest, but it seemed to me that Jonas had just brought a case like this not too long ago. It was another case of jealousy that would put the 'law of jealousy' into effect. Although he said that he had all of the evidence that he needed, he had to prove that his jealousy was rightly called for, so he needed to put his wife/virgin through the procedure of the curse. And now this curse that I administer will produce evidence if she has been unfaithful. This ceremony will rectify or support his suspicions. Jonas waits while I take the case, that he brought in today, before the Lord.

I will bring her (the one under his authority) near the Lord,

take the holy water in the earthen vessel that I had prepared and

take some dust that is on the floor of the tabernacle and put it into the water.

I will dishevel the beautiful woman's hair as she sits before the Lord

and place in her hands the offering that her husband had brought.

In my own hand I will have the water of bitterness that brings the curse. I will say:

'If no man has lain with you,

if you have not turned aside to uncleaness while under your husband's authority,

be immune to this water of bitterness that brings the curse.

But if you have gone astray while under your husband's authority,

if you have defiled yourself and some man other than your husband has had intercourse with you,

the Lord make you an execration (accursed) and an oath among your people, when the Lord makes your uterus drop, your womb discharge;

now may this water that brings the curse enter into your bowels and make your womb discharge,

your uterus drop!'

After I make the woman take the oath of the curse, she shall say Amen. Amen.

I will then take the grain offering, of jealousy, from her hand,

and elevate the grain offering before the Lord.

I will bring it to the altar.

I will take a handful of the grain offering and turn the memorial portion of the offering into smoke.

Then the woman must drink the water that causes bitter pain.

I execute the law. The innocent and guilty all get the same treatment from me. They all hear and drink the same. I just administer. I don't have to decide if the woman is guilty or innocent, the words of the curse will. (And if an unborn child is present, it too will be part of the price that is paid.) The words that the accused must eat and the water that she must drink will produce the truth." (See Numbers 5:11-31 for original translation.)

Judah was headed for the same trial. Her actions have put the law of jealousy into effect. She will drink the water of bitterness. Jeremiah 9:15 says, therefore thus says the Lord of hosts, the God of Israel: I am feeding this people with wormwood, and giving them poisonous water to drink.

Compare God's people today to the accused bride that must go through the painful ritual. The Word of God, which we eat and drink by way of Jesus, will abort all of the elements that are foreign to God. It is a bitter cup for all, but the cup will be most painful for those who are willingly and continually unfaithful.

This presents a portrait of Jesus as the water, though bitter, it cleanses within.

Compare Answers For Chapter 9

A-1: O that my head were a spring of water, and my eyes a fountain of tears, so that I might weep day and night for the slain of my poor people! (Jeremiah 9:1 NRSV.) God will need a continual source from which to produce all of the tears that will be needed for mourning.

A-2: the tribe of Levi which He claimed as His own (see Numbers 3:11-12 and 44-45)

A-3: the great flood

A-4: It did not cleanse the inside.

A-5: At that time it will be said to this people and to Jerusalem: a hot wind comes from me out of the bare heights in the desert toward my poor people; not to winnow or cleanse- a wind too strong for that. Now it is I who will speak in judgment against them. Look! He comes up like clouds, his chariots like the whirlwind; his horses are swifter than eagles— woe to us, for we are ruined! O Jerusalem, wash your heart clean of wickedness so that you may be saved. How long will your evil schemes lodge within you?

A-6: obedience

A-7: disobedience

A-8: they were just like an adulterous wife and cheated on Him

A-9: his leaders who were supposed to be carrying out His word

B-1: bended tongues are like bows shooting arrows

B-2: proceed from evil to evil

C-1: Beware of your neighbors, and put no trust in any of your kin; for all your kin are supplanters, and every neighbor goes around like a slanderer. They all deceive their neighbors, and no one speaks the truth; they have taught their tongues to speak lies; they commit iniquity and are too weary to repent. Oppression upon oppression, deceit upon deceit! They refuse to know me, says the Lord (Jeremiah 9:4-6).

C-2: Jerusalem would be the place to find truth, righteousness and justice.

C-3: (2Kings 23:27 NRSV) The Lord said, "I will remove Judah also out of my sight, as I have removed Israel; and I will reject this city that I have chosen, Jerusalem, and the house of which I said, My name shall be there."

C-4: supplant- uproot; eradicate and supply a substitute for

C-5: too weary, even too weary to repent

C-6: wandering

C-7: They *refuse* to know the Lord.

D-1: The violent overthrow or alteration of an existing government by a small group

D-2: they all speak friendly words to their neighbors, but inwardly (the words) are planning to lay an ambush

D-3: In Jeremiah 9:9, God asks: Shall I not punish them for these things? ....shall I not bring retribution on a nation such as this? (NRSV)

E-1: Take up weeping and wailing for the mountains, and a lamentation for the pastures of the wilderness, because they are laid waste so that no one passes through, ...(Jeremiah 9:10 NRSV).

E-2: For a sound of wailing is heard from Zion: "How we are ruined! We are utterly shamed, because we have left the land, because they have cast down our dwellings" (Jeremiah 9:19 NRSV).

E-3: Thrones (judgment?) surrounding all the cites of Judah

F-1: Because they have forsaken the law that God set before them. They did not obey His voice or walk in accordance with His voice. They stubbornly followed their own hearts and went after the Baals as their ancestors taught them.

F-2: wormwood and poisonous water

F-3: They will be scattered among nations that neither they nor their ancestors have known. The sword will come after them until they are consumed.

F-4: law and God's voice

G-1: raise a dirge over the people so that their eyes may run down with tears and their eyelids flow with water

G-2: All of these sounds are coming from Zion: "How we are ruined! We are utterly shamed, because we have left the land, because they have cast down our dwellings."

H-1: The bad and the good still remain.

H-2: "Death has come up into our windows, it has entered our palaces, to cut off the children from the streets and the young men from the squares" (Jeremiah 9:21 NRSV).

H-3 (OPTIONAL QUESTION): teaching, (even) the wickedest of women, how to seek lovers

H-4: It does not matter if you are the dung (manure) on the field or the sheaves in the field; nothing will be gathered. The sheaves are no better that the manure.

H-5: No one is promised safety everyone is given a warning. (2Chronicles 15:5 NRSV): In those times it was not safe for anyone to go or come, for great disturbances afflicted all the inhabitants of the lands.

H-6: current government leaders

H-7: future as they had planned

H-8: fathers and sons who go to war (their military defenses)

H-9 (OPTIONAL QUESTION): A mark had been put on the foreheads of those who sighed and groaned over all of the abominations and the mark on the forehead (sorrow), at that time, saved their life.

I-1: circumcision

I-2: but let those who boast boast in this, that they understand and know me, that I am the Lord; I act with steadfast love, justice, and righteousness in the earth, for in these things I delight, ….(Jeremiah 9:24 NRSV).

J-1: Egypt, Judah, Edom, Ammonites, Moab, all those with shaven temples

J-2: You shall circumcise the flesh of your foreskins, and it shall be a sign of the covenant between me and you. Throughout your generations every male among you shall be circumcised when he is eight days old, …. (Genesis 17:11-12 NRSV).

J-3: No- Every male was to be circumcised even home-born slaves and those who were bought.

J-4: No- anyone who was uncircumcised was cut off because he broke the covenant.

J-5: There had been no circumcisions among the Israelites for forty years. The Scripture says: for they were uncircumcised, because they had not been circumcised *on the way.*

J-6: I personally might consider the act of baptism as a test of obedience.

J-7: Circumcise yourself to the Lord, remove the foreskin of your hearts, O Judah and inhabitants of Jerusalem, (Jeremiah 4:4 NRSV). Some issues were only skin deep but there were other issues of the spirit and these important spiritual issues is what separated God from His people.

J-8: I am still not sure; but I can see this circumcision issue to be a lot like the issue of baptism today. Many living within our nation, who identify themselves as Christians, are baptized and many are not. Some are baptized but that is where their obedience to the Lord stops and their salvation becomes questionable. Many will say they have obtained salvation but choose not to prove it through baptism. Then there are some that are baptized because it is (to them) handed down as a requirement to *belong*. And then there are those who put off being baptized. I think God has a lot of issues to attend to within our modern day world too.

J-9: I hope that He could write: 1. showed compassion for hurting neighbors and kin 2. knew the truth and spoke the truth 3. Knew Me and that I act with steadfast love, justice and righteousness in the earth.

J-10: The message informed the leaders of the control that God had over the powers of the nations. It charged the leaders to serve Nebuchadnezzar (until the time of his land comes). The message was sent by the hand of envoys. The message was sent to the king of Edom, the king of Moab, the king of the Ammonites, the king of Tyre, and the king of Sidon.

J-11: (Jeremiah 44:30 NRSV): "Thus says the Lord, I am going to give Pharaoh Hophra, king of Egypt, into the hands of his enemies, those who seek his life, just as I gave King Zedekiah of Judah into the hand of King Nebuchadnezzar of Babylon, his enemy who sought his life."

J-12: He was appointed over nations and kingdoms, to pluck up and to pull down, to destroy and to overthrow, to build and to plant.

J-13 (OPTIONAL QUESTION): through dreams

J-14: This is a running list from the previous chapter.

Number 1: You shall have no other gods before me (broken law according to Jeremiah 1:16)

Number 2: You shall not make for yourself an idol (broken law according to Jeremiah 1:16)

Number 5: Honor your father and mother (broken law according to Jeremiah 2:27)

Number 6: You shall not murder (broken law according to Jeremiah 2:30b and 34)

Number 4: Remember the Sabbath day and keep it holy (broken law according to Jeremiah 2:32)

Number 7: You shall not commit adultery (broken law according to Jeremiah 3:6)

Number 3: You shall not make wrongful use of my name (broken law according to Jeremiah 5:2)

Number 10: You shall not covet anything that belongs to your neighbor (broken, see Jeremiah 5:8)

Number 8: You shall not steal (broken law according to Jeremiah 7:11)

J-15: Sometimes we are punished. Sometimes we receive mercy. Both are gifts from God. Whatever gift we are receiving we should always trust God and always love our neighbor.

Chapter 10

Chapter 10 Prelude

Consequences of Resistance

In Isaiah 41:8 God calls Abraham His friend. How does a person become recognized by God and gain that status: friend of God? Friends are easy to come by when you shower them with all good things, but try keeping a friend who has experienced hard times that you seem to be ever responsible for. When your friend finds out that you had the power to make things different but allowed him/or her to suffer, that person will probably not remain your friend for long.

But it seems that Abraham was the kind of friend that stuck with God no matter what God did or what God said. Even when God delivered the worst, Abraham trusted Him. Abraham never asked God "why?" or equated God with being too demanding, uncaring, or inconsiderate. Many mortals associate these kinds of words with God as disasters take place in this world and repeated tests-of-time arise in our lives. Human minds and hearts that have a disconnect with Him wonder about Him and ask: why does God let this-thing or that-thing happen? These little questions may seem innocent enough but in them (those little questions), we judge God. It must be offensive to God, and dangerously close to sinning, when we put God next to our own human measure. But Abraham was different in that way. God could speak with Abraham honestly and openly without regret. I think that's why God calls Abraham His friend. The next paragraph gives just one example of Abraham's way.

One evening Abraham heard something from his Friend, God, that must have been disturbing: "Know this for certain, that your offspring shall be aliens in a land that is not theirs, and shall be slaves there, and they shall be oppressed for four hundred years" (Genesis 15:13 NRSV). Most friends might have said something like this: "Now just wait-a-minute God! That is not how friends treat each other! You promised me blessings and kings and multitudes and all that great stuff! (Compare Genesis 17:4-8.) How can you just stand by and let this happen to your friend's family!" But that was not the course that Abraham's conversation took. Abraham trusted God completely. Even though there had been and would continue be many obstacles that seemed to get in the way of the great promises that God made to Abraham, God kept making-good on His word to His friend. And I suspect Abraham died knowing that. So right now (as we go back picking up some of Israel's history before she reached the Promised Land), getting Abraham's offspring out, from under the confinement, of Egypt was just one more step that God had to take to fulfill His said-promises to His friend.

There was about to be a war between God and Pharaoh and the battleground was Egypt.

The pain, loss of lives, and suffering that the war brought
to the land could have been averted.

But as Pharaoh made one bad decision after another, the inhabitants suffered.

Their leader would not fear the word of God.

Communication is vital if you want to use a peaceful approach and prevent the outbreak of war. So God needed a liaison between Himself and the Egyptian pharaoh. He tracked down a man named Moses and told him about the plan. Maybe God chose him because he was a man who had roots in Egypt. Moses had been born in Egypt and left Egypt as a fugitive (Exodus 2:11-15). When God called him, Moses had been living a far different life style than that of his blood relatives who were still there in Egypt living under great oppression. Though far removed from the heavy burdens of his kin, he had seen and known about their way of life.

So Moses went to Egypt and found his long lost brother Aaron. They had God's demand in their mouth as they approached Pharaoh. God wanted His people to go out to the desert for a festival (Exodus 5:1). But when Pharaoh heard the demand pertaining to the festival he just became angry and made the people, who God was calling out, work harder. More task masters with more whips and less supplies to work with, is how Pharaoh answered the demand from God concerning the slaves. And the people that God would rescue suffered even more.

So the Lord, being the warrior that He is (Exodus 15:3 NRSV) started lining up His armies and each time that Moses and Aaron approached Pharaoh with God's demand, God attached a warning of an attack. God even told Pharaoh the details of each attack before it happened! But Pharaoh was stubborn and kept ignoring God's demands and the Egyptians, old and young alike suffered pain and loss with each attack.

The first attack through God's word came on the waters of Egypt. The waters were all turned to blood but Pharaoh would not comply. Then God (through His word) sent an army of frogs, then an army of gnats; and these attacks were followed up by an army of flies. Each army attacked only after Pharaoh refused to comply. Next a disease, by the word of God, attacked all of the field animals and then there was the deadly attack of boils that affected men as well as animals because of their leader's refusal. Then God, through His word, warned about an approaching hail storm that was on the way. It would not be diverted unless Pharaoh let God's people go. The people of Egypt were, by now, fearing the word of this God of the Hebrews; and began to take cover in order to save themselves and their remaining livestock. They had to take this step themselves because their stubborn leader would not make peace with God and the war continued.

So God sent an army of locusts and on the heels of this army were warriors that carried deep darkness to the land. Egypt had been attacked with great signs and wonders from God's say-so but Pharaoh still dared to resist God and His mighty armies. God would have to call on the only power that would break Pharaoh and that was the power of death. All of the firstborn (man and animal) in the land would be taken by, what some refer to as the grim reaper, if the chosen people were not released to Him.

When the distraught Pharaoh counted his losses after this devastating battle with death, he let the people go. The, soon to be, nation would exit the land that had been destroyed by the many armies formed by God's word. But not long after the people departed, Pharaoh's heart spoke again. It was clear, (by the evidence of its instruction to him), that the hot wind of God had not melted anything in Pharaoh's heart. His actions proved that he feared the signs, not God who was author of the signs. Though the signs had finally gained the power to move him, the spoken word of God did not hold that power over his life. He bent for only a little while. He relented for only a little while. The hot wind, from God, that services the hearts of men served only to make his heart harder still. So being defiant to the Lord, Pharaoh gave the command to his army that his heart gave to him. Now there will be a showdown at the Red Sea; but God's own army would be there in full force to face the Egyptian army that pursued those in the great exodus.

This is where God's word commanded the powerful waters and they obeyed. They (the waters) separated and the once water-soaked path, made by the two walls of water dried up. The now dry path, like a red carpet, ceremonially ushered in the new nation. But this dry path was only for the nation of God. When Pharaoh's unrecognizable army followed in pursuit, they were swallowed up as the waters fell back into place.

But many generations have passed since then. It seems that at this point in time, God's people have acted a lot like Pharaoh. They resist the word of God too. And God has continually, for hundreds of years, warned His people that bad things were going to happen to them if they would not heed His word. But the warnings have stopped and armies are moving into the land; and the people have been well informed of all the tactics that will be used against them. Warnings come and God's armies follow; but just like Pharaoh, they continue to ignore God's demand. They will not make peace. They will not comply.

Israel had a written treaty with God and by overstepping the boundaries of the treaty, they are in breach of contract and they open the door to war and destruction. But the destruction that God's armies will leave behind in Israel goes far beyond the destruction that God's armies left behind in Egypt. Deuteronomy 28:59-61 (NRSV) says: then the Lord will overwhelm both you and your offspring with severe and lasting afflictions and grievous and lasting maladies. He will bring back upon you all the diseases of Egypt, of which you were in dread, and they shall cling to you. Every other malady and affliction, even though not recorded in the book of this law, the Lord will inflict on you until you are destroyed.

Chapter 10 Study

The Care Package

CHAPTER 10 READING, COMMENTS, AND QUESTIONS

📖READ JEREMIAH 10:1-5

A. ADDITIONAL COMMENTS FOR VERSES 1-5

The exiled bride receives a package. It is addressed to: *The House of Israel*. When God sent her away with a decree of divorce (Jeremiah 3:8), she was thrown into cultures with strange beliefs and customs, so God has wrapped up the truth, in a care package, and sent it to her. The package holds the key to a special kind of freedom. It is the only freedom available to her at this point in time as she serves her sentence in the strange land.

ANSWER QUESTIONS FOR VERSES 1-5

A-1: The first law in Israel was: You shall have no other gods before me. The second law was: You shall not make for yourself an idol. These two laws laid the original foundation that Israel was built on. But when social status and economics situations change in a nation, amendments are made to the structure in order to serve the people. What is the meaning of the word: amendment?

A-2: Israel was no longer living in the Promised Land and God's law was not recognized in the foreign lands where she now lived. Israel was no longer the head but she was the tail (Deuteronomy 28:13 and 44). She could no longer walk as she did before. She was now bent and under new pressures that she had never personally experienced. According to Daniel 9:10, the prophets carry God's law to His people. And here in chapter ten He, once again, sends Jeremiah. As God continues to send His up-to-date commands, ordinances, and laws, He shows His desire to still be Ruler of Israel. What is the amendment? (See verse 2.)

A-3: God made an even bigger amendment to His law (His word). What was it? (See the gospel of John 1:15.)

A-4: Describe the production and transport methods for idols? (See verses 3 and 4.)

A-5: When God looks at all of these man made idols amongst the nations it reminds Him of scarecrows in a cucumber field. The peoples of the nations (represented by the cucumbers) use the idols (represented by the lifeless scarecrows) for protection against foolish crows. If God's people realize that they are like the foolish crows, they are on their way to finding peace and wisdom for their current situation. When the crows (God's people) learn the truth about the scarecrows (the idols) they can put their fear away and then they (the crow) will not go hungry. Who really has all of the power in the field full of delusion?

📖READ JEREMIAH 10:6-10

B. ADDITIONAL COMMENTS FOR VERSES 6-10

God's power and might, which had been taken for granted, is now newly recognized. As eyes and ears are opened, the people realize the sharp powers of God in this dull land. But they are in a quandary. It is hard to break a bad habit like the one back in Jeremiah 6:13 (NRSV): For from the least to the greatest of them, everyone is greedy for unjust gain.

ANSWER QUESTIONS FOR VERSES 6-10

B-1: Read the parable in Luke 19:11-28. What should God's people do when they are trusted with valuables?

B-2: Daniel is one of the exiles that will (in the near future of Jerusalem) be carried off by Nebucahdnezzar, king of Babylon. (See the book of Daniel.) When Daniel used his God-given wisdom in the foreign land, it not only benefited the foreign land but how did using His God-given wisdom benefit the Lord? (See Daniel 4.)

B-3: God will continue to send new direction. God will amend His plan to ensure the survival of His people. What message will be going out (in the near future) to the leaders in Jerusalem? (See Jeremiah 27:12-15.)

B-4: We will find that things have not changed much, over time, for God's people. As we cross into the New Testament, they are still under foreign rule. What is the message (amendment) from the following New Testament verses?

(Titus 3:1-2 NRSV): Remind them to be subject to rulers and authorities, to be obedient, to be ready for every good work, to speak evil of no one, to avoid quarrelling, to be gentle, and to show every courtesy to everyone.

(1Peter 2:13-17 NRSV): For the Lord's sake accept the authority of every human institution, whether of the emperor as supreme, or of governors, as sent by him to punish those who do wrong...For it is God's will that by doing right you should silence the ignorance of the foolish...As servants of God, live as free people,...Honor everyone. Love the family of believers. Fear God. Honor the emperor.

(Romans 13:1-3 NRSV): Let every person be subject to the governing authorities…whoever resists authority…will incur judgment.

B-5: They are both stupid and foolish; the instruction given by idols is no better than wood! (See Jeremiah 10:8 NRSV.) The truth will be made known. What, can we only assume, is going to happen when the instruction given by idols comes face to face with the instruction given by God? There is a description of God's word (God's instruction) back in Jeremiah 5:14. That description will help you answer this question.

B-6: There is nothing super natural about these wooden idols. They are mass produced here on earth. They are clothed with man made material. According to the following verses, what is God clothed with?

(Psalms 93:1 NRSV): The Lord is king, he is robed in majesty; the Lord is robed, he is girded with strength….

(Psalms 104:1-2 NRSV): …You are clothed with honor and majesty, wrapped in light as with a garment.

B-7: Even though God's *instruction* (written law) was also, at one time, kept inside wood that had been carved and cut-out (see Exodus 25:10-16), Israel is told that the instruction coming from these man made idols is no better than wood. Why is the idol-instruction no good? (See the first part of verse 10 in this chapter.)

B-8: This ark of the covenant has been held in high regard but what is going to happen? Go back to Jeremiah 3:16. (You may want review section E of chapter 3 also.)

B-9: If Israel fears God instead of fearing false customs in the strange land, she will have the strength to stand strong through the time of God's wrath. God must put a stop to the destroyer of nations. God will do whatever it takes to destroy the lion (Jeremiah 4:7) that has gone up from its thicket.

Who, because of living by instruction that comes from the 'woody man made idols' (false customs), will not be able to endure God's indignation as it thunders, the earth over, on the great lion-hunt? (See last part of verse 10.)

📖READ JEREMIAH 10:11

C. ADDITIONAL COMMENTS FOR VERSE 11

Verse 11 of Jeremiah chapter 10 is noted as being a gloss in Aramaic. Although God's people do not speak Aramaic, God wants them to learn a message in that language.

ANSWER QUESTIONS FOR VERSE 11

C-1: When the Israelites were taken into exile, the daunting words that the enemy spoke were probably not understood. If the exiles did understand and speak the language; they, by human nature, may have responded to the dismaying remarks. But they do not speak Aramaic. So God teaches them a few words in that language and there is actually a message in the words that He teaches them. God's people will finally speak some truth and the whole earth (places where God scatters them) will finally hear some truth about the God of Israel. What did God teach Israel to say in Aramaic?

C-2: Isaiah 10:5 speaks of the time when God's club of anger was in the hand of Assyria. Then later in Isaiah 36 we see that God's club of anger is still at work. At the time of Isaiah 36, God's club of anger (we might recognize the club, in part, as the covenant curses) has severely affected the northern kingdom of Israel. And many fortified cities in the southern kingdom of Judah have also fallen under its brutal blows. The capitol of Jerusalem is next in line. As we read about this standoff between Jerusalem and Assyria, in Isaiah 36, we see proof of the existing language barrier.

Taunting words are sent, by the Assyrian king through one of his army leaders, to Jerusalem. Hezekiah, being the king of Jerusalem at that time, is mocked and ridiculed. He is mocked for trusting in a neighboring power (the then-friendly Egypt) that will not help them and he is mocked for taking down the altars of their God. They have no power at all against the king of Assyria. The Assyrians continue to mock and ridicule Jerusalem by offering the city two thousand Assyrian war horses if the men inside the city of Jerusalem will come out, get on them, and fight.

All of these mocking words had been spoken loudly and boldly, in the dialect of God's people, outside the city walls. There were three representatives of Jerusalem, who also, were outside the city walls, with the Assyrian army. They referred to themselves as servants and said to the Assyrians: "Please speak to us in Aramaic; for we understand it. Do not speak to us in the language of Judah within the hearing of the people who are sitting on the wall." Of course this is how the leaders of Jerusalem have always handled things. They keep the people in the dark about everything, including the things God had to say. Now they want to cover this up too.

Then the leader of the Assyrian army answers with this: "Has my master sent me to speak these words to your master and to you and not to the people sitting on the wall, who are doomed with you to eat their own dung and drink their own urine?" (See Isaiah 36:12.) The leader of the Assyrian army continued to call out to the people on the wall in their own language, warning them that Hezekiah was deceiving them by saying the Lord will deliver.

The king, officials, and senior priests all covered themselves with sackcloth. The king went to the house of the Lord and sent his representatives to Isaiah the prophet for word from God (Isaiah 37:2-5). God gave Isaiah words of hope for Jerusalem that day. Jerusalem would be safe for now but it was too late for sister Israel and the other strongholds in Judah. They were captured.

When God's own people (God's prophets and priests) will not speak the truth about God but show partiality in their message, God must use other sources. His old route of transport has become corrupted. We have seen two alternatives in C-1 and here in C-2. What are the two methods that God used to get the truth out when His own people would not speak it?

C-3: Do you think that we allow our own knowledge, what we personally feel about something or someone, and what we think needs to be said or done, get in the way of God's truth? How did God (again) get the Truth out and overcome the obstacle course, of human-ness, when men's hearts and minds were trained to be partial in dealing with and dealing out, God's word? (See Acts 2:1-14.)

C-4: Can you think of a time when you were in God's way, hindering His will by your own words? Have you ever done what He says instead of doing what you wanted?

READ JEREMIAH 10:12-13

D. ADDITIONAL COMMENTS FOR VERSES 12-13

As Israel continues to unpack the care package, she finds that God has enclosed a picture of Himself.

ANSWER QUESTIONS FOR VERSES 12-13

D-1: What does God want His people to see when they look at Him? Describe His word-portrait.

READ JEREMIAH 10:14-15

E. ADDITIONAL COMMENTS FOR VERSES 14-15

If Israel is looking for some wisdom and the meaning of life, the wooden idols have nothing to give.

ANSWER QUESTIONS FOR VERSES 14-15

E-1: What will the idols do for the goldsmiths, that have made them, and why?

E-2: God's people will look at two kinds of relationships:

The first relationship is between man and the forms that he creates (man creates idols).

The second relationship is between God and the forms that He creates (God creates man).

The first relationship which was initiated by man will come to nothing but the second relationship which was initiated by God is not the same. The image which God created has life. But strange as it may seem His living and breathing creation has proven itself to be a lot like the lifeless wooden idols. How has God's creation become like the abominable idols? (See verse 14.)

E-3: What does God compare His people to back in Jeremiah 5:14?

E-4: Idols were carved-out forms that represented gods. Priests and prophets were created beings that represented God. When the time of punishment comes the idols will perish. What will happen to the priests and prophets according to Jeremiah 6:15?

📖READ JEREMIAH 10:16

F. ADDITIONAL COMMENTS FOR VERSE 16

From the very first day that God and Israel entered into their partnership by way of covenant, God's position has never changed. He has always honored and obeyed (feared) the words of the covenant/contract and kept in close contact with the other party (the bride) who is also bound to, and by, the legal work.

ANSWER QUESTIONS FOR VERSE 16

F-1: What makes Israel's covenanted God different from the other gods that these nations fear?

F-2: When a new nation is born, the birth pains are great and usually come in the form of war and much suffering. But when the Hebrews came out of Egypt, it was not accomplished because of some mighty human soldiers who carried shields and swords and sacrificed their lives to free some heavily burdened slaves. And they were not freed by any of their own efforts or the toil of their hands or the sweat from their brow or the shedding of their blood. They were not freed by any sort of wisdom that they possessed. Israel is 'a people' brought out and formed as a nation by the hand of God and there has been no other nation established in this manner by any other god.

(Deuteronomy 4:34 NRSV): Or has any god ever attempted to go and take a nation for himself from the midst of another nation, by trials, by signs and wonders, by war, by a mighty hand and an outstretched arm, and by terrifying displays of power, as the Lord your God did for you in Egypt before your very eyes?

(Deuteronomy 26:8 NRSV): The Lord brought us out of Egypt with a mighty hand and an outstretched arm, with a terrifying display of power, and with signs and wonders;

(Jeremiah 32:21 NRSV): You brought your people Israel out of the land of Egypt with signs and wonders, with a strong hand and an outstretched arm, and with great terror;

Jeremiah 10:16 (NRSV) says: 'the Lord of hosts is his name'. Look up the word host. What is the meaning?

📖READ JEREMIAH 10:17-18

G. ADDITIONAL COMMENTS FOR VERSES 17-18

God now shifts His attention to the 'nervous and highly anxious' who are probably sleeping with their eyes open now-a-days (the remaining fortified cities of Judah).

ANSWER QUESTIONS FOR VERSES 17-18

G-1: The people have been sitting on packed bags waiting expectantly for their salvation to show up. They know that the day is near. They keep uttering the same words to each other:

"Peace, Peace! No evil will come upon us", "Peace, Peace! No evil will come upon us." Finally God gives the instruction: 'Gather up your bundle from the ground, O you who live under siege! They are cheering, hugging each other, and crying tears of relief, until they hear what else God has to say. What else does God say to those who have bought the idea that they are going to be taking a ride on the 'peace train'? (See verse 18.)

G-2 (OPTIONAL QUESTION): These are words that seem to bring comfort to many Christians: "I don't know what the future holds but I know who holds the future." If God had to do to you what He had to do to His people in Judah, could you still say those words with the same praiseful attitude?

📖 READ JEREMIAH 10:19-21

H. ADDITIONAL COMMENTS FOR VERSES 19-21

As the warnings become reality so does the pain. God had patiently reached out. They did not respond. Then He called. They did not answer. He followed them. They did not slow down. He chased them. They ran even faster still. He has done everything possible (within the limits of the covenant) to get their attention. But the stubborn people would not return. What happens next will not only be painful for God's people but it will be God's punishment to bear also.

ANSWER QUESTIONS FOR VERSES 19-21

H-1: The pronoun 'My' in verses 19 and 20 indicates ownership. List all of the things that God has received (or gained as a burden) and all the things He has lost because of His rebellious people. (All answers will be found after the pronoun 'My'.)

H-2: Here in Jeremiah10:20 (NRSV), God says 'my tent has been destroyed'. Turn to Numbers 3:25-37. Three out of the four divisions of Levi served as God's parabolic (spiritual) tent. Describe who represented the different parts of God's tent.

H-3: After answering the last question; what do you think became the greatest national loss in this war?

H-4: Where is it that Israel's problems began, according to the picture that God has painted in verse 21?

H-5: I have come to understand how important and effective, 'getting the message out to the public', really is. When I was a kid, I was what became known as a 'litter bug'. I thought nothing about throwing a bubble gum wrapper or candy wrapper out the window of our car and no one stopped me when I did it. And from the looks of things then (when I was young), no one else felt guilty about throwing their unwanted trash from their car windows either. But today because of all the campaign messages, on billboards and TV, against littering, I have become conscious of the error. I realize it was an error and by the looks of our clean and litter-free highways now, others realize the error too. And enforcing fines for those who littered helped the campaign.

The campaign against littering began in 1953 when corporate and civic leaders (people who had some power) met to discuss the idea of keeping America beautiful. The first public service announcement on litter prevention appeared in 1956. In 1960, works began for ongoing public service announcement campaigns. In 1965, when I was throwing paper wrappers out of our car, one of the *First Ladies* joined the project in promoting highway beautification campaigns. In 1967 a canine TV star appears as a mascot for anti-littering campaigns. Even though I was still being a litterbug at this time, the popular canine mascot quickly gained the attention of all the young children like me. I don't know exactly when, but I was beginning to feel a little guilty and tried to litter when no one was looking. The service announcements were working (at least on me). Then in 1970 the most successful public service campaign in history: the iconic symbol of 'the Indian'. I saw him crying on the TV screen and I realized that I was making him cry. My attitude change was due to a lot of hard working leaders who were wisely and actively concerned. Only after all of this campaigning (for about 20 years) did Americans, including myself, realize their responsibility for our environment.

The campaign would not have been a success if leaders had not kept promoting and educating the people through the public service announcements. It took quite some time and effort but people finally began to realize their responsibility and that the future of a 'clean America' began with the person in the mirror. Everyone was responsible.

Israel desperately needed a campaign to 'Keep Israel Clean'. But the campaign slogans, from the mouths of the leaders (who served as the billboards and TV in those days), ran a different service announcement to the public: 'No evil will come on us' and 'We will not see famine or sword'; while all of the Promised Land was a garbage heap, full of idols and full of words that praised other gods. The leaders were practicing partiality as they chose their 'Public Service Announcements' from God's word. They chose to only advertise the promise of well-being and prosperity. They neglected to focus in on the things that needed to be changed. They did not focus in on *ridding the problems* that lead their nation to its destruction. What does Malachi 2:7-9 say?

READ JEREMIAH 10:22

I. ADDITIONAL COMMENTS FOR VERSE 22

Judah is finally obeying God. She is now doing *exactly* what He told her to do: "Gather up your bundle from the ground." As they stand with heavy bags in hand, they are weeping because they have to leave home. And then someone hears the whistle blow. "I hear the noise! Listen its coming." And it's true, the train that arrives is not the train of salvation that she was hoping and praying for. God has not relented this time. It is that dreaded train from the north and everyone, who is still alive, will have to get onboard.

ANSWER QUESTIONS FOR VERSE 22

I-1: What will happen to the land of Judah because of the train from the north?

I-2: When parents send their children out into the world, they hope that they have missed no important instructions to get them through life. It is the same with a dedicated teacher who instructs a student who will enter the work force. It is their responsibility is to equip their students to be ready for all circumstances in their field, whatever that might be. The leaders in Judah have not been good caretakers or instructors. What is the spiritual condition of those exiles leaving Judah? Turn to Isaiah 5:13 for the answer.

📖 READ JEREMIAH 10:23-24

J. ADDITIONAL COMMENTS FOR VERSES 23-24

God's leaders in Jerusalem will not change their ways. Through their actions, they continue to choose death and adversity but search for life and prosperity in all the chaos.

ANSWER QUESTIONS FOR VERSES 23-24

J-1: A statement is made that men are not in control of the way that life takes them. That statement might turn out to be quite debatable. But according to the written records, God's people could have changed their future drastically, just by obeying God. According to the written records, they *did* have power and control and according to the written records, God gave it to them. They had the power to choose life or death. The power to receive blessings instead of curses lay at their own front door. There are witnesses to prove it. See Deuteronomy 30:19 NRSV: I call heaven and earth to witness against you today that I have set before you life and death, blessings and curses. Choose life so that you and your descendants may live.

While Jerusalem is still safe, the rest of Judah, now like Israel, is in tears. She is whining. She is crying. She is wringing her hands. She is rocking back and forth on her knees. She wants God to judge her in what she calls a "just measure." In this request, she tries to tempt God. She does everything that she can to get Him to break the rules outlined in the legal covenant. She asks God for things that are not lawfully available to her or permitted. Temptress! Temptress! Get on the train!

(Deuteronomy 6:16-19 NRSV): Do not put the Lord your God to the test, as you tested him at Massah. You must diligently keep the commandments of the Lord your God, and his decrees, and his statutes that he has commanded you. Do what is right and good in the sight of the Lord, so that it may go well with you, and so that you may go in and occupy the good land that the Lord swore to your ancestors to give you, thrusting out all your enemies from before you, as the Lord has promised.

What do you try to talk God into doing for you? (How do you tempt God?)

📖 **READ JEREMIAH 10:25**

K. ADDITIONAL COMMENTS FOR VERSE 25

God thought the weeping and wailing would change her heart, but it didn't. She thought the weeping and wailing would change her circumstances, but it didn't.

ANSWER QUESTIONS FOR VERSE 25

K-1: Now she has become like a finger pointing child who is bitter over the severe punishment being delivered. She won't accept the truth. What is the truth? (See Jeremiah 4:18.)

K-2: When there is an attack of terror, many terrorist groups will claim responsibility for the catastrophic event. Anyone and everyone wants to gain power and recognition. How does Izzie's (Israel's) finger pointing become an enemy act in the sight of God? (See Deuteronomy 32:26-27.)

K-3: According to my record keeping, there was only one Commandment (of the ten written in stone) that had not been broken by *His people* yet. That *was* number 9. How has she (the broken body of Israel) managed to add that to her criminal record too? (See her statement in Jeremiah 10:25.)

> - 1 You shall have no other gods before me.
> - 2 You shall not make any idols.
> - 3 You shall not wrongfully use the name of the Lord your God
> - 4 Remember the Sabbath Day and keep it holy.
> - 5 Honor your father and mother.
> - 6 You shall not murder.
> - 7 You shall not commit adultery.
> - 8 You shall not steal.
> - 9 You shall not bear false witness against your neighbor.
> - 10 You shall not covet anything that belongs to your neighbor.

A FINAL THOUGHT FOR CHAPTER 10 STUDY

After all of this heart-searching (in all the land of Israel),

it seems to me that God has discovered one thing for sure...

Instituting this new form of government on earth is going to be an uphill business venture

especially with an 'ex' as a partner (Jeremiah 3:8) and

all of her rebellious children running the show...

Chapter 10 Tag-A-Long

Growing Trouble

Noah was a man who (like God) planted a vineyard. He had a vineyard which (like God's) produced trouble. In Genesis 9:20 (NRSV) we are told that Noah was the first to plant a vineyard. It seems that he, too, did not know what his produce was capable of because he drank some of the wine and became drunk. Because of the wine, Noah, like most, probably did not have full control of his actions. The bible says that he lay uncovered in his tent. As you read the story, you find Noah in a very vulnerable state. He desperately needed assistance. Ham, one of Noah's sons, saw the nakedness of his father. Ham could have restored to his father that which the wine had stolen. He could have restored his father's honor by covering him up. But he didn't. He walked away and left his father in a condition that invited ridicule, laughter, and disrespect.

I think that there is a good reason that we, for generations, have read this embarrassing story about Noah. Maybe God wants us to have some sympathy for Noah. If we can do that, we can also understand something about God. God is a lot like Noah for two reasons.

- The first: Having control over your own actions when you are in a drunken condition is not possible. God (like Noah) knew that things were not right but He was in, what seemed to be, a helpless situation. The binding covenant between Him and Israel restricted and policed His actions. The covenant gave Israel the power to control that which flowed from her Lord. God's people controlled His actions by their actions. When they were obedient He blessed them. When they were not obedient, He cursed them. That is what the legal covenant demanded.
- Second: God like Noah was left uncovered by one of His children. Levi was His covering (His tent). God had called out to Levi and, at that time, Levi could have done something to restore God's reputation. Levi should have protected his perpetual gift instead of wandering off and leaving it unprotected. But he didn't. When you are left naked and uncovered by those who are supposed to care about you, you might do one or two things. You might get angry or you just might wonder if everyone, who passes by, is blind to your need and deaf to your call. I think that we have seen and will continue to see both of these reactions from the Lord when it comes to *His people*.

✄ Scrapbook Page For Chapter 10

The Making of an Idol

Meihlan's name was well known among the kings, queens, and priests in many nations. He was almost as famous as his made-to-your-order idols. If your city or town wanted a grand idol, he could carve and decorate one for you that would make your town famous. If you wanted your town to be 'the place everyone should go to worship', Meihlan was the man you wanted to see. He was a great crafter who was religiously devoted to his work and you could tell by the finished product. It was hard to believe, that at first, the idol that he carved was just a tree from the forest. As he worked on it day by day, hour by hour, minute by minute, the wood that was brought into his shop flourished falsely into something else.

First he caved the wood. He loved the sweet smell. Meihlan always knew what kind of wood he was working with and he especially liked to work with the mulberry. His hands were kind and gentle as he brushed away the dust from the smooth parts of the body. Why must the tools, that his hands had to use in order to form the image, be so invasive and cruel? But in all of his years of producing the idols, he knew that perfection only came through pounding, cutting, and sawing. And then, after all of that, he had to send the idol down the street to be bathed with hot molten gold.

When the shining idol was returned to him, that's when he really came to know it and that's when the beauty of the idol, made for worship, stole his heart. He was the one who would detail every part of the 'god form'. First he always, worked on the eyes. That way the god would know just how it was put together. They, the two eyes and all the frontal teeth, were of flattened pearl. Sapphire and onyx completed the decoration of its face. Golden strands, which he had braided, were nailed to the top of the idols hollow head. The nails which affixed the strands of hair were hidden under the magnificent jeweled crown. This idol would have no ears, but who would know?

He then pounded ruby, diamond and jasper rings onto the detailed fingers. He clothed the idol with blue and purple linen and then attached strands of silk to secure the clothing. He slid golden embossed bracelets onto the arms. He hung thick beaded medallions around the neck and glued leather sandals on the carved feet. The idol looks like it can walk and talk. Meihlan's work was majestic. The rough cut log that was carried into his shop will be carried out with a magnetic charm that most people do not even possess.

It was always hard for him to let go once the idol was finished. He was always fearful that it would be dropped or tumble off the wagon as it was transported to its destination. Tears welled up in his eyes as he thought about such carelessness from those who would move his crafts. He always made sure to instruct the carriers how to tie down the idol in order to keep it safe.

He could find only one comfort as he safely bundled the image for shipping. He knew full and well that thousands of people were anxiously waiting to worship and adore the new arrival. It would be loved and receive all kinds of affection. People would make sacrifices and bring bountiful offerings to the deity as they attempt to show their loyalty. It was better for the idol not to stay, but go, and rule in the hearts of its worshippers. The followers had the ability to give the idol more power than he as one man alone could do. He sadly gathers up all of the wood chips and scraps from the floor of his shop. Tonight the remainder of the god image would provide him with warmth and it would be kindling to prepare his supper.

Over time, men made images of their gods out of carved wood and stone.

But God would not have it that way for His people.

His image would not be created by the hands of man.

He, Himself, *El* Shaddaih, *Elohim* (*El* meaning, the highest exulted) created his own image

and it wasn't of wood or stone.

It was made of flesh, skin and bone.

His image could walk and talk and think and feel.

He gave His image a power that was real.

We call His image Jesus.

(Acts 17:24 NRSV): The God who made the world and everything in it, he who is Lord of heaven and earth, does not live in shrines made by human hands,

I now submit my last snapshot of Jesus to you for this part-1 project of Jeremiah: the first No-EL

Compare Answers For Chapter 10

A-1: process of altering something; the process of changing, correcting, or improving something

A-2: Thus says the Lord: Do not learn the way of the nations, or be dismayed at the signs of the heavens; for the nations are dismayed at them. (Jeremiah 10:2 NRSV).

A-3: And the Word became flesh and lived among us, and we have seen his glory, the glory as of a father's only son, full of grace and truth (John 1:14 NRSV).

A-4: A tree from the forest is cut down. It is worked with an ax that is held by an artisan. People decorate it and then use a hammer and nails to stabilize it.

A-5: The crows (God's people who have His word in their hearts)

B-1: God's people should use what they have to bless the Lord's kingdom always wanting to gain good repute for the Lord.

B-2: Nebuchadnezzar recognized the power of God and (by his public power) published the notice throughout the nations.

B-3: (Jeremiah 27:12-15): …Bring your necks under the yoke of the king of Babylon, and serve him and his people, and live. Why should you and your people die by the sword, by famine, and by pestilence…Do not listen to the words of the prophets who are telling you not to serve the king…I have not sent them…they are prophesying falsely in my name…

B-4: Be righteously submissive to ruling powers.

B-5: God's word is fire. It will burn up the woody words.

B-6: He is clothed with majesty, strength, honor and light.

B-7: The Lord is the God who is true, living, and the everlasting King

B-8: The ark will be forgotten about and not missed.

B-9: the nations and the whole earth

C-1: …The gods who did not make the heavens and the earth shall perish from the earth and under the heavens (Jeremiah 10:11 NRSV).

C-2: God gave the exiles a message that they could not add any words to it because they knew no other words in that language. They could not change the words or interpret the words in their own way because they did not have the knowledge, of the other language, to do so. And secondly God sent the truth to the people through the mouth of a foreigner from other nations.

C-3: I think that we allow our own personal convictions, personal interpretations of His written word, and personal profile of other lives, affect the words that we use to speak on behalf of God. We add all of those together and get a hodge-podge message which may not be the message that God wanted to be heard.

God kept His message pure in the book of Acts by anointing others with the ability to speak in another language. The anointed who were speaking in languages that they had never known, came to learn, that their words had meaning. The foreigners there in the city that day were hearing about God and His wonders.

C-4: I was in the grocery store one day. I asked a lady at the meat counter for a pound of lunchmeat. She must have been having a bad day because she said or did something that was not nice. I wanted to give her rudeness right back but there was one thought that stopped me. I thought: What if she comes to church next week, how could I walk up, smile, and shake her hand if I acted like that today? Thinking about what would hurt God's reputation has always helped me to do and say the right thing. I want to always let God have His way.

D-1: It is God who made the earth by His power. He established the world by wisdom. By His understanding He stretched out the heavens. When He utters His voice, there is tumult of waters in the heavens. He makes mist rise from the ends of the earth. He makes lightnings for the rain. He brings out wind from His storehouses.

E-1: The idols will put the crafters and makers to shame because their hand made images are false and there is no breath in them.

E-2: God has been put to shame by what He made. His people do not possess true life.

E-3: wood

E-4: The idols will perish whereas the priests and prophets will be overthrown.

F-1: He formed all things. These gods are formed by the hand of the Creator's creations.

F-2: army, a very large multitude

G-1: … I am going to sling out the inhabitants of the land at this time, and I will bring distress on them, so that they shall feel it (Jeremiah 10:18 NRSV).

G-2 (OPTIONAL QUESTION): Jeremiah has opened my eyes and I now have a different fear of

God. I can only ask for strength to stay faithful to Him through thick and thin, like Abraham. I hope that I can accept what He does knowing that it is all with purpose and reason.

H-1: This was God's gain: My hurt, My wound, My punishment. This was God's loss: My tent, My cord and My children.

H-2: Gershon was to be the tabernacle, the tent with its covering, the screen for the entrance of the tent of meeting, the hangings of the court, the screen for the entrance of the court that is around the tabernacle and altar, and it's cords- all the service pertaining to these.

Kohath was to be the ark, the table, the lamp stand, the altars, the vessels of the sanctuary with which the priests minister and the screen- all the service pertaining to these.

Merari was to be the frames of the tabernacle, the bars, the pillars, the bases, and all their accessories- all the service pertaining to these; also the pillars of the court all around, with their bases and pegs and cords.

H-3: I think it is Levi (at this point) under attack (while others are in the line of fire).

H-4: The shepherds are stupid and do not inquire of the Lord.

H-5: For the lips of a priest should guard knowledge, and people should seek instruction from his mouth, for he is the messenger of the Lord of hosts. But you have turned aside from the way; you have caused many to stumble by your instruction; you have corrupted the covenant of Levi, says the Lord of hosts, and so I make you despised and abased before all the people, inasmuch as you have not kept my ways but have shown partiality in your instruction (Malachi 2:7-9 NRSV).

I-1: The cities of Judah will be desolate. The cities will become lairs for jackals.

I-2: (Isaiah 5:13 NRSV): Therefore my people go into exile without knowledge; their nobles are dying of hunger, and their multitude is parched with thirst. (I think the hunger and thirst is spiritual.)

J-1: I ask Him to forgive for me for the same sin over and over. Instead of making changes about myself I want Him to turn away from the truth. I want Him to lie, to Himself, about what He sees. I don't want to change. I want Him to change.

K-1: Your ways and your doings have brought this upon you. This is your doom; how bitter it is! …(Jeremiah 4:18 NRSV).

K-2: This may sound strange, but when she blames someone else for her downfall (which no one except she and her Lord share that power jointly), she gives 'glory' (that belongs to God, it was His plan by His power) to someone else. Her reason for her downfall falsely becomes the fault of another, instead of her own, when the false rumors are uttered (sold and then bought by many).

K-3: She is bearing false witness against her neighbor by saying that they (are the ones who) have devoured her when in truth, this whole thing has been between her and her Lord.

Printed in the United States
By Bookmasters